THE REVOLT OF THE PENDULUM

ALSO BY CLIVE JAMES

AUTOBIOGRAPHY

Unreliable Memoirs   Falling Towards England

May Week Was In June   North Face of Soho

FICTION

Brilliant Creatures   The Remake

Brrm! Brrm!   The Silver Castle

VERSE

Peregrine Prykke's Pilgrimage Through the London Literary World

Other Passports: Poems 1958–1985

The Book of My Enemy: Collected Verse 1958–2003

Angels Over Elsinore: Collected Verse 2003–2008

CRITICISM

The Metropolitan Critic (new edition, 1994)

Visions Before Midnight   The Crystal Bucket

First Reactions (US)   From the Land of Shadows

Glued to the Box   Snakecharmers in Texas

The Dreaming Swimmer   Fame in the Twentieth Century

On Television   Even As We Speak

Reliable Essays   As of This Writing (US)

The Meaning of Recognition   Cultural Amnesia

TRAVEL

Flying Visits

CLIVE JAMES

THE REVOLT OF THE PENDULUM

ESSAYS 2005–2008

PICADOR

First published 2009 by Picador
an imprint of Pan Macmillan Ltd
Pan Macmillan, 20 New Wharf Road, London N1 9RR
Basingstoke and Oxford
Associated companies throughout the world
www.panmacmillan.com

ISBN 978-0-330-45738-5

Typeset by SetSystems Ltd, Saffron Walden, Essex
Printed in the UK by CPI Mackays, Chatham ME5 8TD

Visit www.picador.com to read more about all our books
and to buy them. You will also find features, author interviews and
news of any author events, and you can sign up for e-newsletters
so that you're always first to hear about our new releases.

To the memory of

Pat Kavanagh

A commentator has indeed great temptations to supply by turbulence what he wants of dignity, to beat his little gold to a spacious surface, to work that to foam which no art or diligence can exalt to spirit.

Johnson, Preface to Shakespeare

Many times, unsettled by his own astonishment, Golo Mann returned to the question of how, in the 1960s, there could have been such a remarkable renaissance of Marxism, whose recipe for health had already, for a generation, been laden with intellectual compromise and victims by the million. To him, it was as if a spectre had reawakened. And if that filled him with anxiety, he also had the counter-spectre before his eyes, together with the knowledge that it had been in their competition with each other that they had both first grown strong. From the common experience of the older generation, the ruins and the traces of suffeirng were still visible, indeed written in the wind. Most frightening of all, it had become obvious that no historical disaster could quell the longing for one or another of the world-burning ideologies; that even the bloodiest of evidence could do nothing against it; and that there seemed to be no horizon where such a no-man's-land might end.

Joachim Fest, Begegnungen

A Note on the Text

Most of the essays in this book appear just as they were first printed by various publications whether in Britain, Australia or the United States. To all those many generous editors, my thanks, and I mean them no disrespect by having occasionally restored production cuts, undone the rigours of house style, or reversed the effects of supposedly beneficial changes in the prevailing version of the English language. In Australia, for example, the Symphony Orchestra, in any major city that has one, is nowadays called the Symphony: a clear case of needless confusion introduced through the itch for improvement. A symphony is something composed by, say, Beethoven. A symphony orchestra is something that performs it. To restore such distinctions I counted as a simple duty, like clarifying my own prose where it seemed necessary. But on the whole I have tried to leave a piece exactly as it was, following my established practice of adding afterthoughts only in a postscript. An updated essay would be torn loose from its time, and the resulting claim to prescience would falsify everything in it, because my main aim as a cultural commentator is to help define the connections between the past and the present, in the sure conviction that the future is uncertain. The date given at the end of each piece is therefore the first clue to its beginning.

Contents

Introduction

Originating in my homeland, like the smile of Kylie Minogue and Rod Laver's cross-court running forehand, the phrase 'the revolt of the pendulum' is an invention surely destined to conquer the world. In Australia in late 2007, when the Liberal government of John Howard, after eleven years in power, was finally replaced by the Labor government of Kevin Rudd, a Liberal Party politician said that the change had not been a landslide victory for the incoming party. He said that it was just 'the revolt of the pendulum'. He was right, but his language was imprecise. A pendulum doesn't revolt. But it does swing, and a swing of the pendulum was the most that had happened. The change took place within the limits of modern democratic politics, in which one party concerned with national wealth and public welfare contends against another party concerned with the same two things, but in different proportions.

This is the balance which obtains in the three leading English-speaking democracies, the US, the UK and Australia, and we usually measure the other English-speaking democracies, and all the non-English-speaking democracies, by the extent to which they come near equalling it, or at least aspire to. There may be more than two main parties, but if there are fewer than two, namely one, then we are usually talking about an elected dictatorship which won't be liberal, and will be democratic only in the sense that the people periodically get a chance to re-elect their oppressor. A free liberal democracy in its full sense is governed by the pendulum. It might fall short of the principles of justice enunciated by John Rawls in his *Theory of Justice*, but if its government can be changed at the whim of the people then it fulfils the minimum requirement of a liberal democracy set by Karl Popper in his years of exile to faraway New Zealand, an open society where he was free to consider how human liberty could best hold its enemies at bay. When Francis Fukuyama announced the end of history, he was really talking about the arrival of a general recognition

– spurred by the full development and final discrediting of the horrors unleashed by some of the alternatives – that the free liberal democracy was the most desirable state. He was right to the extent that the argument was settled. He was wrong only in supposing that history might listen.

Devoid of a mind of its own, history doesn't care about a reasonable conclusion. Unfortunately both parts of that sentence apply to many of the public intellectuals who concern themselves with world affairs. For them, a political system which has attained a condition of vibrating stasis provides an insufficient resonance. Briefly, they find it boring. Bored, they play with fire. Those on the left, almost invariably living in a liberal democracy or something like it, would prefer to believe that the liberal democracies, by their nature, are invariably the instigators of any contrary forces that might arise. In the same free countries, those on the right would prefer to believe that liberal democracy must modify its system of justice in order to defend itself against extremism. (They don't see themselves as extremists, although they patently are.) Faced, in the democracy we happen to inhabit, with these two contrary aberrations, we are forced to conclude that the old system of placing the intellectual life of liberal democracy on a continuum from left to right is obsolete.

Such a conclusion, if all could reach it, would usefully reflect the facts about the whole life of liberal democracy, the chief fact being that it can no longer be viewed as being on a continuum either: ever since Nazi totalitarianism and Communist totalitarianism stood revealed as being essentially similar, the old tripartite horizontal distinction, with liberal democracy in the middle, has looked less and less realistic. Better to think of liberal democracy as the breathable atmosphere of a planet. Above the breathable atmosphere there is an unbreathable stratosphere called extremism, trying to get in. In this stratosphere of extremism, suffocating and invasive, what used to be the far left and what used to be the far right are continuous. The extremes not only touch, they blend. In that sense, and in that sense only, totalitarianism has finally become global. On the ground, it has only a few states left to call its own. But in the air, it is everywhere.

It would be a good thing if the word 'extremist' could be taken up more widely to denote any movement which wants to deal with a contradictory opinion by silencing the voice that dares to utter it. Among my own friends, there are several who would have been less likely to be falsely branded as 'Islamophobes' if they had inveighed, not against Islamism, but against Islamic extremism. The word 'Islam' and the word 'Islamism' are easily confused, especially by those who have an interest in confusing them. The term 'Islamic extremism' more intelligibly says what is meant. Islamic extremists want to silence all opposition. Especially they want to silence opposition within Islam. By saying that Islamism is the enemy of Islam you are positively asking to be misunderstood. By saying that Islamic extremism is the enemy of Islam, you are clearly opening the way for a salient fact: there are more than a billion Muslims in the world who don't want to kill you for your opinions. Those who do are a minority, which can just as easily – more easily, one would have thought – be called uncharacteristic as characteristic. As minorities go, it is quite large, but it is a very small proportion of the total population from which it emerges. That fact should gives us cause for hope. The Islamic extremist minority's depredations against the interests of the hated West might get a less clear run if they are seen to injure the interests of the Islamic majority as well. Some evidence for the hope's being well founded is already in, and has been generated under conditions that could scarcely be more intense.

When people are ready to risk their lives to argue for tolerance, those of us who are running no risk at all should be slow to insult them by treating our freedom to conduct reasoned argument as if it were of negligible value. Better to think of it as valuable beyond price: the only guarantee of a decent life for all. If those of us growing old behind the safety of a desk are still hungry for adventure, there is a battlefield before our eyes. It comes to us as an unrelenting barrage of print and images. It won't kill us any faster than time does, but if we don't play our part then others will surely suffer, because although comprehension might have no direct effect, incomprehension will always have its consequences. Either we make the best sense we can of what we see and hear, or we have done less than nothing. Not a very daring aim, perhaps, but it has sustained me while I have been putting this book together. My own story, as usual, is the wellspring of what I have written: my own story with all its trivialities, petty ambitions, sad deficiencies, ludicrous failures and negligible victories, all these things the product of a curiosity that has been allowed to operate without restriction. What has changed, as that story winds to an end, is my inclination to call it mere good fortune. It has been a blessing, conferred by a social and political fabric that it took the whole of history to assemble. Trying to analyse how that might have happened is like trying to analyse the structure of providence. It can't be done, but it can't be left alone either. Even the smallest success is a lot to wish for, but one feels obliged to try.

Most of the essays in this book were written as book reviews or commissioned pieces since my last collection of critical prose, *The Meaning of Recognition*, came out in 2005. Some of them, in their origins, date from slightly earlier, because they were begun while my later book *Cultural Amnesia* was being composed, and for a while I thought that the themes they contained might be incorporated into it. In each case, after I decided that an essay deserved a separate life apart from that book, I developed it as an individual piece and found a home for it in a suitably receptive periodical, whether in Britain, Australia or the USA. If I received any requests from periodicals in Ireland, Canada, South Africa, India or New Zealand I would certainly consider them. The idea of an Anglosphere, or international English-language commonwealth, seems very real to me: a sign, in fact, that the old Empire was something better than an aberration, if somewhat less than an ideal.

One of the privileges of my position as a living relic of literary journalism is that I can sometimes peddle a finished article rather than just wait to be offered a commission. The range of publications in which I might pull such a trick has thankfully widened in recent times, and not just because my market value has gone up pro rata with the increasing curiosity generated by my continued ability to breathe. The actual number of suitable publications has increased. In Australia, for example, the *Australian Literary Review*, in its latest form, has at last been given the editorial resources befitting its status as a supplement to the country's leading newspaper. Rupert Murdoch will be able to brandish a copy of it when he arrives at the pearly gates and St Peter asks him whether he really thinks his proprietorship of the *News of the World* qualifies him for entry. And the current-affairs magazine the *Monthly*, carrying the flag of the new and vigorous Black Inc. publishing empire, has room for the longer article in a way that the now defunct *Bulletin* rarely did. It's always good to know that such specialist magazines as the *Australian Book Review* and *Quadrant* and the *Griffith Review* are widely read in the universities, but the *Australian Literary Review* and the *Monthly* are right out there on the newsstands, and the newsstands are where I like to operate if I can. Australia, by now, does the intellectual magazine well, but it's the commercial magazine for the general audience which carries the bigger prize: a readership whose attention is not automatically conferred, but has to be won.

In Britain, *Prospect* now has a rival, called *Standpoint*, on the other side of the political centre; so now there are two newsstand magazines in search of the longer essay. Two buyers are enough to create a seller's market. Sometimes it takes only one: under their current editorship, the cultural pages of the *New York Times* are wide open to critical prose written at the highest level, and a literary journalist would have to be crazy not to try getting in. The question remains, however, of what one is trying to sell. I hope the pieces in this book add up to an answer. One either does this kind of thing as journey-work, or else one tries to convey a viewpoint. For the old sweat, the chief advantage of having been around the block a few times is that he develops a viewpoint anyway, just to make sense of the era that he has succeeded in living through. Sometimes he has succeeded in nothing else, but a grizzled enough veteran will congratulate himself on having survived to be issued with a Freedom Pass.

Armed with such experience – which, appropriately nuanced, can be made to sound edifying if not dramatic – it becomes difficult to avoid writing essays. The obituaries alone would keep me busy, and there is also the necessity to bark for the various activities by which I supplement my pension now that I am no longer a wage-earner on main-channel television. Whether I go on stage alone or tour with my song-writing partner Pete Atkin, I have to send out my handbills if I am to do my share of filling the house in the next town. Writing such material could be treated as a formulaic chore but I prefer to give it the works. Some of the results are here, and to any readers who find the intensity of self-promotion embarrassing, I can only say that it seemed to me like a matter of sink or swim. As for my website, www.clivejames.com, it makes no money at all but I have to publicize it if it is not to make even less, and besides, I value my twilight folly too much to sell it short: I have never been more sure of being on to something, even if I still don't know what it is. Perhaps it's what Prospero called a midnight mushroom. Anyway, my web-spinning needs promotion in the MSM (mainstream media: yet another set of initials to cope with) along with anything else I get up to in these crowded days of retirement. The wares of Autolycus rattled on his cart, but he still had to cry out that he was there. So writing the next essay is something that one is always doing, like writing the next poem. I just hope I'm getting better at it. Encouraged by the worldwide reception for *Cultural Amnesia*, I have a second volume of the same proportions in mind, and perhaps even a third, if there is time: but the difference between those projected books and the essays that appear in this book will mainly be a difference of scale. If I hadn't thought that the pieces here assembled could contain the utmost of what I have to say on their subjects, I wouldn't have written them. That, in fact, was the attraction: the chance to prove that one's freedom to reflect on life has not been wasted.

Being so occupied has helped to make for a quick few years. Some of the world events during this period might have seemed slow to unfold. Barack Obama was a full two years on the campaign trail before he won a victory which will seem to history like the work of a moment. The events in Iraq, between 2003 and 2008, gave critics of allied intervention plenty of opportunity to say that an unending nightmare had been unleashed. And indeed, for the parents and relatives of the dead soldiers and innocent civilians, there could be no quick end to the agony. But the events themselves, despite every possible blunder having been made by the forces of salvation, turned out to be finite. The decisive moment was in early 2007, and almost all the international commentators missed it. They had made such an investment in the idea of an irreversibly catastrophic intervention that they were disappointed, rather than chastened, by any evidence that Iraqi democracy might be establishing itself even though the word-blind President Bush said it was. When the zealous leaders of the Sunni and the Shia finally started showing less interest in killing each other and more interest in fighting off the attentions of al-Qa'eda, pundits accustomed to placing all blame on America were stuck with a conundrum: reluctant to admit that the Pentagon's famous 'surge' might actually have made a positive difference, they were obliged to entertain the possibility that the Iraqis had their own opinions about the inevitability of a civil war. The blogs coming out of Iraq sent a clear message that for any citizen free to act, the aim was to rebuild. But for most commentators outside the country, the conundrum was too much, and they lapsed into echolalia. To put it bluntly, they had a theory, which was proof against any facts.

The pervasive effect of just such a blind obduracy was one of my themes for *Cultural Amnesia*. It was also a theme, steadily growing more dominant, in my previous collections of essays, and once again it is a theme here. It's a perennial theme. I wish it wasn't, and by that wish I state my difference from all those negligent vigilantes who profess a grand vision of how the world must go. (I wish I had thought of the term 'negligent vigilantes', but it was Alain Finkiel-kraut: fine phrases should never be borrowed without acknowledge-ment.) In the twentieth century, many among even the best-qualified intellectuals thought that liberal democracy either had a natural outcome in Nazi-style fascism or was helpless to oppose it, and that Communism might therefore have credentials as an historical force to shape a just future. Only slowly was the conclusion drawn that fascism and Communism were merely two different forms of totali-tarianism, and that they were far less the enemies of each other than they were the common enemy of democracy. In the twenty-first century, a further form of totalitarianism, which does not depend on nation states, was quickly enough identified – by its own proclama-tions, its intentions were hard to miss – but it was thought to be an inevitable consequence of how the liberal democracies behaved. From any sensible viewpoint, it should be clear that this latest form of the murderously irrational would be determined to expand its power even if the liberal democracies did nothing except exist.

But a sensible viewpoint is not glamorous enough for those who are commanded by a vision, and the vision of the culpable West is now the dominant vision among the intellectuals of the world, and all the more dominant if the West is where they come from. Those of us without that vision must content ourselves with having a viewpoint, which even at its most coherent is nothing more ambitious than a set of views. Any set of views should logically begin with the view that there is something desirable about a political system that leaves us free to have them, even if that system finds it difficult, as it should, to deal with views that are inimical to its existence. In any free nation, for example, there will be eloquent voices to proclaim the virtues of isolationism. And indeed that view is considerable: it can always be plausibly said that the United States would be better off if it had never gone near Iraq. But to say that Iraq would be better off, you need to be pretty detached about what Saddam Hussein and his ineffable sons might have done next, let alone about what they had done already. And to say the same about Darfur, if and when the cavalry rides to the rescue, will take something beyond detachment: it will take a wilful forgetting, a rewriting of the past which will involve yet further reconstruction of the language, so that nothing can be called evil if it is not caused by the only forces that have the power to correct it. Interference will always have a moral cost, and to accept that cost without question will always be callous. The moral cost can even be too high: in retrospect, it might have been better if the people of South Vietnam had been left to their fate, which they would have voted for anyway, just as the people of Czechoslovakia once voted for it, postponing their freedom into the generation after next. But the idea that there need never be a moral cost in leaving things as they are is one that only a visionary could hold. Charles Lindbergh had a vision of isolationism that would have kept America out of World War II. But he could express his vision only as one view among others: the surest sign that his country, when it was drawn into a war against evil, was not entirely evil in itself. It could have been said at the time that America's only aim was to secure its oil supplies, but it could equally have been said that the GIs were on their way to save the life of Harold Pinter, and that second thing would have been true.

My own views begin with the welfare of the common people, to which I prefer to make subsidiary any total scheme of historical necessity. Born and raised in the industrial proletariat, I have a long memory for the forces which once exploited it, and one of them was left-wing ideology, which never ceased to believe that manifest destiny was an ally fit to command any sacrifice, including the sufferings of the very people who were meant to benefit from the march of progress. But historical necessity, if such a thing exists, can be analysed by intellectuals only to the extent that they are ready to deal with reality, and their best way of doing that is to begin by staying alert to the language in which they speak. If eleven million Iraqis turn up at the voting booths despite their being threatened with death for doing so, the commentator may call them dupes if he likes, but he should know that his terms of expression prove that he is more concerned with his own wish than with their hopes. If he calls the brave women of the Iraqi provisional government Quislings, he should at least know who Vidkun Quisling was. He should know where his own words come from, and what they were once meant to mean. That should be his first alertness, because the area of language is the only area where he is ever likely to effect any change, and it will be a change for the worse if all he can say compounds an illusion. So constant an attention to the use of mere words is a finicky business with small apparent reward, and the world's vast supply of expert onlookers get understandably impatient when they are reminded of their true and only role. But I would rather offend them than further insult the vast numbers of comparatively voiceless people they ignore while proclaiming their concern for humanity.

'All I have is a voice,' said Auden, 'to undo the folded lie.' Coming after a decade of flirtation with romantic politics, it was one of the best things he ever said, a permanently valuable demonstration of how a true confidence connects with a sense of duty. The operative word is 'folded'. The writer, if he wishes to write about current affairs – and ideally he should wish it only because he is forced to – must have the confidence to regard the unpicking of language as a proper job, and he must have the patience to do it. It is hard work for low returns, but the same condition is true for almost everyone in the world. The workers building the luxury hotels in Dubai get fifteen minutes for lunch. They look like the lucky ones to untold millions of people elsewhere who are doing even worse. It's all too easy to think of poor people in the mass, and it takes only a modicum of compassion to start blaming it all on us. But the feeling is as foolish as the thought. They *are* us: a multitude of individuals. They are just leading less fortunate lives, and anyone who writes about justice from his privileged position as a citizen of a Western democracy will be able to do very little for them if he fails to realize that his own fortune begins with his freedom.

London, 2009

LITERATURE

THE QUESTION OF KARL KRAUS

'A liberated woman,' said Karl Kraus, 'is a fish that has fought its way ashore.' Even at the time, there were women, some of them among his cheer-squad of beautiful mistresses, who thought he was talking through his hat. Agree with him or not, however, you wouldn't mind being able to say something that sharp. Kraus was famous for being able to do so whenever he wanted, but eventually, as with his hero Oscar Wilde, his fame as a wit was there instead of the full, complex, tormented and deeply contemplative man. As a writer and practitioner of the higher journalism, he is still up there with all the other great names of literary Vienna – Arthur Schnitzler, Robert Musil, Joseph Roth – but up there for what, precisely?

The risk run by the aphorist is that people will grow restless between aphorisms, because they aren't getting enough of what it says on the label. Even while he was alive, most people didn't want any more of Kraus's world view than would fit into a fortune cookie. Though he had no computer on his desk, Kraus was essentially a blogger before the fact: his basic technique was to write a couple of hundred words about something silly in the newspaper. He sometimes wrote at length, but his admirers preferred him to keep it short. The kind of thing they liked best from him might have been designed to pop up on a BlackBerry today. 'An aphorism can never be the whole truth,' he once wrote: 'It is either a half-truth or a truth and half.' Yes, but that's an aphorism. So is it true?

Outside the German-speaking lands, Kraus is now known mainly for having been the Viennese café pundit who brilliantly fulfilled a self-created role as the scourge of loose language. Serious readers, even if their serious reading does not often include him, know that Kraus, from before the turn of the twentieth century until a couple of years before the Anschluss in 1938, was the linguistic health inspector who searched through what was said for what was meant, and was particularly scathing about the jingoistic propaganda that helped drive a generation of young men irretrievably into the mincing machine of the Great War. Kept out of it by his distorted spine, he was the pacifist on the warpath, the libertarian grammarian. Whether in the pages of his magazine *Die Fackel* (The Torch) or by means of his celebrated readings on stage, he constantly pointed out the connection between official bombast and the suffering of the people, between journalistic mendacity and political duplicity, between fine writing and foul behaviour. Some of those serious readers also know, or think they know, that Kraus finally fell silent because, on his own admission, Hitler had left him speechless.

Not true. The facts say that Kraus, immediately after confessing that the Nazis left him with nothing to say, went on to say quite a lot. There are thousands of facts like that in Edward Timms's biography *Karl Kraus*, a two-tome desk-breaker which can be taken as the instigation of the piece I am writing now, because such a big, factually precise yet historically approximate biography brings to a focus some of the problems that Kraus's brilliant career exemplified. Such a biography can also be a problem in itself, if its interpretations come to define its subject. Something like that, I believe, has happened in this instance, and it might be worth attempting a short historical account of Kraus's career without wasting space by decorating the narrative with the usual sprinkle of aphorisms. There are a dozen different anthologies of those, quite apart from the compendia of his writings that Kraus put together himself. What we need, however, is a picture of the mind behind the fragments. Was that fragmentary too?

Timms's first volume, with its Margaret Mead-sounding subtitle 'Culture and Catastrophe in Habsburg Vienna', covered the years 1874–1918 and was published to acclaim in 1986. The second volume, 'The Post-War Crisis and the Rise of the Swastika', covering the years 1918–1936, came out late in 2005. I had meant to write about it before this, but first I had to read it. As with its predecessor, ploughing through it took time. Timms has done a lot of reading, and takes a lot of reading in his turn: far more than most non-academic students will ever give him. It should be said that he makes that demand with good credentials. Though his hulking double whammy of a book is further burdened by an ultra-post-modern vocabulary and by his apparent conviction that having become an expert on the European

politics of the early twentieth century has somehow given him
automatic insight into the world politics of the early twenty-first
century as well, he has done a good job of bringing subtlety to the
accepted picture of Kraus, the picture we thought was adequate.

It wasn't. But it wasn't all that untrue either. Kraus, in the end,
might not really have run out of things to say, but he did run out
of hope that they might be relevant. His business had been to criti-
cise high-flown speech that concealed base motives. Now, with the
Nazis mouthing off in all media, he was faced with gutter talk
that concealed nothing, or else with lies so blatant that they were
clearly weapons in verbal form. There was nothing to uncover. Like
Othello's, his occupation was gone. Although Timms has the smaller
facts to say otherwise, the larger fact remains: Kraus spent a lifetime
thinking that euphemistic talk led necessarily to evil, as exemplified
by the Great War, which he had thought the most evil thing
imaginable. But the Nazis, who largely said exactly what they meant
– and even their euphemisms were meant to be decoded as the threat
of murder – brought an evil even worse than that. Though it's a
conclusion Timms doesn't reach, his facts reach it for him: Kraus
had been wrong from the start.

This, however, is a conclusion we should not reach too early.
Today, there is no excuse for failing to see that the avowedly irrational
doesn't yield to reason. Kraus had every excuse, because total irrationality was not yet in charge of a modern European state. Even
before the Great War broke out, Kraus had ample cause to think
that he was already dealing with enough madness to keep him busy.
Kraus was a Jew, but if he had not sought baptism in 1911 he
would have faced a lot of closed doors. He wanted those doors to
be open. He wasn't against the Austro-Hungarian social order, he
merely wanted it to be less stupid, and indeed it wasn't until quite
late in the war that he began blaming the Empire for having driven
its various constituent populations into a slaughterhouse. Kraus
preferred to blame the newspapers. He blamed them no less if they
were owned and/or edited by Jews. Indeed he seemed to blame them
more, a fact which left us obliged to deal with the question of Kraus's
anti-Semitism.

Timms deals with it in torrential detail, but seems to be in two
minds when dismissing the usual accusation against Kraus of *jüdische
Selbst-Hass*, Jewish self-hatred. Timms can only partly dismiss it,

because Kraus really did seem to reserve a special virulence for Jewish artists he didn't admire – the list went back to Heine, on whose grave Kraus regularly danced – and really did seem to go out of his way to accuse the Jewish bourgeoisie of money-grubbing, especially if they had taken baptism in order to increase their opportunities. (Kraus found it convenient to forget that he himself was living on an unearned income: it flowed copiously from the family firm in Czechoslovakia, a source that made it inflation-proof.) The question was already omnipresent in Timms's first volume, and in the second volume, which takes up the Kraus story from the end of the First World War, through the disintegration of the old Empire and on into the various phases of the new Austrian republic, the question attains something worse than mere omnipresence: a focused virulence that takes it out of culture and society and puts it into the heart of politics.

Timms might have reached an answer on the subject more easily if he had realised, going in, that it was Hitler who gave the question new life – or, rather, new potential for death. Before being Jewish became unequivocally an issue of race rather than of religion, any Jew who vilified another might indeed have been aiding and abetting an institutionalised prejudice. But he wasn't complicit in mass murder. Very few Jews, no matter how clever, even dreamed that such a day could ever come. At the turn of the century, Theodor Herzl had guessed it, but most Jews thought he was just a nut. The playwright Arthur Schnitzler had half guessed it, but most Jews thought he was just a playwright. Freud, the master of dreams, never dreamed of it. Kraus, whom Freud admired for his insight, never dreamed of it either. The multi-zero deaths of the First World War were racially unspecific. That there might ever be, in modern Europe, such a thing as a racially specific extermination was unthinkable.

It should be said, however, that Kraus sometimes sounded as if he might be trying to think of it. In 1916 Kraus wrote a poem naming 'Israel' as the 'cosmic enemy'. You can strain to believe that he was using 'Israel' as a symbolic analogy for 'Germany', but it seems more plausible to take it that by 'Israel' he meant the Jews. And in 1918 Schnitzler was surely right to complain that Kraus, when denouncing the war-profiteers, seemed only to notice them when they were of Jewish origin. The fact awkwardly remains, though, that a Jew could

as yet flirt with anti-Semitism and still convince himself that he was
being merely rhetorical.

For a man nominally at war with rhetoric, this was a strange
flirtation to indulge, but no doubt the causes went deep. It could
have been that like so many Jewish rentier intellectuals living on
incomes they had never had to work for, Kraus just despised the
bourgeoisie for their materialism, and that the bourgeois people
he knew most about were Jews. In Germany during the thirties, the
same lofty distaste for his personal provenance drove Walter Benjamin to become a Marxist, even as the Nazis were busy proving all
around him that their own views on the Jewish question were free of
class bias, in no way theoretical, and immediately effective.

In post-war Austria there were all kinds of contending views
among the Jewish population about who they actually were, how
they fitted into the state, and what kind of state they should favour.
There were even Jews who backed the idea of Austria's joining itself
to Germany (Anschluss) as soon as possible. Kraus never really made
his mind up on the subject of what the state should be. Even as he
lost faith in the ability of the old social order to revive, and began to
favour socialism, he still wasn't sure, under his crisp air of certitude,
that democracy could bring about a reasonable society. Like young
radicals almost fifty years later, he began to nurse a fantasy about
China. In his case there was no sweet smoke involved, but it was the
same pipe-dream. In a letter to his great love, Sidonie Nadherny, he
said 'but really there remains only China.' It scarcely needs saying
that he had no idea of what China had been like, was like then, and
might be like in the future. He just wanted a cloud-cuckoo land to
console him from the stress of living in his actual surroundings.
Sidonie had already gone a long way towards providing him with
that.

The Baroness Sidonie Nadherny von Borutin was elegant, sexy,
clever, and loaded. Her country seat, Schloss Janowitz in Bohemia,
was the full arcadian dream. Kraus was no hick – several great ladies
had been among his mistresses – but he was still pleased by such
lavish access to gracious living at top level, whereas Sidonie, with the
delightful charm of a Euro-aristo bluestocking whose malapropisms
came in three languages, enjoyed having her grammar corrected by
the man who could make her laugh. In private, Kraus had a sweet

nature to ameliorate the biting sarcasm he deployed in public, and
he had the key element of a way with women: he found them
interesting. Under the style and gloss, the baroness had a wanton
nature and Kraus knew how to set it loose on the overnight train
from Vienna to Trieste. Well aware that he was a great man, Sidonie
was as flattered by his attentions as he by hers. Timms began to tell
the story of their long, on-and-off romance in the first volume, but
in the second he could have told us more about how it petered out.
In a work whose chief characteristic is to tell us more than the doctor
ordered on almost every topic, this is an annoying deficiency, because
the romance between Kraus and Sidonie was something much bigger
than a love affair: it was a meeting of history running at two different
speeds.

Sidonie stood for inheritance, for noblesse oblige, for a long-
standing social tradition that contained all its contending forces in
a recognised balance, if not a universal harmony. Kraus stood for
intellectual merit, which, in a rapidly developing political explosion,
was only one of the contending forces, and possibly among the
weakest. Even if the crisis had never come, the two lovers would have
been star-crossed enough. Sidonie was one of the rulers of a Bohemia
with a capital B. Kraus was a different kind of bohemian: no capital
letter. However brilliantly, he lived outside the walls she owned.
There have always been liaisons between the two realms but it works
best if the participants respect each other's individuality even when
their physical union is intense. Sidonie quite liked his possessiveness,
but the day came when she found herself gasping for air.

Kraus somehow overdid it. He got all the love she had to give but
wanted more. The dynamics of the breakdown are hard to specify
because his half of their correspondence is missing. But we should be
careful not to underrate the significance of the part played by Rilke,
who warned Sidonie, at a time when she might have been considering
marriage to Kraus, that Kraus was essentially a stranger. Possibly
Rilke, a schmoozer *de grand luxe*, had his eye on a solo guest spot at
Janowitz: his talent for scoring free board and lodging from titled
women was up there with his talent for poetry. But there can be no
doubt what Rilke meant by his warning word '*fremd*'. He meant that
Kraus was a Jew. Timms is well aware of this, but doesn't make
much of it. And possibly it doesn't tell you much about Kraus and

Sidonie, who, after all, went on being loving friends. But it does tell you an awful lot about Rilke.

And Sidonie's tolerance for what Rilke said tells you an awful lot about the insidious prevalence of anti-Semitism even among the enlightened international *beau monde*. There is no reason to think that mass murder would ever have got started anywhere in Europe if the Nazis hadn't come to power in Germany. But the Nazis, on their way up, had a lot of prejudice to draw upon, and it doesn't need a very big minority to look like a majority when it comes parading down the street. Military force transferred to civilian life was the revolutionary new element that would eventually paralyse conventional political expression and Kraus's critique along with it. After the war, Kraus realised almost as soon as Hitler did that if the war's unfettered violence were to be unleashed in peacetime politics, private armies could enforce a new and criminal legality. Unlike Hitler, however, he had little idea of what to do about it. He can scarcely be blamed for that. Apart from the psychopaths, hardly anybody had. Sticking with the old legality looked like the only civilized option. The realisation that the civilised option, even with a professional army at its command, had little hope of prevailing against the uncivilised one was slow to dawn. By the time it did, the sun had set. Comprehension came after the fact.

Kraus saw the menace, however, and should be respected for his insight. From 1923 onwards he had no doubts that the Nazis were out to wreck everything. He just had trouble believing that they could. On the eve of the First World War, Kraus had said 'violence is no subject for polemic, madness no subject for satire.' Here was a new and madder violence, a reign of terror. When it came to power in Germany, in 1933, Kraus was faced more acutely than ever with the question of what form of government in Austria might stave it off. His Social Democrat admirers were horrified when he failed to condemn the authoritarianism of Dollfuss, but Kraus was choosing the lesser of two evils: a choice that evil always demands we make, revealing itself in the demand.

In his long paper 'Third Walpurgis Night', Kraus pilloried the Social Democrats for not realising that only Dollfuss's illiberal measures could keep the Nazis out. Timms gives a long and valuable analysis of 'Third Walpurgis Night' – it was the speech about the

Nazis that Kraus gave after saying they had left him speechless –
but doesn't make enough out of the fact that Kraus never published
it. It was meant to appear as a special issue of *Die Fackel*, but it
didn't. In effect, Kraus was already retreating from his public role.
After the assassination of Dollfuss, he gave up altogether.

He was through with politics. The sophisticated reasoning of a
lifetime had come down to the elementary proposition that anything
was better than the Nazis. After Kraus's death, the plebiscite that
Schuschnigg called for would probably have shown that the majority
of Austria's population thought the same. Aware of this, Hitler
terrorised Schuschnigg into calling off the plebiscite, and the Nazis
duly marched in. A lot of them were already there. Austrian citizens
put on swastika arm-bands and set about their vengeful business.
Kraus was lucky enough to breathe his last before they took power
but he already knew that his long vigilance over the use of language
hadn't changed a thing.

The dying Kraus could congratulate himself that he had at least,
at last, seen things clearly. He had discovered the limited effectiveness
of telling people they are fanatics when they think fanaticism to be
a virtue. The full force of totalitarian irrationality had become plain
to him: the real reason why 'Third Walpurgis Night', *pace* Timms,
was not only unpublished, but incoherent. It was a piece of writing
that knew that it was useless. Kraus might have reached the same
conclusion about all his previous satirical writings had he lived long
enough. His German equivalent, Kurt Tucholsky, had the same
trouble sinking to the occasion. Asked why he had not said more
about the Nazis, he said, 'You can't shoot that low.'

In exile, before he committed suicide, Tucholsky was heard to
wonder whether being satirical about the Weimar Republic had ever
been a particularly good idea, in view of what was coming next. But
even the brightest people – in fact especially them, and especially
those who were Jews – had been slow to form a view of what was
coming next until it actually came. Even then, some of them still
couldn't believe it. Rational people expect rational outcomes. In
exile in London, Freud said in a letter that there was still a chance
the Catholic Church would straighten the Nazis out. Not long ago
I heard that letter read aloud, at a literary soirée in his Hampstead
house. If one of the great analysts of the human mind was capable of

that degree of wishful thinking, we can only imagine what drove him to it. But imagining that, of course, is still the hardest thing.

The First World War had confirmed Kraus in his pacifism, but by the time he died he knew that peace, in the face of Hitler, had ceased to be credible as a principle, and could be espoused merely as a desirable state of affairs. He had been blind-sided by events, but at least he changed his mind. Many of his admirers were to prove less flexible. Kraus preceded Orwell in the notion that the lying language of capitalist imperialism was the cause of all the world's evils. Orwell also was obliged to change his mind in the light of events, but once again there were epigones who never gave up on the idea: it was too attractive as a catch-all explanation. And there is something to it, after all. But the idea has an imperialism of its own, which we can now see most clearly expressed in the patronising assumption that nobody would behave irrationally unless driven to it by the dominant West, with America to the forefront. In its extreme form, this mass delusion of the intellect comes up with brain-waves like the one about President Bush having arranged the attack on the World Trade Centre. Since it was always clear that President Bush was barely capable of arranging to recite his own name with the words in the right order, it seems a bizarre notion.

It is quite possible to imagine Kraus having a fun time with Bush's use of language, although first it would have to be translated into German, and before that it would have to be translated into English. Commentators who amuse themselves today with the verbal output of Bush are following Kraus. If Kraus were here, he might point out that their target is a sitting duck. Kraus, before Orwell and even before H. L. Mencken, was the ancestor of many of our best sceptics, and almost all of our best bloggers. (The blogger technique of glossing some absurdity highlighted in a mainstream publication was what Kraus did in every issue of *Die Fackel* and even in his enormous play *The Last Days of Mankind*, which consisted almost entirely of citations from newspapers and periodicals.) But his biographer, who has gained a dangerous authority by the sheer magnitude of his labours, takes a lot on himself when he assumes that Kraus would have been against armed intervention in the Middle East as an example of our being led into folly by 'propaganda for war'.

The phrase is of Timms's coinage, and rings like pewter. By the time Kraus died, he knew that there could be an even bigger danger in propaganda for peace. Some of the brightest people in Europe, up to and including Bertrand Russell, preached non-violence up to and beyond the day Hitler invaded Poland. The British Labour Party, sitting in opposition to the Conservatives, denounced fascism but also denounced any proposed armed opposition to it as warmongering. In service to the great analyst of cliché, Timms is hampered not only by his Cultural Studies jargon (the leaden word 'discourse' riddles the text) but by an untoward propensity for not spotting what a current cliché is. The two drawbacks are connected, by his tin ear. Kraus, whom Timms tacitly invites to join in the widespread practice of putting jokey quotation marks around the phrase 'war on terror', might have pointed out that the quotation marks are a cliché in themselves, helping as they do to disguise a brute reality: terrorists are at war with us, and don't care who they kill. The reason terrorists don't use those risible cosmetic terms of ours such as 'collateral damage' is that they not only have no intention of sparing the innocent, they have no more desirable target in mind.

The terrorist can talk a pure language: it's purely violent, but still pure. His opponent is bound to equivocate, and sound silly doing so. That was the point Kraus missed because it had not yet become apparent by contrast with something worse. A liberal democracy, of any kind or degree, is bound to deal in hypocrisy and lies, simply because it has a measure of real politics, and is not unified and simplified by an ideology. Totalitarian irrationalism can say exactly what's on its mind. Hitler had genocide on his mind, and said so. But only his nuttiest colleagues believed he would actually do it. Samantha Power, in her excellent book *Genocide: A Problem from Hell*, reached a conclusion she didn't want to reach, as the best analytical books so often do. After showing that no genocidal government in the twentieth century had ever been stopped except by armed intervention, she reluctantly concluded that the armed intervention usually had to be supplied by the United States.

Those among us who sincerely believe that the Iraqis are killing each other in fulfilment of an American genocidal plan might think that her conclusion is no longer true. We would have to ignore the implicit opinion of the eleven million Iraqi adults who voted in the last election, but most of us would rather do that than be taken for suckers. The Vietnam War dulled the Stars and Stripes in our eyes.

But Power's idea was certainly still true when Kraus was alive. And there can be no question that he would have eventually spelled out the same conclusion himself. In effect, he had already reached it. In 1930 he published a piece called 'SOS USA' predicting that America would have to step in if Europe were to be saved. And in 1933 he renewed the provision in his passport to include travel to the USA. Timms, who makes little of that development, could safely have made more. He could have said, for example, that in making of itself a refuge so difficult to reach, America had abetted the efforts of the maniacs. It would have been true, or at any rate half true.

Kraus had no particular love for America – it wasn't China – and he definitely overestimated what America would have been able to do in the short term, when its armed forces were still considerably inferior even to those of Czechoslovakia. But he guessed how the balance of forces was shaping up. Can there be bad violence and good violence? But of course there can. It's a tragic perception, though, and the day is always sad when a comic perception must give way to it. Kraus had a comprehensive sensitivity to all the abuses of society. Injustice angered him. He was way ahead of the game on questions of race. Nobody ever wrote more powerfully against capital punishment. Despite his famous pronouncement about the fish that fought its way ashore, he understood what women were facing, and why they had to fight. He was their champion. He was a serious man, and a piercing satire was his weapon. But it worked only because he was funny. And then, first gradually and then suddenly, being funny wasn't enough.

Australian Literary Review, March 2007

Postscript

When Kraus was alive there was no need for a word like 'media' because the press was the main thing, with radio only just on its way up. Had he been reborn into the television age, he would have had a vastly increased range of mendacity to debunk. In the 1970s, when I began reviewing television, I was well aware that I was following in his footsteps, and since that time his attitude has become universal. The main reason that his name now means so little outside the German-speaking countries is that an implacable scepticism towards the media onslaught seems a self-evident requirement: nobody intelligent thinks any other way. It would be an unwarranted assumption, however, to suppose that if Kraus were here now he would agree with what the majority of professional sceptics think, or even find them sceptical enough. He was a pioneer in his suspicion of power, but he lived long enough to realize that the only answer to the force of the irrational is a democratic state with a realistic determination to defend its liberties. Edward Timms is symptomatic in his confident retroactive prediction of what Kraus might have said today. Kraus might well have said, for example, that few official statements coming out of Washington in the last ten years, even those that stumbled from the lips of the second President Bush, have ever attained quite the lethal fatuity of Osama bin Laden's *fatwa* of 1998. He wouldn't have been able to read it in Arabic, but his analysis of the German translation could have been scathing. The consensus that the Western democracies are responsible for any threat aimed at them might not have convinced him.

JOHN BAYLEY'S DAILY BREAD

Collected under the fitting title *The Power of Delight*, forty years of John Bayley's book reviews have given us a book almost too rich to review. Where to start? Bayley himself at one point conjures the threat of 'reviewer's terror, a well-known complaint like athlete's foot.' Tell me about it, mutters the reviewer's reviewer. There are more than six hundred pages in the book, and after reading it this reviewer finds that he has made almost four hundred notes. Every reviewer knows that, for a thousand-word review, a mere ten notes are enough to induce paralysis. So either this is going to be a forty-thousand-word review, or there will have to be a winnowing. It could start with a mass crossing-out of all the phrases and sentences transcribed merely because they are excellent. Since we don't seem to need William Gerhardie's novels any more, do we really need what Bayley says about Gerhardie's life? 'Like most butterflies, he was far too tough to be broken on a wheel.' But no, it's too good: we do need it. And maybe we need Gerhardie's novels as well, if they could inspire a critic to a sentence as neat as that.

In this respect, if in no other, Bayley resembles the more slavish of the old-time bookmen memorialised by John Gross in *The Rise and Fall of the Man of Letters*. Hacking away week after week, they either enjoyed most of what they were force-fed or else they choked on its abundance. George Gissing was only the most famous victim of piecework literary journalism. Others did worse than fail: they succeeded, earning the tiny immortality of termites. For them, delight was compulsory. Bayley's delight is compulsive: a different thing. He revels in everything that has been written well, and he himself writes so well that he adds to the total. Reviewing a writer's biography, he reads, or re-reads, the other books by the biographer, every book by the biographee, and brings in all the other relevant writers he can think of. Talking about a novel, he has not only read all the other novels by the same novelist, he has read all the novels by other novelists that are remotely like this novel. (Sometimes very remotely: the resemblance of *The Unbearable Lightness of Being* to *Northanger Abbey* hadn't occurred to me before, and I wonder if it will again.) He sees no end of connections, but the best thing about them is that they are not theoretical.

Apart from his intellectual objections, the main reason Bayley has no time for literary theory is that he is absorbed in literary practice. Praising Fred Kaplan's biography of Dickens, Bayley endorses Kaplan's 'all-around attention,' adding that the understanding of Dickens is 'probably best served . . . not by theories about him but by the facts – all the swarming lot of them.' Among the swarming lot are the facts about how the good Jew Riah got into *Our Mutual Friend*. It was because a deputation of London's Jewish citizens had pointed out that the bad Jew Fagin in *Oliver Twist* had worked mischief in their lives. Kaplan supplied that fact. But Bayley, with a typically resonant epithet, supplies the further relevance. 'Dickens promised like royalty to put the matter right.' The word 'royalty' conveys an insight, based on real events in Dickens's life. Risen to great rank, Dickens had dispensation to bestow. The author's achieved position in the real world, and the other world he created while occupying that position, were in complex interplay. Social duty and artistic impulse didn't always coincide – Riah, a better role model than Fagin, is a far less interesting character – but there is no understanding Dickens without acknowledging the connection. Concern with such a thing puts Bayley back not just beyond Cultural Studies (in which there are no authors, only texts) but beyond the New Criticism (in which the text tells all). The latest and perhaps among the last in a native line of artist-critics that stretches back through V. S. Pritchett, Cyril Connolly and Desmond McCarthy by way of Matthew Arnold to Hazlitt and even further, he exemplifies the old tradition of socio-literary commentary, with all its benefits and dangers. The chief danger is to lapse into the sweet distraction of gossip. But the chief benefit is so valuable that we would be foolish not to welcome such a lavish demonstration of what it is. The literary past comes alive, sheds all the schemata that have been imposed on it, and teems with contingency, like now. The effect is of a glass-bottomed bucket dipped into the water beside the boat, so that the tourists can suddenly see the living colours and incessant traffic of the reef beneath.

Dickens is a good place to start with Bayley, who is fully familiar with everything Dickens wrote, takes his supreme importance for granted, and can draw on the perceptions of every scholar who has done the same. Humphry House is commended, as is John Carey. (The professor's son, Leo Carey, is the able curator of this book, which must have taken some curating: Bayley, by all reports, was never a man to keep orderly files of anything, least of all his own articles.) Dr Leavis is duly twitted for ever having held the 'unreal' opinion that Dickens, except for *Hard Times*, was a mere entertainer. Leavis revised that opinion later, but it was amazing that he should ever have advanced it. Elsewhere, Bayley is generously ready to concede that the irascible Leavis could say pertinent things, but generosity exceeds itself when Bayley says that 'attitudes have changed a good deal since then.' They have only changed back to what they were before Leavis made his bizarre strictures. Not only was Chesterton, whom Bayley mentions, fully aware of Dickens's true stature, so was Shaw. Bayley doesn't mention Shaw at all in that context, but Shaw mentioned Dickens habitually. Shaw assumed that the readers of his Prefaces would recognize his profuse allusions to the Dickens characters. It could be daunting if you didn't, as I well remember; but there was no mistaking Shaw's love of Dickens, which exceeded even his love of Wagner. Many years later, when I finally got round to reading the capital works of Dickens instead of merely pontificating about them, it was because Shaw's enthusiasm had niggled in my conscience too long. If I had not done so then, Bayley's enthusiasm would make me do it now. The personal theme is worth touching on because one of the things reviewing does, or should do, is to transmit an appreciation, sometimes to the point of sending an ignoramus to the bookshop.

Or even back to Trollope. For those of us to whom Trollope matters but not a lot, Bayley sends the message that he should matter a lot. How did we convince ourselves, after reading half a dozen of Trollope's novels, that the other umpteen could be safely put off until we had overcome the same impression about Balzac? Bayley synthesises the answer from the facts assembled in three different books about Trollope that he is reviewing. Trollope damaged his own reputation by being too honest in his autobiography. The picture he painted of himself, getting up early in the morning to knock off a few new chapters before lunch, gave even those readers who wolfed down his books a chance to belittle him as an artist. Tolstoy adored him and later so did Yeats, but a long roster of eminent readers has never been enough to get him taken seriously. Bayley thinks the very idea of 'seriousness' is a blind alley anyway, but he particularly objects to it when it draws attention away from what he regards as any writer's best tactic, to present an attractive surface while delving deep, to grow a pleasure garden over the mine. In his view, 'serious-minded persons from Dr Johnson to Dr Leavis' were bound to miss the point about Sterne: if he hadn't been a court jester for the *beau monde*, he would never have been able to tell so much truth. The aristos were less shockable than the upcoming bourgeoisie. Bayley takes the same line with the novelist at the apex of all his admirations, Jane Austen: treating matters of life and death in a manner that did *not* match their solemnity, she proved that 'light is the best foil for the dark.' We could add that Henry James thought he was doing the same thing in *The Awkward Age*: he honestly believed that the style he chose was a babbling brook, even though it strikes us as an invitation to suck up a sand dune through a straw. But before adding our own observations on the point, we had better deal with some of Bayley's. The idea of a seductive context for profundity looks a bit less useful when George Eliot leaves him cold. Once again he has read all of her and all about her. Edmund Wilson, notoriously, reached his harsh judgement about *Middlemarch* without having read it. Bayley knows what he is talking about, but that just makes what he actually says about her more of a poser. 'The fate of lawgivers and sibyls, in literature if not in life, is to have no lasting influence.'

Well, *Middlemarch* still has an influence on some of us. Even if all you remember about Casaubon is his Key to All Mythologies, you have remembered a powerful symbol for busy futility, and if you remember that his still-born summa was 'as endless as a scheme for joining the stars', you have equipped yourself with a pretty good line to mutter the next time you make an unassisted attempt to update the software on your laptop. Those of us who will always need instruction in goodness are bound to go on recalling Dorothea once we have read about her, and to recall also that the story of her example is why the clinching line about the 'unvisited tombs' has its plangent force. Such an impact on a modern reader sounds like a lasting influence to me. What was Bayley expecting her to have a lasting influence on? The Novel? But his preference for talking about all those hundreds of considerable novels in all languages, rather than about that abstraction The Novel, which exists only in the meta-language of theory, is one of the best things about him. So we quarrel with him on behalf of his best self, using his own principles to do so. There are things in this book that can make you fume. What would John Bayley say about them? Wait a second: he wrote them.

In fact, Bayley's fondness for paradox can carry him away. Usually it carries him away in the right direction. It's an unexpected but useful thing to say about Keats that he didn't really want to write some of the poems we most admire. He would have preferred to avoid what was then thought of as 'women's' romance. But, says Bayley, when Keats got his genius fully in line with his intentions, the result was only 'Hyperion'. Keats did better when 'The Eve of St Agnes' trapped him into the kind of emotional turmoil that women wanted to hear about. Bayley is slyly funny about the good Madeline's unlikely fate at the hands of Porphyro the noble voyeur. 'Keats has boxed himself comically in . . . by his insistence that his hero make love, like an incubus, to a sleeping girl, and without waking her up: an undeniably difficult feat, even if the girl were not, as Madeline is, a virgin.' Good on the actualities of sex, Bayley knows that not all of them are physical. He sounds more paradoxical than he really is when he defends the 'sex in the head' of John Cowper Powys against D. H. Lawrence's supposedly piercing idea that a romantic longing could only be a deception. In our love lives, it's 'Romance' (Powys's capital letter and Bayley's quotation marks) that carries the real erotic charge, although Lawrence might have been right to think that it's also what does the damage. In another part of the forest, Bayley calls Stendhal's treatise on love abstractionist, and his women characters 'pillow-dreams'. Too much sex in the head, perhaps? But taken either way, this point about the material and spiritual in carnal knowledge is a focal point for argument about almost every novelist we care for. It isn't for Conrad, whom Bayley admires, but it is for Hardy, whom he admires even more, and for Tolstoy, whom he admires with a discovering purity reminiscent of Matthew Arnold's when he read Tolstoy in French translation and wrote the pioneering articles in English about the Russian's greatness. Bayley asks the question about

human passion that we can't help turning to our own use. What
exactly happened to Anna Karenina and Vronsky? Did they lose a
dream when it came true? Quite often we get annoyed with him for
forgetting to ask it. Shouldn't he have seen that Casaubon is Dorothea's Karenin? Isn't the agony of Scobie in *The Heart of the Matter* a
genuine possibility in any man's conscience, and not just a dilemma
cooked up by a Catholic apologist who is out to scare us? If Bayley's
book, glittering with perceptions, sometimes seems as big as a small
universe, this oscillating point about idealism and desire is one of the
worm-holes that take you everywhere in it: a scheme that really does
join the stars.

Sometimes the angle of approach is so unexpected that it spoils
the party, like a waiter who overdoes the fancy footwork and delivers
the soup into your lap. Evelyn Waugh, we are told, was short on
humour. 'But humour in fiction is about an interest in real people,
and Waugh had no such interest.' One is reminded of Stephen
Potter's classic ploy for reviewers: if an author is famous for a
particular characteristic, accuse him of not having enough of it.
Speaking as one whose spirits can be revived at the mere thought of
little Lord Tangent's incremental demise in *Decline and Fall*, I can
only say that I think Evelyn Waugh was short of humour the way
that Sir Richard Branson is short of confidence. But what, the reader
sputters, about the young man who vomits into the room instead of
out; and Mrs Stitch's little car going down the lavatory steps; and
Apthorpe's thunder box; and . . . the list goes on like moments from
Dickens. Isn't Mrs Melrose Ape up there with Mrs Jellyby in *Bleak
House*? You could deny that Waugh had amiability – his version
of *Nicholas Nickleby*'s Ninetta Crummles, the Infant Phenomenon,
would have been a lot nastier – but to deny him a comic gift sounds
like comedy in itself. Such moments from Bayley prove that the
knack for paradox should always be set to fire single shots, and never
switched to automatic. His indulgence of it, mercifully infrequent, is
the only way he ever reminds you of those desperate commentators,
omnipresent now in our multiple media outlets, who must always
advance an outlandish opinion because they don't write well enough
to make a reasonable opinion interesting. Since Bayley writes more
than well enough to advance reasonable opinions indefinitely, you
sometimes wonder how he could let the Devil get into him. Perhaps,
on occasion, even he gets bored.

Or perhaps the Devil gets into Bayley when God gets into art. Bayley much prefers Anthony Powell to Evelyn Waugh. Quoted almost as often as Auden, Powell is treated as a friend throughout the book, and clearly revered as an artist, even when the critic likes some of his novels more than others. (Bayley favours the peace-time volumes of the *Music of Time* sequence over the war-time ones, thus reversing the usual preference: the reader is left to decide whether the reviewer might be saying this because too many people said the opposite.) Bayley correctly points out that Powell's chief concern, unlike Waugh's, was less with the landed gentry than with the higher bohemia and its population of misfits. Powell would never have bothered to revisit Brideshead, even though he lived in a house quite like it, if on a smaller scale. But probably Bayley's main reason for preferring Powell to Waugh is that he prefers humanism to mysticism. He just doesn't think that art and religion make a good match, especially if the religion is an adopted one, as in the case of Waugh – and the case of Graham Greene, by whom he is enthralled even less. Without precisely calling those two eminent Catholic converts perpetrators of a put-up job, he makes it clear that he thinks their religiosity detracts from their scope of vision rather than adding to it. This emphasis on Bayley's part will ring a bell with anyone who thinks that not even Dante was able fully to subject his human comedy to divine judgment, and couldn't have written it if he had. A work of art exists to occupy the whole space between tumultuous reality and the artist's attempt to give it shape, with no supervening providence to nullify the order of what has been achieved. Bayley is at his very best when he is pushing his insistence that the mundane is sublime enough. ('Boots and shoes', 'the detail and the dailiness': the phrases keep on coming.) He is surely right. Art, by making bearable sense of the world, is out after religion's job, which is probably why no religion in its fundamentalist phase has ever liked it. Art is its own ideal state, which is probably why Plato didn't like it either.

Plato wanted the poets thrown out of the ideal Republic. For Bayley, they are the way in, the entrance to the only habitable civil order, which can never be ideal. Poetry comes first and fiction follows. The poetry of Pushkin, as you might expect from a critic who would be well known if he had written about nothing else, is the key subject of the book's Russian section, whose wealth we should not allow to daunt us just because he can read the language. Speaking about the Russian poets from Pushkin through to Akhmatova, Tsvetaeva and Pasternak, he is equipped to assess them right down to the level of their technique, and he can do the same for those prose stylists who will always present difficulties to a translator because they either inhabit the musicality of their language or else gain in effect by deliberately damping it down: Gogol, Turgenev, Bunin, Chekhov, Babel. Modest about his attainments as a linguist, Bayley would not want us to be astonished by his capacities with Russian. We should try to agree with him. Though it is a full-time job to speak any language except our own well enough to stay out of gaol, we ought to expect from any critic a reading knowledge of the standard European languages, and Russian would have been one of those if things had gone differently in 1917: it took the Revolution to stem the onrushing force of Russian culture, and even as things turned out, the accumulated achievement up to that time demands by right as close a familiarity as possible. Bayley would be the first to admit that only a native speaker can get to the heart of, say, Gogol, whose babyishly playful verbal inventiveness was at the source of a torrential imagination that not even his most madcap works could fully find room for. (Gogol convinced his mother that he had invented the steam engine: a pertinent fact that Bayley, for once, fails to record.) But our critic reads the language well enough to know whether Gogol's 'primal power of creation' has been well translated or not. So deep a feeling for the historic background, when it comes to assessing post-Revolutionary literature, gives Bayley both an advantage and a drawback. The advantage is that he can get right in amongst the details of the professional jostling that goes on between writers even when the state is bearing down on all of them equally: Pasternak, we learn, was daunted by Mayakovsky's 'zany felicities'. The drawback is that Bayley tends to share, or seem to share, Isaiah Berlin's genial belief that Russian culture, just because it was not entirely stamped out, somehow came through. The power of delight trumps the power of disgust.

Not that Bayley is politically insensitive to the twentieth-century European disaster in its awful multiplicity. Nobody has written better about such an immediate victim as Bruno Schulz, or such an eventual victim as Paul Celan; and about an exile such as Witold Gombrowicz he gets into the secret of how a modern Pole could echo Conrad by taking his country's history of dislocation with him into a world of his own. A pity, here, that Bayley's piece is mainly about an English translation of Gombrowicz's pre-war surrealist novel *Ferdydurke*, rather than about the many wonderful volumes of his *Journal* and *Varia* that until recently were still coming out in French year after year. Holed up in Buenos Aires while his lost homeland went to Hell two different ways in succession, Gombrowicz lost interest in the Novel, including his own novels, and even lost interest in any form of art: he wanted a formless art, a genre beyond the genres. He came to think that you could just write, as long as you wrote well enough. It's a view that Bayley himself exemplifies. His essay about another displaced Polish-speaker, the Lithuanian Czeslaw Milosz, would be my pick for the most thrilling item in the collection, perhaps the best place to start in a book you can start anywhere. He exults at Milosz's confident readiness to work in all the literary fields, as poet, critic, historian and philosopher. 'By writing in every form, he writes virtually in one: and he instructs in all.'

But poetry is where it starts, even for Milosz. 'The self in his poetry is not impersonal but effortlessly manifold.' Poetry is language at its closest to the world, and incorporates automatically an acceptance that the things of this world are actually there. For Bayley, Barthes's confident insistence that 'the fact can only exist linguistically, as a term of discourse' is a sign of madness from the one theorist he regards as even half-way sane. He might have quoted T. E. Hulme in rebuttal: 'Philosophy is about people in clothes, not about the soul of man.' Bayley is good about people in clothes. Wordsworth's poems 'are like one's parents' clothes – always out of fashion.' But our critic, an accomplished poet himself when he was young, has the tools of technical analysis to tell you why Wordsworth will always be current, and why Tennyson deservedly became 'a pop star, one of the most successful and famous ever.' Bayley can tell whether his subject poets have the palpable earth for a launch-pad when they lift off for higher realms. That useful emphasis runs out of road only when he gets to John Ashbery. According to his own principles, Bayley ought to be powerfully delighted by the later Ashbery's unflagging determination to blend all of America's vernacular tones into 'the natural voice of the contingent present,' a nice way of describing a slow avalanche of verbal hamburger. But scepticism shines through the praise. 'Ashbery in his own way often *sounds*

memorable . . .' The italics are a deliberate giveaway. Ashbery is out
to mean everything by saying anything, and Bayley clearly suspects
that the attempt is in danger of adding up to nothing, because
there is nothing to keep in your head. Finally Bayley believes that
all writing should aim to be remembered. It can't happen, but the
possibility should be there. It is there everywhere in this fabulous
flea-market of a book, which might have the additional merit of
finally putting an end to the tediously recurring contention that book
reviews should never be collected. Book reviewers who say that are
right about themselves, but couldn't be more wrong about a man
like this.

TLS, May 27, 2005

Postscript

John Bayley was always too modest about his qualifications as a poet.
I had read a lot of his criticism before I even found out that he had
once written any poetry at all. One day at lunch Kingsley Amis gave
me a copy, which he himself had typed out, of a poem by the young
Bayley about *Salammbô*. I found it brilliant: rhythmically stately,
packed with meaning, a lyrical argument of fully mature authority.
Plenty of critics have written poetry in their youth but seldom on
that level. It was a huge gift to repudiate. Similarly he was too shy
about the work he put into learning to read languages. He should
have said outright that he had found time to do so only because he
hadn't wasted time with literary theory. He could also have pointed
out that the London literary world was enfeebled by its provincialism.
One of the heroes of my book *Cultural Amnesia* is the above-
mentioned Witold Gombrowicz. Only in London would a reviewer
have reinforced his demonstration of my book's frivolity by jokily
supposing that Gombrowicz might be a made-up name, and only in
London would a literary editor have let him do it. Gombrowicz
didn't go through all that, and create so much, in order to have his
very existence questioned in the *Sunday Times* Culture section. The
Culture section! If Bayley had taken his proper place as a whip-
cracking literary ringmaster, he might have kept the boys up to the
mark. But he was too nice for that.

KINGSLEY AND THE WOMEN

In his early role as Lucky Jim, Kingsley Amis declared the awkward essence of his personality. 'I'm the boredom detector.' That ability, or affliction, qualified all his other propensities, even the one for multi-targeted amorous desire. In Zachary Leader's long, thorough and generally judicious new biography, its hero's spasmodic quest for emotional satisfaction is rarely out of the picture. The novelist, poet, critic, teacher and bibulous clubman we more or less frequently meet, but the man with sex on his mind we seldom escape. Journalists understandably find this material an alluring compost in which to burrow.

But even here they tend to miss the spiritual element, signalled by how easily the universal lover – Roger Micheldene in *One Fat Englishman* was one of these, and clearly a disgusted portrait of his author – could be put off by an ill-considered remark from the object of his quest. In missing that, they miss half the secret: it wasn't just an itching id that made him restless. The truly dedicated bedroom operator is seldom daunted by a cliché emanating from the mouth he longs to kiss. With Kingsley Amis it was obviously otherwise. A word out of order from the fair face on the pillow could set him reaching for his trousers soon afterwards. It was touch and go.

The man who feared the dud phrase as he feared the dark night is now beyond the first threat, if not the second. But if he could hear himself being talked about in his absence, he would find, to his horror, that his very name has become a cause of boredom. Dunces of restricted growth are hopping in a circle around his tomb, singing their tiny songs. One can only hope that this condition will be temporary. Prominent literary reputations quite commonly lapse for a while after death, but it is mercifully uncommon that a prominent literary reputation should be entirely replaced by impertinent gossip. Quite a lot of the first reviewers of this book were so caught up in its anti-hero's supposed moral turpitude that they seemed to forget the extent by which his literary achievements outstripped their own. The most eminent of them, Professor Carey, seemed to forget that there had been any literary achievements at all.

In his time, Professor Carey had called *Lucky Jim* a funny book; or had at least implied that it was, by saying that its author's autobiography, *Memoirs*, was his funniest book since the one that made his name. Professor Carey, a true wit in his own right, is well aware that a funny book is always an achievement. But in his review of this biography – a review that amounted to placing a corpse under arrest and charging it with a misspent life – no achievements were mentioned. At least that omission left room for a scrupulous and influential critic to remind himself, at some future time, that there might be beginners listening, and that the starting point of a critical essay should therefore always be the subject's gifts, and not his crimes. If the subject did not possess the first, there would be no point discussing the second. One lesser critic – he had initials instead of a Christian name, and I have forgotten his surname – managed to do even worse than not mention Amis's work. He presumed, in the yellow light of all this sulphurous information about the author's moral transgressions, to reassess the work, pointing out that Amis's poetry, in particular, was a glacial reflection of his heartless attitude towards women.

This reassessment was so perfectly fatuous that it wasn't even boring. The general assumption among the reviewers that the man was more real than what he wrote should have been detectable even by them as the sort of platitude that drove the choleric latter-day Kingers back to a bottle already three-quarters empty: being forced to inhabit a world in which literary journalists could promulgate such tedious opinions was probably one of the chief reasons that he drank. But it was beyond boring, it was bizarre, to suggest that the cold view of women in some of Amis's poems reflected a view that Amis actually held. In the Dai Evans poems, Amis finds Evans reprehensible both in his behaviour and in his mentality. We could tell that just by the way those particular poems are written, even if there were not so many other poems by the same author ('A Bookshop Idyll', for example) to prove that he valued the integrity of women, and that he thought any man in physical thrall to his mental condition as a roué was in no great shape to lead a worthwhile life.

Amis's poems about sexuality continually reveal that the obligation to behave well, as against the difficulties of doing so posed by a libido about whose power he felt equally obliged to be realistic, was one of his abiding concerns. Far from being detached from the question of sexual morality, his poetry had almost no other subject. His depth on the matter, and his capacity to dramatise an inner conflict and make it vivid through his mastery of phrase and rhythm, would have made him, had his friend Philip Larkin never existed, a good contender for the title of the most accomplished and least self-satisfied poet of his generation. But of course there was a connection there: self-satisfaction can be defeated only by taking thought, and without thought there is no real technique, only the making of patterns. In Amis's poetry, for all its formal virtuosity, there is not even one instance of a pattern being made just for the sake of it, and the same might be said of his best prose. The sure sign of his greatness as a comic writer is that nothing interested him less than mere word-play. If he ever gave into it, it was a sign that he was on the ropes, and that his peculiar gift for self-examination had been protectively switched off, perhaps through fear of what it might reveal.

Obeying the rule that we should start from the work, we can start at that very point, and observe that at the height of his art he was always worried about himself, and especially on the level where we might think he was insouciant. In the early part of the book, at Oxford and then in Swansea, we find him chasing women, and frequently catching up with them. In Princeton he caught up with all of them. If he hadn't got Hilly pregnant he might not have married her, but having done both those things he found his appetite for further adventure unblunted. The title phrase of *That Uncertain Feeling* was another way of saying that he found it hard to answer for his actions when there were bright and beautiful women around. In academic life they were always around. Hilly seemed to understand, thereby throwing petrol on the fire. We might disapprove of all this but we should remember that we would have difficulty disapproving as much as he did. It's a constant theme of the early novels. In *Lucky Jim*, Bertrand, the high-scoring tail-chaser, is the villain. In *Take a Girl Like You*, Patrick Standish is less repellent than Bertrand but even more dangerous, because in the end he is capable of taking Jenny's virginity while she is drunk: i.e. he rapes her. His urge takes over.

Amis spent a lot of time arguing, in both prose and verse, that an urge should never be allowed to do that. He was against the idea of artist's privileges. He might have been more persuasive on the subject had he always been able to behave well in real life – although he would have been crucially short of inside information – but here again we have something to remember. In real life, it wasn't just a case of him wanting nearly all the women. In the early days, at least, nearly all the women wanted him. He was good looking and he was brilliantly funny. In Princeton there were academic wives who didn't realise that they had been married to a bore until they found themselves in cocktail-fuelled colloquy with the visiting genius. Over they went like nine-pins.

Like most men who have that effect, Amis probably kept a private moral account book in which he gave himself points for all the opportunities he turned down, and used the total to offset how depressingly often he succumbed. There are all kinds of mental tricks such a man can play, but it would be pharisaical on our part to preach as if we could be sure of being abstemious granted the same advantages. Nevertheless we can permit ourselves to echo Amis's belief – evident in all the novels, especially evident in the early novels and vividly evident, throughout his life, in the poetry – that the ungoverned libido was bound to have a wrecking influence, even if everyone involved had joined the circle by consent. The most startling proof of this attitude is in *The Anti-Death League*, where he gives an otherwise virtuous woman a man's promiscuity. She does what all men would do if they could, unless they are candidates to join Plato's Nocturnal Council. She takes on every man she likes the look of. But in the end she agrees to be rescued. We can deduce that Amis thought she needed rescuing. It was a generous conclusion for Amis to reach. After all, he didn't make himself randy, although men who don't suffer from the same affliction can perhaps be forgiven for assuming, in his case, that a trick of fate was a human failing.

A deeper indication of Amis's capacity for self-analysis on the matter of sexual attractiveness is that he was capable of making a subject out of what it might be like not to be attractive: what it would be like, that is, to be not like him. In *Take a Girl Like You*, Jenny Bunn is the fully articulated version of Christine in *Lucky Jim*. Those who thought Christine unreal would have twice the reason to think that of Jenny, but surely, in both cases, the combination of beauty and goodness is not impossible.

You might even say that the beautiful find it easier to be good. It is certainly true to life that Jenny, with her practicality and her sense of fun to go with her looks, would touch the heart of any man, and especially a man like Patrick, who is heartless and knows it. But in the figure of Graham, the decent type who yearns for her hopelessly, Amis pushed analysis into a new area. There had been radiant young lovers in English novels before, from Tom Jones and Sophia Western onwards. And there had been stumbling, hopelessly yearning dim bulbs before: Dickens is full of them. Graham was not even the first of these to bare his soul: Leonard Bast in *Howards End* tells us what it might be like to be a loser. But Graham was the first to bare his soul with eloquence. The scene where Graham tells Jenny what it is like to be a man who has no chance with a girl like her is like nothing else in literature before, and would alone be enough to establish Amis as the moral writer that Dr Leavis said he wasn't. (I was present at the Dickens lecture when Leavis, asserting that Amis had no interest in describing the behaviour of a gentleman, inadvertently defined Amis's central literary interest as exactly that.)

Jenny doesn't want to hear about Graham's despair, and then despises herself for not having wanted to hear. She has perfect moral pitch, but no intention of letting her life be ruined by a quest for justice. In a just world, she would have married Graham. But she wants Patrick. She just doesn't want to sleep with him until they are married. So Patrick, exercising his charmer's privilege, gets in early. To think that Amis does not condemn that privilege, you would have to be dense enough to think that Amis actually approves, in *Girl, 20*, of Sir Roy Vandervane's up-tempo urge to seduce women who get younger twice as fast as he gets older. You would have to think that Amis, when he gives us portraits of men who regard the individuality of women as merely the temporary disguise of a common object, actually endorses that attitude. Instead, he loathed the idea.

He probably made a line out of saying so – sympathy works – but his scorn of the rampant clod was genuine. Leader is good at bringing out how Amis's sensitivity on the subject was one of the very things that made him attractive. Women were interested in him because he found women interesting. Hilly always found him

interesting and would probably never have left him had he not
compelled it. She knew all about his weaknesses but adored him
anyway. And he, despite everything, was basically uxorious and
thought she was the one woman that counted. He thought that early
and he thought it late, but late was too late and much of his life story
that we find truly disturbing happened in the stretch between his two
ménages with Hilly, on the path which at long last led him back to
that fateful fork in the road.

The philanderer often has a better chance of staying married than
the man who is so bowled over by love that he not only marries on
the strength of it, he wrecks his first home when love strikes again.
A measure of how hard Amis was hit by his love for the elegant
and accomplished Elizabeth Jane Howard is that he behaved like an
honest man and changed his circumstances. Finally we don't know
the secret of what brings two people together and keeps them there.
If it was sex, the chances were mathematically slight that Amis had
run into something he had never met before.

What he had run into was romance. The coarse language in
Amis's letters might seem to indicate the opposite of a romantic
propensity, but indicates it so strenuously that it would be wise
to suspect a cover-up. Lucky Jim's interior monologue when he
dances in Christine's arms for the first time (it beats even Larkin's
phrase about 'the wonderful feel of girls') is surely a better testament
of Amis's true feelings. There are good reasons for thinking that
the concept of sex with nothing else to it was foreign to his nature,
and this time there was a lot else to it. The history of the British
Establishment can scarcely be told without due account of how it is
continually replenished by people born outside its walls, but Jane
was an insider: she was the gifted interloper's glittering reward.
On the evidence presented by Leader we are permitted to conclude
that the increasingly illustrious Amis had reached the standard
climacteric where the ascending cultural figure is ready to leave the
vagabond life he has led so far and become a toff.

Not that he wanted to become a Tory: not yet. His politics had
always been on the left. In fact he started out as a Communist, but
his dislike of authority guaranteed that he would not remain in the
party long. His dislike of authority in the army shows up in his short
stories: the title story of *My Enemy's Enemy* is only one example. In
his universities he abominated the prospect of being presided over by

an unfeeling hierarchy. (The abomination is incarnated in Professor Welch, and the precedents for it are outlined by Leader in convincing detail, to the extent that you marvel at Amis's conscientiousness as an academic: how could he have borne the drudgery?) Amis was a natural Labour voter. But he was always wistfully responsive to the prospect of an elect tribe of upper-order males confidently at their ease. (He once told me that he admired the way they were 'not bothered'.) Gore-Urquhart in *Lucky Jim* is one example, and Julian Ormerod in *Take a Girl Like You* would be the moral centre of the book if Jenny wasn't. (It is Ormerod who tells Patrick that he has not behaved like a gentleman.)

Kingers had a soft spot for a gent. Jane was a female gent: noblesse oblige on a pair of killer legs. She had everything, and she could do everything. While independently busy with her own flourishing career, she also knew how to look after him. He liked that idea. It was a bit unfair on Hilly, who had travelled with him over some hard roads. (There are moments early in the book, as Hilly cleans up the widely dispersed kiddy-food while Kingsley marks a towering pile of exam papers, that you wonder if Leader might not be getting it all out of George Gissing.) Hilly was elected by fate to incarnate Cyril Connolly's cruel principle about the woman with whom we share our early struggles rarely being the same woman with whom we wish to share our later successes. Or rather, she was elected by Kingsley. He might have done otherwise. He could have stayed, and kept Jane for a mistress. According to the evidence here, Jane loved him so much she might have settled for that. But he was too moral, or perhaps he was bored.

A book of this length can have few hidden texts, but there is at least one, and it starts with the breaking up of his first marriage. The alteration distorted his life, but he lacked the steel to be unworried. All the subsequent troubles, and a lot of the art left still to be accomplished, flowed from the great man's reluctance to be a complete swine. The born scoundrel never causes more trouble than when he turns sincere. Against his convictions, Amis had taken an artist's privileges, and like most men who unleash such damage he tried to save his conscience by convincing himself that he was facing facts. The disintegration of his family had consequences for the children which Leader explores with tact, but there's enough to make you shake your head. (His predecessor as a biographer, the late Eric Jacobs, though he was rather better than Leader at evoking anything funny, would undoubtedly have been less sensitive about anything that wasn't, so it's a blessing that he is no longer on the scene, from which he departed pursued by the curses of the entire family.) But you might say that Amis's new glory became punishment enough in itself for his having reinforced its outward show with a conspicuous change of wives.

Superficially his circumstances were now ideal, and the book gives ample evidence that the couple were creatively fruitful both separately and together. At the end of the day's work they would read each other what they had written, like Katherine Mansfield and Middleton Murry. Jane, who had a history of accepting burdens and being treated badly, seemed well capable of getting on with her work while doing all the other work as well. Cosseted by a heaven-sent helpmeet cum soul mate, Kingers lived a king's life: nothing was allowed to disturb his concentration. One is reminded of Thomas Mann at home in Munich, where the children had to play at the other end of the garden.

Amis had always been suspicious of the artist who demanded ideal conditions but he knew what they ought to be and was glad enough to accept them when they came. One of his ideal conditions had always been plenty to drink. Jim Dixon dreamed of being able to smoke as much as he wanted. His creator had dreamed of being able to drink as much as he wanted. In his role of squire, Amis made sure that this wish was fulfilled on a scale that it had never been before: there was a keg of upmarket Scotch in his study. All on his own, he had the weekly drinks bill of a whole table at the Garrick Club even before he was elected. After he was, he would get so tight there that he could barely make it to the cab. And this was a man famous for never showing the effects. Visiting him for a long lunch, those of us who were famous for showing them blessed our frailty. With a light head instead of a hollow leg, he would have lasted longer.

The depths of his drinking were achieved after Jane left him, but the bathysphere was well on its way down while she was still there. The low point of his catabasis took time to reach, but the steadily descending trajectory is hard to miss. We don't have to look for it in what seemed to confuse him. We can find it in what he seemed sure of. Though he continued to turn out novels with clearly defined themes, the prose in them – once the initial attraction – became less clearly defined all the time, and eventually, as it was bound to do, this deficiency eroded his comic invention. John Carey was right to say that Amis's style became an instrument for evading meaning instead of conveying it. He might have said 'Amis's style, of all people's.'

All his life, Amis was a stickler for correct English, but the time came when he turned correctness into a kind of spiked truss: his putatively comic prose could hardly walk for its attention to its own detail. By no coincidence (an academic phrase that would have made Amis howl) his attitudes hardened to match the progressive sclerosis of his fictional style. This stylistic petrification did not show up so much in his non-fiction, but that was often because the opinions conveyed by his journalism had become wilfully simplistic. His anti-Communism, for example, became a hunt for reds under the bed. The perpetual dimwit-left consensus will disgust any liberal eventually, but the trick is to reclaim the democratic centre, not to take refuge in the illusion that the traditional right-wing prejudices were a system of thought all along.

Once, Amis had been an effective polemicist, made more so by his winning capacity to disclaim expertise in advance. Now he became an over-confident dogmatist, an advanced instance of what Jean-François Revel identified as the tendency of those who had once believed the wrong thing to claim a monopoly of rectification on the grounds that those who had never believed in it could not have been serious. It was as if Amis had come to find a reasonable position so boring that mania was more interesting. In his long-running friendship and verse-trading double-act with Robert Conquest, the zealot was Kingers, not Conkers. Conquest, whose book *The Great Terror* probably did more than any other single publication from either side of the Iron Curtain to bring down the Soviet Union, was unfailingly polite in controversy. Amis accused honest men of bad faith. This book does not record how thoroughly Amis managed to alienate Karl Miller – who had once given *Take a Girl Like You* one of its most thoughtful notices – by calling him a Communist sympathiser. It might usefully have done so. Miller was only one among many admirers of Amis who were forced to conclude that his public stance had become explicable only by pathology.

Amis the erstwhile enchanter developed a strange capacity to alienate anyone, almost as if he wished to. The notorious incident when he managed to drive Julian Barnes and Pat Kavanagh from the dinner table is recorded here. Pat Kavanagh, who had spent most of her life in protesting exile from apartheid in her home country, was not disposed to hear Amis's late-festering opinions about how the blacks were ruining South Africa. He even developed similar opinions about Jews, though he must have known that this was a form of intellectual suicide.

Proof that he knew this was provided by Martin Amis's story, told in his book *Experience* and duly rehearsed here, of how, after reading aloud from the passage in Primo Levi about the deportees drying their babies' nappies beside the train tracks, he turned around and found his father in tears. To tell this story was a decisive intervention, on the son's part, in the father's legend: and was no doubt meant to be. The stakes were high. Without that moment, a saving grace might have been lost to history. The anecdote gives some much-needed evidence for what must surely have been the truth: that Amis had turned against himself deliberately. A drunken man may speak with a brutality towards nuance that the same man sober wouldn't put up with. Amis's plain aim was to attain that condition even between drinks. Since a civilised mentality consists entirely of nuance, for its possessor to attack his own subtlety is the sign of a war within. What was the war within Kingsley Amis all about?

With due allowance for the requirement that we should be fair to Jane – she never stole him, he made a free choice – it seems fair to guess that the troubled grandee came to disapprove of his own conduct. The artist who invented Sir Roy Vandervane well understood how a figure of achievement could be propelled into stupidity by the anguish of passing time. But Amis, in his second marriage, was no philanderer. There could have been several reasons for that. As any man can note by keeping an eye on the divorces in his generation, the second marriage has to work. But Amis's anxieties with Jane weren't centred on the strain of being faithful. They were centred on the loss of desire. The fiction told the truth, and nowhere more conspicuously than in *Jake's Thing*, where the erstwhile cavalier ends up wearing a dinky little rubber ring to measure the flaccidity of the lance he had once followed into action.

For Jake's creator, the consequences of blaming himself for that indignity would have been drastic. He would have had to admit that he had come to such a pass all for the sake of a passing fancy. The answer was to blame her, a message he wrapped up by blaming women in general. In the strict sense, this was a turn-up for the books. Attacking one of his own best qualities, he produced, in the later novels from *Stanley and the Women* onwards, passages that made you wonder whether he was the same man who wrote the earlier ones. Surely the answer was that he wasn't. In matters of love, the man who goes out of his mind says that he is being true to his heart. Love having vanished, Amis was left with memories of folly, and no feelings left to steer by, except the one that underlay most of his life and all of his art. What could be more boring than marriage? A wrecked marriage. What could be more boring than a wrecked marriage? Another wrecked marriage. Time for a drink. Long after the husk became impossible to live with, Jane walked out on him. She had been noble to stay.

The book ends with the resurrection that preceded death. It was a blow when Jane left him, but also the end of an agony, because now he could go back home. Home has been defined as the place where, when you have to go there, they have to take you in, but Leader's closing account is here to remind us that it wasn't a case of Hilly, now Lady Kilmarnock, graciously allowing the washed-up ex-husband to crawl in through the cat-flap of her castle. Those who need reminding, or telling for the first time, will have swallowed the impression put about by the media that Hilly was exercising retributive generosity. The facts say that there was a lot of generosity on the part of Amis. Lady Kilmarnock and her husband were broke. Amis, now Sir Kingsley, with an earning power that not even he could convert entirely into alcohol, was in a position to help.

There was a lot in it for him – fearing the lonely dark above all other things, he was able to end his days in the crowded light – but he could distribute the seigneurial largesse only because of his commanding position. In his last phase he was no less the grand figure, and to underline the fact he produced a book that brought much of his subtlety back into play. *The Old Devils* marks an artistic recovery not just because the humour is funny again but because something of his tenderness returns – the quality with which he is seldom credited, but which underlay all his literary powers, humour not excepted. In the cast of aged characters, the lovable woman has lost the bloom of Christine or Jenny. In fact she has gained a complete set of false teeth. But Rhiannon is still, or once again, the authentic Amisian love object. She is the proof that while lust might once have mattered too much, it was always love that mattered most. In life, even in his terminal misogyny, the one thing that never bored him was romance: the adventure that was still there at the end, in his mind if nowhere else. What was true for Larkin was equally true for Amis: the love of beauty was high on the list of all the things that made death so terrible. Both men had been sustained all their lives by the ideal of love, and when they spoke coarsely, either separately or together, it was to stave off fear of the oblivion that would take all that beauty from them.

In the journalistic aftermath of both these important lives, evidence of their inner torments is viewed as the sure sign of their defeat. Viewing it as part of their triumph will take time, but it is bound to happen, because finally art wins out. If it hadn't already won out, there wouldn't be any journalistic aftermath anyway: such a fuss is never about nothing. The typical purveyor of Ted-and-Sylvia arts stories to the broadsheets must be excused for trafficking in the marketable theme of reputations unravelling, but the only reason such a journeyman can't hear the all-pervasive voice of Larkin and Amis is that he is speaking with it. Together, the two men gave the next generation the schooled yet bewitchingly conversational tone with which to talk about art as an everyday event, and about artiness as its enemy.

Their combined effect is omnipresent, and of the two it is a nice question which one resounds the most. Quantitatively it has to be Amis: not just because novels reach more people than poems can, but because he was so funny. The last step, and the hardest to take, in assessing any comic writer, is to assert what should be an obvious truth, but one which always shyly hides: humour is not an overlay to seriousness. Humour is the actual thing, compressed and intensified into a civil code. The reason that Amis, when he failed, failed so catastrophically, was the same reason that a jet pilot stunting close to the ground has no negligible version of getting things wrong. Comedy has to be astonishing or nothing, and Amis was astonishing often enough to make even the obtuse momentarily realise that there are truths which only comedy can clarify.

Unless we laugh at nothing, we laugh at truth to life: life in all its complexity, where people, even created people, are not just characters, but individuals. In the full flight of his comic depiction of Margaret Peel in *Lucky Jim*, Amis still paused to remind us, at the moment of her true tears, that all the false tears were products of her neurosis, and that she was a figure of sympathy even though she drove everybody nuts. She was alive, and people are alive one at a time. At which point it is time to revisit all those academic wives at Princeton who threw themselves beneath the visiting Englishman in the splendour and promise of his energy and invention. They weren't nine-pins. They were individual women, and they fell for him because they knew he knew they were.

TLS, February 2, 2007

Postscript

After the death of Philip Larkin I began asking myself just how valuable even the most thorough biography was, if it encouraged the dunces in their victory dance of small radius with pointed toe. A suitably knowledgeable literary journalist could do something to head off the false impressions, but wouldn't it usefully shorten the circuit if the biography were not published at all? I knew it was an obscurantist position but couldn't help flirting with it. Enlightenment came when I read Sara Wheeler's biographies of Denys Finch Hatton (*Too Close to the Sun*) and Apsley Cherry-Gerard (*Cherry*). Those two men weren't literary figures, they were adventurers, but her biography of each was so well written, and so full of pertinent social detail, that there could be nothing wrong with the genre, even though her avowed model was Michael Holroyd, the man who started the craze for the biography a block long. (Actually it had started with the biographies of the composers, pioneered by Ernest Newman's admittedly magnificent four volumes on Wagner, but Holroyd was the first to transfer the overkill to the literary field.) Since then I have been catching up with a neglected cairn of literary biographies and have often felt grateful. Anthony Cronin's *Samuel Beckett*, for example, is full of things that I would never have figured out for myself. It can always be contended that a complete artist should need no explaining, but the answer is obvious: no artist is that complete. One can hope, however, that the actual bulk of the biography might be kept within reasonable limits. My own rule of thumb is that a book is of a decent length if I can remember how it started when I get to the end. Ideally, though, one can't help wanting less than that. Lytton Strachey, unwitting subject of a Holroyd *opus* so excessively *magnum*, got himself on the front end of a paradox when he wrote biographies not much bigger than articles. His *Eminent Victorians* was a meretricious book but it was in a meritorious tradition. One doesn't say that Aubrey's *Brief Lives* set the desirable measure, but it always helps to remember how much got said by Johnson in his *Lives of the Poets*, any one of which is the first thing to read on the poet in question. Not, of course, the only thing: but surely our aim, like Johnson's, should be to get abreast of the essentials first.

CANETTI, MAN OF MYSTERY

As a literary type after World War Two, the German-speaking International Man of Mystery found Britain a more comfortable land of exile than America, where he was always under pressure to explain himself in public, thereby dissipating the mystery. The chief mystery was about his reason for not going back to German-speaking Europe. Before the mysterious W. G. Sebald there was the even more mysterious Elias Canetti. While the Nazis were in power, Canetti had excellent reasons to be in London. But now that the Nazis were gone, why was he still there?

Like Sebald later on, Canetti might have found Britain a suitable context for pulling off the trick of becoming a famous name without very many people knowing precisely who he was. Canetti even got the 1981 Nobel Prize for Literature, and people still didn't know who he was. He was a Viennese Swiss Bulgarian Jewish refugee with an impressively virile moustache; he was Iris Murdoch's lover; he was a mystery. Apart from a sociological treatise called *Crowds and Power* which advanced a thesis no more gripping than its title, his solitary pre-war novel *Die Blendung*, known in English as *Auto da Fé*, was the only book by Canetti that anybody had ever heard of. Hardly anybody had read it, but everybody meant to. Those who had read it said it was about a mysterious man in a house full of books, and that the house, in a symbolic enactment of the collapse of a civilisation, fell down, or almost did, or creaked a lot, or something.

While living in Britain, Canetti wrote three books of memoirs about his life in pre-war Europe. He wrote them in German. (All three volumes are now available in English, although readers are warned that the translations lose some of the effortless pomposity of the original.) They were full of literary gossip: hard material to make dull, even for a writer with Canetti's knack for colourless reportage. He proved, however, that he had a long memory for the frailties of his colleagues. He had a good story about Robert Musil, author of *The Man Without Qualities*. In the circumscribed world of the Vienna cafés, Musil reigned unapproachably as the resident genius. But Musil was eaten up by resentment of the international recognition accorded to Thomas Mann. When, in 1935, Canetti published *Die Blendung* to some acclaim in the press, he entered the café to find Musil, who had previously barely noticed his existence, rising to meet him with a congratulatory speech. Canetti was able to say that he had a letter in his pocket from Thomas Mann, praising him in exactly the same terms. Musil sank back into his chair and never acknowledged Canetti again.

The story shows how Canetti could recognise self-obsession in others. But there is no account of his ever recognising the same failing in himself. His memoirs not only take him to be the centre of events – a standard strategy in autobiographical writing, and often an entertaining one – they proceed on the assumption that no events matter except those centred on him. Hitler scarcely gets a mention. The story is all about Canetti, a man with good reason, we are led to assume, for holding himself in high esteem.

Canetti spent the last part of his life in Zurich. In his last year he was at work on his memoir about London. (Now, in Elysium, he is probably working on his memoir about Zurich.) The unfinished book, *Party in the Blitz*, is the story of his years in and around Hampstead during the war and just after. We are fortunate that there is no more of it, lest we start wondering whether Canetti should not have received another Nobel Prize, for being the biggest twerp of the twentieth century. But a twerp must be at least partly stupid, and Canetti wasn't even a little bit that. Instead, he was a particularly bright egomaniac, and this book, written when his governing mechanisms were falling to bits, simply shows the limitless reserves of envy and recrimination that had always powered his aloofness. The mystery blows apart, and spatters the reader with scraps and tatters of an artificial superiority. Witnessing, from Hampstead Heath, the Battle of Britain taking place above him – the completeness with which he fails to evoke the scene is breathtaking – Canetti, unlike many another German-speaking refugee, managed to take no part whatever in the war against Hitler. He had his own war to fight, against, among others, T. S. Eliot. Canetti's loathing of Eliot is practically the book's leitmotiv: you have to imagine a version of *Die Meistersinger* in which Beckmesser keeps coming back on stage a few minutes after he goes off. 'I was living in England as its intellect decayed,' Canetti recalls. 'I was a witness to the fame of T. S. Eliot . . . a libertine of the void, a foothill of Hegel, a desecrator of Dante . . . thin lipped, cold hearted, prematurely old . . . armed with critical points instead of teeth, tormented by a nymphomaniac of a wife . . . tormented to such a degree that my *Auto da Fé* would have shrivelled up if he had gone near it . . .'

The problem, of course, was that Eliot couldn't have gone near it, because before 1946, when *Auto da Fé* was finally translated, scarcely anybody in London had read it. This might have been one of several practical reasons why Canetti was not accorded the automatic respect he felt due to him, but there was a supreme, spiritual reason which only he, the profound analyst of crowds and power, could detect: English arrogance. The English intellectuals, his antennae told him, were being arrogant even when they strove to seem tolerant. Tolerance, in fact, was the surest sign of their arrogance. 'Arrogance is such an integral part of the English, one often fails to notice it. They take arrogance to new, unsuspected levels.' Eliot, for example, was such a master of arrogance that he could conceal it completely. 'There he sat, the very famous man among all those others, amidst whom there were certainly many bad poets whom he must despise from the depths of his being, and he gave no indication of the fact . . .' Always keen to seem at home in British polite society, where zeal is rarely worn on the sleeve, Canetti found it politic to forget his earlier history as a Brechtian radical, but passages like this remind you that he was a born Vyshinskyite prosecutor, forever taking the ability of the accused to defend himself as proof of guilt, and the ostensible absence of a fault as a sure sign of its lurking presence.

It should be said in his favour that Canetti, by his own reluctant account, did manage to meet at least a few Englishmen who were not reduced to 'desiccation' by the national trait. Herbert Read, Bertrand Russell, Vaughan Williams, Arthur Wayley: each is forgettably evoked, with perhaps an extra touch of specificity for Wayley, because he had read Canetti's novel in the original language. But as a general rule, Englishmen neither realised Canetti's importance at first glance nor managed to conceal their arrogance even when adopting an elaborate guise of congeniality. Take T. S. Eliot (did we mention him?) as a case in point. The fact that Eliot had been born and raised in America was only a further proof of the pervasive nature of English arrogance: having gone native, he had taken on the local characteristic, and indeed would not have been a success in England had he failed to do so. But he probably managed to acquire it so easily because his ancestors had been English in the first place. It was 'the acquisition, so to speak, of an American returned to the home country after many generations. It will be difficult to describe Eliot as the quite abysmal character he was . . . His costive-minimal work (so many spittoons of failure), the poet in England and among the Modernists of emotional impoverishment, which became fashionable through him . . .'

The continually recurring diatribe about Eliot is made almost piquant by the fact that Canetti is talking about a time in his enemy's career when the sequential poems later to be known as *Four Quartets* were being published to universal praise for their magnificence. There were plenty of English intellectuals who had no particular respect for Eliot's conservative intellectual position but could see that he was writing the greatest poetry of his time. For Canetti, however, it was out of the question to separate man and work. The man *was* the work: it was the way, after all, that he felt about himself. 'My chief trait, much my strongest quality, which has never been compromised, was the insistence on myself . . .' Canetti measured himself against other men according to the adamantine strength of his self-regard, so it can be imagined what he was like when he was measuring himself against women.

Or, rather, it can't. Just when you thought you had been handed the complete picture of a louse, you read how he rewarded the young Iris Murdoch for having bestowed her favours on him. Here we need to make a distinction. His abusive opinions on her qualities of mind were delivered long after their affair was over, and might even seem reasonable to those of us less than convinced about her status as a philosopher. 'I don't think there is anything that leaves me quite as cold as that woman's intellect.' But his comments about her qualities as a mistress bring into question his own judgment at the time. 'I could not ignore the ugliness of her feet. She had a bearlike walk, but it was a repulsive bear . . .' It was also a passive bear, for whom love was 'an indifferent act'. You might have thought that this drawback would have become apparent to him fairly quickly, but not so. 'This went on . . . for a couple of years.' Their love affair (one of the

inspirations behind her second novel *The Flight from the Enchanter*)
became famous as an event submissive on her part and dominant
on his, but on this evidence he did his own share of the suffering,
simply by having known her. 'Everything I despise about English life
is in her.' Except, strangely enough, arrogance. With typical gallantry,
he sums her up as being 'ambitious as a master criminal. But she's
too fixated on love to be arrogant . . .' The bitch, she couldn't be
depended on even for that.

Regulars in Canetti's extensive harem pop up wanly throughout
the book, usually doing exactly what he wants and almost invariably
being patronised for their compliance. The historian C. V. Wedg-
wood, as 'the student who loves her teacher', is given a few points
for translating *Auto da Fé* but earns a conclusive demerit for not
being enthusiastic about – for possibly (whisper this) not even having
read – *Crowds and Power*: 'she was unoriginal, had no ideas about
anything.' It could be said that she had enough original ideas to go
to bed with an unmitigated creep, but it isn't said by Canetti, who
never awards women credit for choosing him. What choice do they
have? It's fate. Abject devotion from the poet Kathleen Raine is first
welcomed ('It did not seem to matter to her that she didn't know the
first thing about me') and then scorned for the usual reason ('I had
no idea at the time of the arrogance there was concealed behind such
modesty'). That was a close one.

Intelligent beauties lined up to be treated like dirt. The International Man of Mystery was also the Man with Power over Women.
In Hampstead there was only one Vienna-style coffee house. It was
called the Coffee Cup. Canetti was still to be found hanging out there
when I was introduced to him in the first summer after I got to
London in the early sixties. He didn't even pretend to be polite, and
I couldn't blame him. After only a few minutes in his company it
was clear to me what attracted him about the passing parade: trainee
bluestockings, of the stamp nowadays known, in Britain at least, as
posh totty. Today they would be dressed exclusively out of the Toast
catalogue, but even then they were dreams in suede and cashmere.
He didn't move his head to track them as they wafted by, but I could
see his eyeballs swivel. Suffering from the same proclivities, I was in
no position to despise him, and I might say that the same goes for
the characteristic that he projected on to the local population because
he had so much of it himself.

Arrogance is the natural condition of a mind in exile. If history had never torn Canetti loose from his first context, he might have flourished as a type well recognised, and even cherished, in the European world of the literary cafés: half know-all, half clown. It was being a displaced person that made him preposterous, and those of us in the post-war peace who chose to roam the world could have no warrant to look down on those among our elders who had been forced to. For the German-speakers, especially, there was never any easy undoing of the damage. Of the two undoubted masters of modern German prose, the novelist Thomas Mann and the essayist Alfred Polgar, neither ever really came back to the main German-speaking lands. Each was offered every enticement, but they settled for Switzerland. So, in the course of time, did Canetti, if not to find a final home for his mastery, then at least to give one extra twist to his mystery, and to gain the perspective for writing a memoir so delightfully awful that it makes his self-satisfied literary personality palatable at last.

Canetti had some reputation as an analyst who could skewer people in a paragraph. Here is the proof that he was too pleased about himself to be truly perceptive about others. The striking aphorism, said Polgar, requires a stricken aphorist. On the threshold of death's door, Canetti saw nothing to be worried about when he examined his conscience. On this evidence, he couldn't even find it. Instead, he wrote a book fit to serve every writer in the world as a hideous, hilarious example of the tone to avoid when the ego, faced with the certain proof of its peripheral importance, loses the last of its inhibitions.

New York Times, October 2, 2005

Postscript

Ever since the imprecations of Coleridge failed to cure them of the habit, the second-rank literary editors of London have indulged their proclivity for 'lively copy', so Canetti always attracted more coverage than the Man of Mystery who really counted: W. G. Sebald. It was Sebald who used his years of exile in England to write European masterpieces. In his great book *Austerlitz* you get walking tours of London that show you what a foreign-born viewpoint could do to register detail and bring it alive. With a Leica lens in each eye, Sebald could turn Liverpool Street railway station into Chartres. Sebald, too, had his limiting quirks: he was all wrong about Germany's post-war memories of the Allied aerial bombardment. He said that the Germans had wilfully repressed the traumatic recollection. In fact, the kind of pop magazines that he never read were full of stories about night-fighter pilots, and a whole generation of young men grew up dreaming of tearing Lancasters in half with the upward-angled cannon batteries of their Ju-88s while lakes of fire boiled far below. In that case, Sebald's taste was too refined to catch the raw material. But on his own beat, with his Proustian gaze scanning photographs, documents, abandoned fortifications and all the resonant detritus of the past, he had a generosity that left a posturing snob like Canetti next to nowhere.

CAMILLE PAGLIA BURNS FOR POETRY

Clearly designed as a come-on for bright students who don't yet know very much about poetry, Camille Paglia's new book anthologises forty-three short works in verse from Shakespeare through to Joni Mitchell, with an essay about each. The essays do quite a lot of elementary explaining. Readers who think they already know something of the subject, however, would be rash if they gave her low marks just for spelling things out. Even they, if they were honest enough to admit it, might need help with the occasional Latin phrase, and they will find her analysis of individual poems quite taxing enough in its upper reaches. 'Having had his epiphany,' she says of the sonnet 'Composed Upon Westminster Bridge', 'Wordsworth moves on, preserving his estrangement and solitude by shutting down his perception.' Nothing elementary about that.

She flies as high as you can go, in fact, without getting into the airless space of literary theory and Cultural Studies. Not that she has ever regarded those activities as elevated. She has always regarded them, with good reason, as examples of humanism's perverse gift for attacking itself, and for providing the academic world with a haven for tenured mediocrity. This book is the latest shot in her campaign to save culture from theory. It thus squares well with another of her aims, to rescue feminism from its unwise ideological allegiances. So in the first instance *Break, Blow, Burn* is about poetry, and in the second it is about Camille Paglia.

One measure of her quality as a commentator is that those two subjects are not in the reverse order. In view of her wide knowledge, her expressive gifts, her crackling personality and the inherent credibility problems posed by looking too much at her ease on top of a pair of Jimmy Choos, it is remarkable how good Paglia can be at not putting herself first. From this book you could doubt several aspects of her taste in poetry. But you couldn't doubt her love of it. She is humble enough to be enthralled by it; enthralled enough to be inspired; and inspired enough to write the sinuous and finely shaded prose that proves how a single poem can get the whole of her attention. From a woman who sometimes gives the impression that she finds reticence a big ask, this is a sure index of her subject's importance to her, and one quite likely to be infectious. My own prescription for making poetry popular in the schools would be to ban it – with possession treated as a serious misdemeanour, and dealing as a felony – but failing that, a book like this is probably the next best thing. If she doesn't make a poem sound like something dangerous, at least she makes it sound like something complicated. Students grown wary of pabulum might relish the nitty-gritty.

The term 'a poem' is one we have to use, because our author is strong on the point that a poet should be measured by individual poems, and not by a 'body of work'. To a reader from outside America, she sounds tremendously right about this, but inside America her view is likely to go on smacking of subversion for some time to come. One can only hope that the subversion does its stuff. Good poems are written one at a time: written that way and read that way. Even the Divine Comedy is a poem in the first instance, not part of a body of work: and even in Shakespeare's plays there are passages that lift themselves out of context. ('Shakespeare the poet,' she says, 'often burns through Shakespeare the dramatist, not simply in the great soliloquies but in passages throughout his plays that can stand alone as poems.') The penalty for talking about poets in universal terms before, or instead of, talking about their particular achievements is to devalue what they do while fetishising what they are.

This insidious process is far advanced in modern America, to the point where it corrupts not just the academics but the creators themselves. John Ashbery would have given us dozens more poems as thrilling as his *jeu d'esprit* about Daffy Duck if he had never been raised to the combined status of totem pole and wind tunnel, in which configuration he produces one interminable outpouring that deals with everything in general, with nothing in particular, can be cut off at any length from six inches to a mile, and will be printed by editors who feel that the presence in their publication of an isotropic rigmarole signed with Ashbery's name is a guarantee of seriousness precisely because they don't enjoy a line of it. Paglia, commendably, refuses such cargo-cult status even to Shakespeare.

Working chronologically from then to now, the book starts with him: Sonnet 73, Sonnet 29 and the Ghost's speech from *Hamlet*, each individually explicated. The Ghost's speech counts as a poem because we not only experience it as an especially intense and coherent episode, we remember it that way. A poem's demand to be held in the memory counts for a lot with Paglia. Notably sensitive to language, rhythm and technique as devices for getting meaning into your mind and making it stick, she persuades you, throughout the book, that she has her poems by heart, even if she doesn't favour the idea of memorising them deliberately like a trainee spy scanning a room. Her readings of Shakespeare are close, fully informed by the scholarship, and – a harder trick – fundamentally sane, thus auguring well for her approach to Donne, whose Holy Sonnet XIV supplies the book's title. But her sensitivity to George Herbert is the best early sign of her range of sympathy.

With Shakespeare, Donne and Marvell she has merely to convince her students, fresh from their gender studies, that a poet could call a woman his mistress without belittling her. With Herbert she has to convince them that a poet could feel the same passion about God. ('We follow the path of the all-too-human quester as he advances towards God, then retreats in confusion.' That 'we' could be a bit optimistic, but she might get lucky.) One of her best attributes is well brought out: her refusal to modernise the past. Her thorough background in cultural history – the Italians, who should be proud of her parentage, would call her *preparatissima* – is always in play. Her entertaining wealth of up-to-date pop-culture allusion is merely the top dressing, and she is usually careful not to strain after a faddish point. In her exemplary analysis of Shelley's 'Ozymandias', for example, she could easily have referred to the last scene of *Planet of the Apes*, when Charlton Heston looks up at Liberty's head just as the Traveller from an Antique Land looked up at the truncated legs of stone. I was rather expecting her to. Perhaps she has realised, however, that the pace of forgetfulness is always accelerating, and that we have moved from an era of people who have never heard of Shelley to an era of people who have never heard of Charlton Heston.

When she calls Yeats's 'Leda and the Swan' 'the greatest poem of the twentieth century' she makes one of her few sweeping statements. It isn't a bad one, but it doesn't do enough to offset an equally sweeping question from us. When the book moves towards modern times it moves towards America. Whatever happened to the old world it left behind? After Coleridge (a bold and convincing interpretation of 'Kubla Khan'), Yeats is the last European, living or dead, to get an entry. Still, there are probably copyright reasons for choosing nothing by, say, Auden, and meanwhile there is the compensation of the way she can treat great American poets as accomplished artists without merely abetting the worship of icons. This coolly enthusiastic emphasis shows up clearly in her detailed admiration for Emily Dickinson. Paglia can see the epic in the miniature: an especially important critical gift when it comes to a poet who could enamel the inside of a raindrop. One would be glad to have a complete Dickinson annotated by Paglia. An utter contrast of destinies, it would be a meeting of true minds. Paglia, too, has a kind of solitude, though it might not sound that way. The media attention she attracts does little to modify her opinions. That might be partly why she attracts so much of it. The proud motto of every suckerfish is: we swim with sharks.

But the most threatening thing about her, from the American viewpoint, is that she refuses to treat the arts as an instrument of civil rights. Without talent, no entitlement. She has the powers of discrimination to show what talent is – powers that add up to a talent in themselves. A critical scope that can trace the intensity uniting different artistic fields is not unprecedented in America, but she is an unusually well-equipped exponent of it. Making a solid attempt to pin down the sliding meanings of Wallace Stevens's little poem 'Disillusionment at Ten O'Clock', she brings in exactly the right comparison: a piano piece by Satie. She compares the poem's 'red weather' with a Gaugin seascape: right again. These comparisons help to define the post-Impressionist impulse from which all the verbal music of Stevens's Blue Guitar emerged, while incidentally reminding us that Paglia, before she made this bid on behalf of poetry, did the same for painting, and with the same treasury of knowledge to back up her endeavour. But above all, her range of allusion helps to show what was in Stevens's head: the concentration of multiple sensitivities that propelled his seeming facility. 'Under enchantment by imagination, space and time expand, melt, and cease to exist.' Nobody has a right to a creative mind like his. It's a gift.

Students expecting a poem by Maya Angelou will find that this book is less inclusive than the average line-up for Inauguration Day.

But there is a poem by Langston Hughes; and, even better, there is 'Georgia Dusk', by Jean Toomer. A featured player in the Harlem Renaissance of the early 1920s, Toomer transmuted the heritage of southern slavery into music. So did the blues, but Toomer's music was all verbal. He was a meticulous technician, which is probably the main reason why his name has faded. Paglia does a lot to bring it back, but she might have done even more. She concedes too much by saying his 'flowery, courtly diction' was more Victorian than modernist. The same might have been said of John Crowe Ransom, and with equal inaccuracy. Toomer sounds to me like a bridge through time from Elinor Wylie, whom Paglia doesn't mention, to Richard Wilbur and Anthony Hecht, neither of whom she mentions either.

If she has a deaf spot, it lies on that wing. Favouring, with good reason, the American vernacular, she tends to set it up as something that supersedes European formality, as if it were possible for a poem to be over-constructed. But it can't. It can only be underpowered. If she had paid the same pin-point attention to the complex interplay within Toomer's four-square quatrains as she pays to William Carlos Williams's free verse in 'The Wheelbarrow', she would have been able to show how a superficially mechanical form can intensify conversational rhythms by the tightness with which it contains them. It would have been a useful generosity. Anthony Hecht's reputation was injured when Helen Vendler found his forms limiting. On the contrary, they were limitless. As for Wilbur, his fastidiously carpentered post-war poems were part of the American liberation of Europe. Whether that liberation was a new stage in American cultural imperialism's road to conquest remains a nice question. One would like to have heard her answer. Such a discussion would lie well within her scope. But our disappointment that she stops short is a sign of her achievement. It we want a book to do more than what it does, that's a condemnation. If we want it to do more *of* what it does, that's an endorsement.

Occasionally there is cause for worry that her young students might listen too well. Three short poems by Theodore Roethke are praised without any warning that most of his longer poems, if the reader goes in search of them, will prove to be helpless echoes of bigger names. Ambition undid him, as it has undone many another American poet infected by the national delusion that the arts can have a Major League. The short poem by Frank O'Hara should have been marked with a caveat: anything longer by the same poet will be found to have a lot less in it, because the urge to find a verbal equivalent for the apparent freedom of New York abstract expressionist painting led him to believe that he could mean everything by saying anything. Nor are we told that Robert Lowell would spend the later and incoherently copious part of his career making sure that he would never again attain the rhetorical magnificence of the opening lines of 'Man and Wife'. But Paglia knows why, and how, those lines are magnificent: and in Lowell's case, among her specific remarks, there is a general one that typifies her knack of extending an aesthetic question into the moral sphere. Lowell's 'confessional' streak insulted his loved ones. The same question is posed again by Sylvia Plath's 'Daddy', an agonised masterpiece by which Paglia is driven to a stretch of critical writing that stands out for its richness even in a rich book.

Applying her particularised admiration to rescue the poem from those who cite it as a mantra, Paglia points out an awkward truth about Plath as a feminist Winged Victory: that her poetry was in 'erudite engagement with canonical male writers'. A still more awkward truth is that the manner of Plath's suicide helped to set up her husband Ted Hughes as an abuser of women. Paglia defends Hughes against Plath, a defence that few feminists have dared to undertake. She also defends Plath's father against Plath, which might seem a quixotic move in view of the poem's subject matter, but does help to make the point that Plath, by calling her father a Nazi and identifying herself with millions of helpless victims, was personalising the Holocaust in a way that only her psychic disturbance could excuse. Leaving out the possibility that Plath might have been *saying* she was nuts, Paglia does Plath the honour of taking her at her word. But you can't do her that honour without bringing her down off her pedestal. The poet used her unquestionable talent to say some very questionable things, and there's no way out of it. Paglia is tough enough to accept that conclusion: tough enough, that is, not to complain when she winds up all alone.

She seems to enjoy being alone. It's a handy trait for the sort of thinker who can't see an orthodoxy form without wanting not to be part of it. Google her for half an hour and you will find her fighting battles with other feminists all over cyberspace. Telling us how she became, at the age of four, a 'lifelong idolator of pagan goddesses' after seeing Ava Gardner in *Showboat*, she tells us why she is less than thrilled with Madonna. It's a view I share, but at least Madonna manufactured herself. Ava Gardner from South Carolina was manufactured in a Hollywood studio, as she was the first to admit. And what is Paglia doing, saying that an actress as gifted as Anne Heche has 'the mentality of a pancake'? How many pancake brains could do what Heche did with David Mamet's dialogue in *Wag the Dog*? And what about her performance in *One Kill*? No doubt Heche has been stuck with a few bad gigs, but Paglia, of all people, must be well aware that being an actress is not the same safe ride as being the tenured University Professor of Humanities and Media Studies at the University of the Arts in Philadelphia.

Paglia by now should be famous enough to start throttling back on some of the stuff she is famous for. She might make a start with bitchery, for which she has a taste but no touch. The media want snide remarks from her the same way that the Sahara wants rain. But writers capable of developing a nuanced position over the length of an essay should not be tempted into believing that they can sum it up in a sound-bite. Liberal orthodoxy will always need opposing, but not on the basis that all its points are self-evidently absurd. According to Paglia, gun abuse is a quirk of the sexually dysfunctional. That might be right, but people aren't necessarily deluded when they want a ban for the sort of gun that can kill a dozen people in half a minute. Waiting until everybody is sexually functional would be a long time to hold your breath.

Nor does Paglia's useful conviction that feminism, as an ideology, is as debilitating for individual responsibility as any other ideology make it true that women are now out of the woods. Only the misapprehension that she can be wise like lightning could explain her brief appearance, in *Inside Deep Throat*, to tell us that the cultural artefact in question was 'an epochal moment in the history of modern sexuality'. On the contrary, it was a moronic moment in the history of exploitation movies made by people so untalented that they can't be convincing even when they masturbate.

But all these posturings by the madly glamorous Paglia happen only because, in the electrified frenzy of the epochal moment, she forgets that the light-storm of publicity makes her part of the world of images. In her mind, if not yet in her more excitable membranes, she knows better than to mistake that world for the real one. This book on poetry is aimed at a generation of young people who, knowing nothing except images, are cut off from 'the mother ship' of culture. The mother ship was first mentioned in her 2002 lecture called 'The Magic of Images'. In the same lecture, she put down the marker that led to this book. 'The only antidote to the magic of images is the magic of words.' She can say that again, and let's hope she does, in a longer edition of a book that shows her at her true worth. When you have proved that you can cut the mustard, it's time to cut the malarkey.

New York Times, March 27, 2005

Postscript

One way of summing up Camille Paglia would be to say that she looks like the classiest number in the bar until the fight breaks out. It isn't that she doesn't watch her words: she watches them to make sure they are going the wrong way. One is forced to conclude that publicity is the sea in which she swims, beating it to a phosphorescent froth. But we should not let her effulgence blind us to her import- ance. *Break, Blow, Burn* is an important book in a movement we should all favour: the movement to restore the ideal of the self- contained poem to a superior position over the more marketable notion of poetry as a generalized and infinitely teachable commodity. I thought my review had unmistakably praised her for this initiative, so I was quite stunned to find some of the American cultural bloggers accusing me of having done a knife-job. The noisiest bloggers are often the most stupid, and probably the worst you can say of Camille Paglia is that she sometimes sounds as if she might like to hang out with them, always granted that hanging out is something they ever do. You would expect someone with so formidable a mind to fight shy of petty quarrels. I can think of no contemporary cultural figure who would so benefit from being less available. She should stay in more.

THE GUIDEBOOK DETECTIVES

If you've spent a couple of years being unable to get past the opening chapter of one of the later novels of Henry James, it's hard to resist the idea that there might be a more easily enjoyable version of literature: a crime novel, for example. After all, quite a few literary masterpieces spend much of their turgid wordage being almost as contrived as any crime novel you've ever raced through. On page thirteen of my edition of *The Wings of the Dove*, Kate Croy is waiting for her father to appear. 'He had not at present come down from his room, which she knew to be above the one they were in . . .' But of course she knew that; knew it so well that she wouldn't have to think about it; she is only thinking about it so she can tell us. If a narrative is going to be as clumsy as that, can't it have some guns?

It's been a long time since Sherlock Holmes cracked his first case, and by now every country in the world must have at least one fictional detective with half a dozen novels to his name. Some countries seem to have half a dozen fictional detectives with twenty or thirty novels each. Can't even one of these current sleuths be surrounded by classy prose like Raymond Chandler's Philip Marlowe, so that we can get the art thrill and the thriller thrill both at once? *Down these mean streets a man must go who is not himself mean.* Great idea, great sound, great sociological significance. But above all, an eventful narrative to make you read on. Something unputdownable, to make you feel less bad about the unpickupable, such as *The Wings of the Dove*, which surely deserves everlasting blame for the kind of sentence it so wilfully refuses to include. 'Kate Croy looked up at the fully dressed but headless corpse hanging from the ceiling fan and realised with a surge of fear that unless there was another equally well-tailored man with the same cuff-links, this was her father . . .'

If the author does that kind of stuff well enough, he starts counting as literature. That's the possibility that keeps us, the readers, on the case: the search for the gripping story that counts as good writing as well. It could be that we are dodging our obligations to high art, but for as long as Patricia Highsmith brings a poetic touch to the narrative details of how the central character of *Deep Water* just happens, in the swimming pool at night, to lean on the rival for his wife's affections and hold him under, are we really going to kick ourselves for not having finished reading that novel by Willa Cather? There can be no question that the best genre fiction has always aimed, and sometimes successfully, at usurping literature's place. The question is about the extent to which the crime writers have dominated genre fiction. In answer to that, even the science-fiction writers would have to admit that the crime writers have pretty well taken over. Magic sells more copies because magic includes J. K. Rowling, but crime has more writers, with a different crime-fighter for every writer.

In all the European languages, there were many famous fictional crime-fighters after the demise of Sherlock Holmes and before the advent of Maigret, but it was Maigret's prolific inventor, Georges Simenon, who really started the crime novel on the way to its current aspiration to seriousness. Supposedly helping to fuel the aspiration, but perhaps also helping to ensure that it can rarely attain its object, is the presence of a recognisably characterised detective. There had always been a space-warp area in which gifted writers wrote *noir* books that hovered trembling between thrills and thoughtfulness, but without a star detective the gifted writers had trouble writing enough of them, and one of the imperatives of the genre-fiction business is that you must publish enough books to survive in a market where everybody else is publishing a lot of books for the same reason. It helps to have your own sleuth and get people hooked on him. Simenon, with the organisation and instincts of a Colombian drug-runner, got the whole world hooked on Maigret.

Not only did Maigret sell by the million in every tongue and in all media, literary critics praised his author's stripped-down style. Though it could be said that the style was stripped-down because Simenon was essentially styleless – he *said* he spent hours taking out the adjectives, but he also said he was irresistible to women – nevertheless he acquired such prestige for Maigret that his action novels without Maigret in them started counting as proper novels, the absence of the star turn being thought of as a sign of artistic purity.

Seriousness is a tag that most genre writers can be counted on to covet, even when they have made a good fist of seeming to despise it. Soon a new, specially commissioned novel by the Edinburgh author Ian Rankin will be serialised in the *New York Times*, a prospect which has already attracted attention in the upmarket British press, as when the occasional British astronaut is deputed by NASA to do the blindfolded bean-counting experiment in Earth orbit. But apparently Rankin's famous Inspector Rebus won't be in the story.

Interviewed by the London *Independent* about this startling act of self-abnegation, Rankin sounded the way Fred Astaire once did when he suggested that his forthcoming appearance in *On the Beach* would be a heaven-sent opportunity not to dance. For Rankin's fans all over the world, Rebus is the ideal sleuth: a maverick (of course) cop who drinks so hard that he gets another hangover from inhaling his current hangover, he keeps his job only by the kind of deductive brain that can operate even when bombed. In Britain he is played on television by Ken Stott, with a magnificently burred accent and a rack of luggage beneath each eye.

Looking and sounding like a man who has slept under a reclining horse, Rebus will be a big absence from this new story. But the new story will still be set in Edinburgh, which has the advantage, even as it becomes more prosperous, of offering, along with plenty of well-preserved classical architecture, an infinite number of equally well-preserved dank staircases leading down into squalid areas where Rankin's reeking hero can find bodies in even worse condition than his own. Other Scots detectives get to operate in the less ambiguous setting of Glasgow, where far fewer classical outlines have survived to frame the rough stuff. To indicate that they are not pampered, the actors who play the Glasgow flatfeet on television say 'murghder' instead of 'murder'. With throats that hurt from the accent, and teeth chipped from being gritted, Glasgow tecs are tougher. But Edinburgh *looks* better, a fact bearing implications to which we might return.

Most lone detectives belong to a police force nowadays, because it gives the writer an easier task: in a police station, there are a lot of other personnel for the hero to interact with. In the days when the lone detective was alone, he interacted mainly with the bottle, *à la*

Philip Marlowe, who had nothing else in the top drawer of his filing cabinet. Even with Marlowe, the action improved when the regular cops showed up, so that Marlowe could hate them and they could hate him back. A requirement of today's lone detective is that the police force he serves in is riven by faction if not corruption. This is where Italy scores heavily. With dozens of differently uniformed Italian police forces jostling for position to get on the take, there are plenty of mean streets available for a man not himself mean to walk down. Also – a factor we should note now in case we need it later – a lot of the Italian streets are lined with attractive old buildings. Against such an inherently interesting background, the swarming lone detectives are in many cases invented by writers who are not native Italians, but just visiting.

My younger daughter, an expert on crime fiction, was the one who tipped me off that the Italian maverick cop who really counted was Inspector Brunetti, created by Donna Leon. Inspector Brunetti operates in Venice. Donna Leon, however, is not Venetian, or even Italian. She might have lived in Venice for twenty years, but she benefits mightily from the outsider's traditional love of the Serenissima. Donna Leon is an American, and although the Brunetti novels are bestsellers in many languages, she has so far not allowed their translation into Italian. Thus her fans are either non-Italians or else Italians who read foreign languages. It seems a fair guess that the factor uniting them all is a sad involvement with Venice. In every fan's first-pick Brunetti novel, *Acqua Alta*, she gives intimate details of the decaying city while never delaying the action for a moment. Hers is an unusually potent cocktail of atmosphere and event. People get addicted. There will be another Donna Leon out imminently, but meanwhile, in our house, everyone is lining up to read the last one.

Always vowing to give up soon, by now I have read at least half a dozen Brunetti novels and have got well past the stage of remembering what happens in which book, even though the author, for the length of time it takes to read the text, is pretty good at not letting background detail overwhelm foreground action. You always know which canal the body is in, but the inspector never takes his eye off the way it has been lashed to the piling. ('Although the fish and crabs had been at her during the high water of September, he knew it must be the Englishwoman, Kate Croy...') Inspector Brunetti is happily married and eats well, the way Maigret used to when Madame

Maigret fixed his lunch. Usually, in this sort of book, the sleuth is divorced, eating badly off a snatched sandwich, and drinking hard, especially if he is Irish. But Inspector Brunetti can't wait to get home to his hot wife and her subtle tricks with the calamari. He is kept on the case, however, by crimes of rare intricacy that would take time to solve even if he were not frustrated all the way by an incompetent senior officer. Meanwhile the beautiful city sinks slowly but irretrievably into a sea of corruption. Down these means streets a man must row who is not himself mean.

Another of the vast crowd of Italian lone detectives, Inspector Zen, is also the creation of a non-Italian, Michael Dibdin: based in Seattle, background in England and Northern Ireland. Typical among Dibdin's several Zen novels, *Vendetta* reveals that Dibdin commands a precisely literate prose. He knows what it means to 'eke out', for example. But he doesn't know that the action would move faster if Inspector Zen didn't take what feels like a hundred pages to get across Rome, mentally noting every detail, as if he were a writer. Since Zen is nominally functioning in the Criminalpol section of the Ministry of the Interior, and is already unpopular with his superiors for being too honest – no wonder he's divorced – this tendency to annotate the atmosphere can only hurt his image. The disadvantage of an author's being a *straniero* is thereby starkly revealed. Non-Italians find Italy too fascinating. There is thus room for the home-grown writer to score on the level of economical evocation.

Featuring prominently in this department is Andrea Camilleri, inventor of the Inspector Montalbano mysteries, which in Italy are put out in an elegant series of paperbacks that any sophisticated family likes to have a couple of neatly displayed on the glass-topped coffee table. Montalbano's bailiwick is Sicily. If mainland Italy is corrupt, Sicily is corrupter, and Montalbano has some plenty-mean streets to walk down. He does so at a brisk pace, and it is because Camilleri knows his background too well to be impressed. He speaks the language. Camilleri's regular translator Stephen Sartarelli has made a well-deserved career out of rendering Montalbano's Sicilian dialect first into Italian, then into English, and then into your living room, where you can back it up, if you like, with subtitled DVDs, because Montalbano is an all-media phenomenon in his land of origin.

A typical Montalbano novel, and one which I recommend heavily for when you can spare a couple of sunlit afternoons from *The Wings of the Dove*, is the impeccably grimy *The Shape of Water*. Hookers, junkies, scary crime, inspired sleuthing, great sexual tension between the happily fixed-up Montalbano and the vampy young female cop Corporal Anna Ferrara. Notable is the way Camilleri can do a character's whole back-story in half a paragraph, and only rarely do you get that giveaway trade trick by which one character tells another what he already knows, so that you can find out. 'You know what he's like,' says A to B about C, and then proceeds to tell B what C is like, as if B didn't know after all. But at least Camilleri is aware that these technical requirements exist, and that it really is a lot easier all round to depict the character outright, rather that plant him in front of a mirror and give him Rembrandt's ability to depict himself.

That last habit is one of the sure signs of the beginner in genre writing. Italy's most recent home-grown crime-fiction wonder boy, Massimo Carlotto, hasn't got even that far yet. But unlike most crime writers, Carlotto has a criminal record, which gives him a flying start with the street cred. In the days of the Red Brigades, he was rounded up in an anti-terror sweep and did time in gaol before being sprung into a life of writing. If only he wrote better. Another dozen novels and he might, but it could be a case of congenital ineptitude that no amount of experience will cure.

Carlotto's latest hit, *The Master of Knots*, is a story of torture, snuff movies and arbitrary death that once again features his free-lance fighter for justice, nicknamed the Alligator. The Alligator drinks Calvados the way the Scots and Irish boys drink whisky, but unlike them, and like most of the other Italian sleuths, he lines his stomach with decent food, evoked in some detail. His friend Max is a cook. 'Max had prepared linguini with a cream sauce containing prawns and aubergines.' Philip Marlowe never ate anything like that. On the other hand, Philip Marlowe never had to listen to anything like the following, which might just possibly sound better in the original Italian, although I wouldn't count on it. ' "We've absolutely got to find a way of stopping the Master of Knots and his gang," Max said angrily.' Those are the moments that make real writers wonder if they shouldn't get into the crime-fiction business and run up a score.

The temptation is as old as the discovery that any real writer can use a cash cow. The British poet C. Day Lewis was once the crime novelist Nicholas Blake, and for a while Julian Barnes was Dan

Kavanagh, whose bi-sexual private eye Duffy patrolled Soho in search of loose change. All over Europe and all through modern history, there have been real writers sending out a sleuth on the same mission. John Banville is the latest to fall for the lure. Banville has adopted the pseudonym Benjamin Black in order to produce a crime novel called *Christine Falls*, starring a pathologist called Quirke.

The action is set mainly in Dublin and Galway of fifty years ago, so that Quirke can smoke and drink all he wants, which is a lot. There can also be poverty, secrecy, fear of pregnancy, bungled abortion and all manner of Catholic scandals of the fine old type. In today's Ireland, as prosperous as Monaco, you practically have to be a Russian au pair girl to get killed, but in Quirke's days of yore there are bodies everywhere. There are also some fine incidental phrases. Banville is a real writer who can really write, and that's the trouble, because the high quality of the incidental prose makes you wonder if his heart is in the main action. Raymond Chandler proved that a gifted writer could occupy himself with genre fiction, but Chandler didn't have all that much gift left over – a serious theme would have left him short of analytical tools. *Christine Falls* actually does face you with the question of whether you really want your crime writer to have that much literary talent – the very question you started off with when you got tired of wondering whether Kate Croy's elaborate description of a house she already knew inside out could not have been juiced up a bit with the presence of a dead body, preferably hers.

In that regard – the question of literary talent – my pick of the current avalanche would have to be Gene Kerrigan's *The Midnight Choir*, starring Inspector Synott. The book is set in today's Dublin, but Synott manages to find a few mysterious bodies in among the parked BMWs. Synott is divorced, drinks whiskey, and eats particularly badly: three scrambled eggs and a couple of slightly off tomatoes when cooking for himself, a cardboard box of Kung-Po-beef takeout when he's in a hurry. But Kerrigan's prose (always supposing that there really is a Kerrigan, and that this isn't Seamus Heaney hustling for a buck) is luxury stuff: brief, funny descriptions, phrases that give you the speaker's age ('*Every move totally ace*'), and a complete financial analysis of a city whose property prices are going up like a flock of flamingos off a lake of money.

I would gladly believe it all, except that Kerrigan doesn't. Synott, his man of integrity, spends the first half of the book being incorruptible, and then the second half trying to frame the perps. Serpico turns into the Prince of the City, and finally we have no hero. Down these mean streets a man must go who is as mean as the streets are? Genre fiction that gets too far into the ambiguous tends to remind us that if we had a hankering for the quasi-meaningless we could have stuck with *le nouvel roman*. It would be nice to think that Kerrigan had got himself lost in a genuine search for complexity, but I fear that he just became impatient with the form.

He was right to. As a form for real writers, the detective novel is bound to be a dry well in the end, because a detective novel, no matter how memorable in the detail, is written to be forgotten. Not even a sure-touch writer like Donna Leon would stay in business if you remembered every bit of every book. You need another meal because you digested the last one: if it had stayed intact in your stomach, you would stop eating. And no matter how carefully depicted, whether by the omniscient author or by themselves looking at length into their own shaving mirrors, the maverick detectives are too consistent to be true characters. As for the action, there is only a finite number of angles at which the hooker's headless corpse can hang from the chandelier. So finally there is nothing left of the books in the memory except the place they are set in.

Essentially they are guidebooks. That's why a maverick detective from Edinburgh outranks a maverick detective from Glasgow, and why we can't get enough of the detective from Venice, and why even Elmore Leonard, who can get so much out of a small American city whose main drag consists almost entirely of franchises – some of which, admittedly, come equipped with a dead body in the dumper out in back – still gravitates towards Los Angeles as the natural stamping ground of Chili Palmer, a criminal with a hankering to bulk large in the film industry, thereby reversing the cliché of the cop with criminal tendencies. Chili Palmer is a criminal with cop tendencies, but even then, his deep-down urge is to have a studio parking space with his name on it in the town they call This Town. Ideally, any author of crime fiction should turn out a sequence of detective novels that will generate a bus tour in the city where they are set.

As a demonstration of that principle, the biggest detective-fiction sensation in Britain in recent years has always been the rather tedious Inspector Morse, because the novels about him and his even more tedious assistant Sergeant Lewis are set in Oxford, and when the Morse mysteries are transferred to television the colleges look wonderful already, even before the enthralled viewer finds out that there is a dead body nailed to an oak door in almost every one of them.

And that's why the undisputedly least fascinating item in the current landfill delivery of detective novels is *The Return*, by the Swedish writer Håkan Nesser. It's set in an unnamed country in Northern Europe, so we don't get to see even the clinically shining pavements of Stockholm. (Down these clean streets . . .) It's just set somewhere out in the countryside, where Inspector Van Veeteren is investigating the mystery of the headless corpse wrapped in a carpet and dumped in a ditch. A transcription of Van Veeteren's thought processes is the main narrative technique. 'Here I am, he thought.' Van Veeteren is profound. 'The world, he thought. Life.' But so is the author. 'What strange worlds there were in existence.' Perhaps so, but not in this part of Scandinavia. There is scarcely a building of any kind to remember. Some spur road into the woods off the highway is the closest the book gets to having any mean streets. As for a man to go down them, Van Veeteren doesn't even remind you of Van Der Valk, the Dutch detective who made a Euro-hit thirty years ago because he was co-starring with Amsterdam. Van Veeteren is playing opposite a ditch. Rarely have I laughed so much at a dead body without a head, hands and feet. It was a male dead body, however, so it couldn't have been Kate Croy. But Van Veeteren himself, though flat as a tack, is not far enough below his many international rivals to stand out, as it were.

No matter how carefully depicted, whether by the omniscient author or by themselves looking into some arbitrarily selected reflecting surface, these purportedly maverick detectives are too much on the one note to be true characters. Given all the other constraints, including the finite number of points in the ceiling from which the hooker's headless corpse can hang, there is by now a looming danger that even the travelogue aspect is fated soon to wear out. In some respects, Henry James had it easier after all. It may be tempting for the reader faced for page after page with one of those placid Jamesian sitting rooms to imagine it being sizzled up with some extra action. 'As the butler entered with her father's head in one hand and a blood-stained Horikawa Kunihiro samurai sword in the other, Kate Croy's nickel-plated automatic coughed once, twice.' But that's just an adventure holiday. The real adventure, less gripping but far more memorable, is waiting to begin again on page fourteen. Real literature is written in the light of the inexorable fact that the mysterious dead body that really matters will one day be ours.

New Yorker, March 17, 2003

Postscript

As Edmund Wilson discovered when he dared to ask the question 'Who Cares Who Killed Roger Ackroyd?', people with a deep commitment to genre fiction are reluctant to concede that their passion might put a question mark over their sensitivity to fiction practised as an art. After I published this piece, I was the target of many letters accusing me of snobbery, when I should have thought it was obvious that I was wide open to the possibility of a genre piece making it on the artistic level: a development always to be welcomed, as long as it actually happens. When Michael Dibdin died, people told me I had been unfair to him, as if there has been a connection between my limiting judgment and his demise. I managed to brush that off, but I am still trying to get over the fact that the excellent Will Self, when he wrote an article about the number of times Raymond Chandler's Philip Marlowe gets hit on the head, seemed never to have seen my article, collected in my book *As of this Writing*, which touched on the same sensitive subject. When one lavishes time and effort on the analysis of the evanescent, one hopes that the cognoscenti will get with the programme. But wait a second: why should they? One of the definitions of genre fiction is that it entertains without benefit of explication. One explicates in the hope of proving that the subject is a bit more serious than that. But if it really were, the point would need no proving. There is a conundrum in there somewhere, and it is permanent.

DENIS HEALEY'S CLASSIC MEMOIR

The unexpectedly high quality of Alistair Campbell's published diary *The Blair Years*, which I came to late and have just finished reading, leads me to wonder if we spend enough time being grateful for living in a post-imperial culture whose politicians and political operatives manage, in a gratifying number of cases, to write their memoirs on a human level. We don't necessarily have to like the person doing the talking. Alan Clarke, for example, would have been reprehensible for his opinions if he had not been so patently unhinged. But his *Diaries* have been compulsory reading ever since they came out. There are so many good books on this particular shelf, in fact, that some of the best ones, after their early fame, forfeit the continuous respect that they deserve.

High on that list, in my opinion, should be placed Denis Healey's *The Time of My Life*. The book is a delight to read, and would be significant even if it were dull, because Healey was such a substantial representative of that generation of British left-wing idealists in the late 1930s who favoured Communism as an answer to fascism, until they found out the hard way that the two brands of totalitarianism were effectively identical. To put it bluntly, they learned that grand plans kill. Idealists of today, though they are less likely to pledge allegiance to a foreign power, are just as likely to be impatient with the imperfections of liberal democracy and its ordinary politics. A reminder that ordinary politics are the only kind that count is always useful. Healey's memoir embodies that truth, as well as providing a model of prose. Since Healey, it seems fair to say, is of an age when we should not hang about if we want to praise him while he is still with us, perhaps it is time for someone to give an account of just how good the book is.

Before discussing its enduring merits, however, we should face the possibility that younger auditors might need reminding of just how big a wheel Healey once was. Let the following few sentences stand as the brief biography that the reader needs in order to appreciate the fact that Healey's autobiography, published in 1989, would have been an event even it had been bad. Healey was born near London in 1917 and raised mainly in Yorkshire, as the Scholarship Boy of a hard-working family. After grammar school he gained a double first at Oxford, spent a brief period as a starry-eyed young Communist, and went on to serve in the British army during World War II. At Anzio, a graduate course for those who survived it, he was Military Landing Officer for the British assault brigade. His experiences in the frustrating Italian campaign, a grim education in the art of the possible, translated readily to post-war British politics. After six years as the Labour Party's International Secretary, he was elected as Member of Parliament for Leeds in 1952, and served for thirty-five years on Labour's Front Bench both in power and out. In Government he was both Defence Secretary and Chancellor of the Exchequer, and in Opposition he was Shadow Foreign Secretary. Whatever the post, he showed such conspicuous ability that many still wonder why he was never Prime Minister, but the best answer is probably the most obvious: though he had the common touch, his superiorities were too striking. Among them was a wide range of learning, worn without pretension but not easily emulated. Delightful from start to finish, his autobiography is an education in itself, disheartening only in its implicit suggestion that it takes the near-breakdown of civilization to produce a generation of politicians who can appreciate the value of what was almost lost. But perhaps we should try to demonstrate its quality with an initial quotation. Try this:

> I was worried by a streak of intolerance in Gaitskell's nature: he tended to believe that no one could disagree with him unless they were either knaves or fools. Rejecting Dean Rusk's advice, he would insist on arguing to a conclusion rather than to a decision. Thus he would keep a meeting of the Shadow Cabinet going, long after he had obtained its consent to his proposals, because he wanted to be certain that everyone understood precisely why he was right.

That comes from page 154 of my paperback edition, and there is something to equal it on almost every other page of the book. One doesn't say that cultivation ensures political acumen. If it did, Neville Chamberlain would have been the most effective Prime Minister in British history. But an empty mind is rarely reassuring. A cultivated man across the whole range of the arts, Healey was a gift from war to peace. If there had been no war, the dazzling double first in Greats might have gone on to be an academic, a scholar, a critic, a writer, a star broadcaster, or any combination of those five things. But the war sent him into politics: real politics, Labour politics, not the Communism he had briefly embraced when too young to know the difference. (Isaiah Berlin said that most of those bright young people who enrolled in the Communist Party in pre-war Britain didn't really want a revolution: they were just liberals who wanted to feel serious.) In parliament, Healey's mere presence on the Labour front bench was enough to make the Conservatives look like philistines. Not all of them were, but few of those who weren't had a mind as well furnished as his. Their culture was part of their inheritance. He had to acquire his, and went on acquiring it throughout his career, out of a passion that was never stilled even by the crushing, necessary boredom of political committee rooms. So it was unsurprising, if gratifying, that he marked his retirement with one of those rare books of political memoirs that connect politics to culture. A book like Noel Annan's *Our Age*, while of comparable quality, is really coming from the other direction, in which the going is far easier. At the end of the war, Annan, as a leading light in the Allied Control Commission, played a key role in fostering the reconstruction of Germany's civilized institutions. It was a difficult task requiring much tact and ingenuity; but that was as far as he went with politics. Post-war, Annan was a cultural grandee, which for a man with his qualifications was easy street. Healey, once he had made his choice, never saw the ivory tower again.

As often happens, the hard road makes for the more revealing journey. There are not many appreciators of Verdi who have been Secretary of Defence. Healey's real university was not Oxford, where he was merely brilliant, but war-time Italy, where he learned the prickly realities of making decisions that could lead to no clear result, but only, at best, to something that might have been worse. The Anzio beach-master's bitter experience (the landing went smoothly, but Kesselring's counter-attack almost undid the whole enterprise) was behind the easy-seeming grace of Healey's slippered prose as old age approached: a grace – and here I switch to the present tense, because his style is still alive – that sins only in its undue fondness for semi-colons, and in the occasional dangling participle. But he isn't being lazy. He is just breathing out. After arguing for a living all his life, now at last he can settle down to be unanswerable.

Nevertheless he is careful to put in plenty of self-deprecation. Opponents are allowed their opinions. If it turns out, as it almost invariably does, that Healey's opinion was better, he tries not to crow. He forgets to record that in 1945 he advised his fellow Labourites not to be panicked by evidence 'that our comrades on the Continent are being extremist'. Annan does not forget: in *Our Age* he quotes chapter and verse of what Stalin was up to, while conceding that Healey changed his mind the following year. But on the whole Healey is convincing when he makes himself sound reasonable. Though he had the reputation of a bully among those he dominated, there was always evidence that the tolerance he claims in retrospect was genuinely there all along, if sometimes well shrouded. I remember that after the first televised session of the House of Lords in 1985, Healey called Lord Stockton's speech 'a lulu'. Since Lord Stockton had started life as Harold Macmillan, and Healey had publicly denounced Macmillan's part in the Suez enterprise as a disgrace, unstinting admiration for a shameless piece to camera was a pretty tolerant reaction to the decrepit lurk-man's latter-day pose as a wise old bird who had seen it all.

Pushing tolerance to the limit, Healey even has good words for Harold Wilson. At the time, Healey's contempt for Wilson's opportunism matched Wilson's fear of Healey's competence: the multilingual Healey was uniquely qualified to be Foreign Secretary, so Wilson kept him busy with every post except that. The good words make Healey's portrait of Wilson even more devastating. In R. H. S. Crossman's long, detailed and hilariously self-approving parliamentary diaries, the portrait of Wilson is devastating too, but Crossman was a zany who amply merited Healey's one-line dismissal: 'A Machiavelli without judgment is a dangerous colleague.' Healey is too well-mannered to argue for his own intellectual superiority over most of his coevals, but the superiority is plain. As with Roy Jenkins, you wonder about the amount of coincidence it must have taken to ensure that he did not become Prime Minister. In a presidential system Healey would have taken the top spot for certain, because he

was dynamite on TV. In the British system, however, the party must
be pleased before the people, and never since Gaitskell has an
intellectual managed to please the Labour Party, unless, like Wilson,
he is ready to wear disguise, or, like Michael Foot, to talk shapeless
waffle on his feet in order to offset his scholarly precision on the
page. Besides, Healey was an unequivocating advocate of nuclear
deterrence, and would have had a chance at the leadership only if he
had equivocated. (Foot, who was helped to the leadership by his
advocacy of the opposite thing, equivocated in the opposite direction
in order to win the general election, and the strain helped to ensure
that he clamorously lost it.) Healey never flaunted his culture, but he
could not conceal it. It was there in the way he talked, and even in
the way he listened. He might demolish somebody else's argument
in a few sentences, but he took it in first.

So Healey had the credentials to detect intolerance in Gaitskell.
Our initial quoted passage is made energetic by the analysis of why
the Cabinet meeting goes on too long: because agreement is not
enough. But the way the passage is illustrated is what shows why
Healey's memoir is of such unusual quality. The reference to Dean
Rusk is not dragged in. It just appears at the right spot with perfect
naturalness. Healey works the same quick magic at least once per
paragraph throughout the book. Other people's observations decorate
his. If his were not so good, the co-opted aphorisms would look like
medals on a dummy. But they are not just worthy of their place,
their place is worthy of them, and so everybody shines. Churchill
never sounded better than when quoted by Healey. As Secretary of
Defence, Healey frequently played host to Montgomery, who would
drop in for a chat when he was up in London visiting the House of
Lords. Montgomery was a lonely man by then, with no object in life
beyond getting the rules changed so that nobody except him could
be called a Field Marshal. The reminiscence is almost touching. But
Churchill's verdict on Monty is quoted to stiffen it up: 'In defeat,
indomitable; in victory, insufferable; in NATO, thank God, invisible.'
Healey had an ear for rhythm, and anyone who has that will hear
rhythm wherever it occurs. He was delighted by every sharp mind he
met. His reputation for brutality might have arisen among those who
knew that they did not delight him. There was a sharp critical ability
at the heart of his wide powers of appreciation, and his excellent
book of memoirs is a reminder that we should value the kind of

public figure more interested in cultivating his mind than polishing his image, even though he is likely to end up being sidelined by the man who is better at the second thing than at the first.

Standpoint, November 2008

Postscript

Somebody wading through Bill Clinton's memoirs, let alone Ronald Reagan's, could be excused for wondering whether the experience of having held public office were not a guarantee against recalling it effectively in print: even the ghost writers sound weary. But there is a contrary tradition of being energized by memory into a captivating summation, and it goes back to Metternich at the very least. (It could be said that it goes back to Clarendon.) From his years at the coal-face of politics, Healey not only remembered the ring of the pick, he got it into his style. The same was true for Abba Eban, whose two main books (*An Autobiography* and *Personal Witness*) were much in my mind while I was reading Healey. It goes without saying that both men knew what they were talking about. What doesn't go without saying is that they knew how to write it down.

ZUCKERMAN UNCORKED

Philip Roth's *Exit Ghost*

In a Moebius striptease, the disrobing stripper is always on the point of getting dressed again, and there is no resolution to the revelation. A Moebius striptease in written form, Philip Roth's new novel *Exit Ghost* is purportedly his long-running character Nathan Zuckerman's new novel, narrated in the first person. During the course of Nathan Zuckerman's new novel, Zuckerman raises the question of just how far an author's personal biography should be drawn into any discussion about his works of art. The answer seems to be that any reader who might want to do so must be a bit of a klutz.

But we get that answer only if we decide that Zuckerman is speaking for Roth when he, Zuckerman, seems to endorse the opinion of Amy Bellette, now old, grey and diseased but once the young mistress, helpmeet and nurse of Zuckerman's mentor and hero E. I. Lonoff, that there is something crassly illiterate about any attempts even by scholars, let alone journalists, to trace the inspiration of her erstwhile lover's works to his actual life. And what if Zuckerman doesn't endorse her opinion? He quotes her at length, but without explicitly agreeing, even though the long letter in which she expresses her objections to biographical reductionism suggests that she can write an essay nearly as well as, say, Philip Roth.

Maybe Zuckerman is withholding judgment. He might well have reason to do so, because in Roth's early Zuckerman works, notably *The Ghost Writer* (first published in 1979, and hey, there's the ghost already), Zuckerman was probing the secrets about the connection between Lonoff's work and his real life even as a character in this new book, Richard Kliman, is hoping, by revealing the facts about Lonoff's real life, to win for the neglected Lonoff the fame that he has always lacked, and thereby get his works republished in the Library of America (the same distinguished imprint which, we alert readers will note, is currently republishing the complete works of none other than Philip Roth – no victim of neglect he). Hoping to? Insisting. There is no getting rid of Kliman. He just keeps on coming back.

As portrayed by Zuckerman, Kliman is irredeemably obnoxious. But room is left for the possibility that the young Zuckerman might once have been a bit less altruistic – a bit more ruthlessly ambitious all round – than he once reported himself as being in the first person, or was reported to be by Roth in the third person. (If you want to go back and check this out, the early, *Zuckerman Bound* sequence of Zuckerman novels is now published in a single, typically sumptuous volume from, you guessed it, the Library of America: but a warning – the name Zuckerman has the word 'sugar' loosely buried within it, and once you give that old hunger a chance to burn again, you might not be able to stop.) What if the decaying Zuckerman, by heaping imprecations on the repellent Kliman, is simply refusing to recognize his pristine young self reborn? Complicated enough for you yet? We're just getting started.

If Zuckerman ever decides that he was once, under his show of Chekhov-loving sensitivity, crassly illiterate to stalk Lonoff, then we might decide that we are crassly illiterate to ask whether Zuckerman's state of health in this new novel has any connection to Roth's in real life. In *Exit Ghost*, Zuckerman, whom we have known since he was young and potent, has had prostate surgery that has left him impotent, not to mention incontinent. (We might not mention it now, but we're going to have to soon.) There is a beautiful young woman in the novel, Jamie Logan, who is willing to be made love to by the avowedly decrepit Zuckerman, but he deliberately fails to keep the appointment, or seems to. (By then he is talking about himself as if he were a character in a play. Maybe he nailed her, but rigged the dialogue to suggest he didn't. See my forthcoming paper *How Unreal was Thereal McCoy? Strategic Female Fantasy Figures in the Disguised Biography of Philip Roth*.)

Is Roth saying, through Zuckerman, that the only reason he, Roth, might fail to show up for such a date is that he is no longer capable of going through with the consequences? Are we allowed to ask whether the real-life Roth, who once had to stave off accusations of providing the model for his character Alexander Portnoy, is no longer in thrall to his virile member, if he ever was? (After all, he never actually *said* he was. He said Portnoy was.) In the last rumour I heard on the subject, one of the most luxuriantly beautiful young Australian female film stars had thrown herself at Roth's feet lightly clad – I mean she was lightly clad, not Roth's feet – and demanded satisfaction.

This rumour might have had no more substance than the one about the famous actor and the gerbil, but it travelled through cyberspace at the same speed, and for the same reason: it fitted the legend. Roth has been catnip for upmarket women all his life, and never not renowned for it. In London, when he lived there, Roth would enter a fashionable drawing room with Claire Bloom on his arm and you would wonder how he had got into the house without a band striking up 'Hail to the Chief'.

Roth might never have been Alexander Portnoy, but the inventor of Alexander Portnoy, unless he was a studious lizard from outer space with limitless powers of telepathic imagination, was a male human being well schooled in carnal relationships with women. It is true that Zuckerman, even when all the books of his saga are taken together, falls short of being a full case of Portnovian satyriasis. Zuckerman lusts after many women, but he does not get to make them all. He gets to make notes on them all. He is a writer. In just such a way, Jay McInerney might have invented an alter ego who was a dietician, and who lured all those fashion models up to his apartment in order to weigh them. How can we fail to ask whether or not Roth still has what it takes, if he presents us with a central character based on himself who has it no longer? But is the character really based on himself? Let's go back to the beginning.

Before we do, we should note that there is no question of abandoning the quest for clarification. *Exit Ghost* is just too fascinating to leave alone. It was designed that way, like the Tar Baby. Actually – leaving all questions about authorial identity aside for the moment – this book is latter-day Roth at his intricately thoughtful best, and a vivid reminder of why a dystopian satirical fantasy like *The Plot Against America* was comparatively weak. Roth has no business making up the world. His business is making up his mind, in the sense that his true material for inventing a pattern is self-exploration, not social satire.

Roth, speaking *in propria persona*, once echoed Tom Lehrer's remark by saying that when Henry Kissinger got the Nobel Prize for Peace it was time to give up on satire. But for Roth it was always time to give up on satire. The world is too obviously out of whack for a writer of his quality to give it the best of his attention. He should reserve that for his own psyche, which is only subtly out of whack, but still would be if he were living in paradise. Unlike the world, his mentality can't be fixed, so a self-assertive rage is inappropriate. Only self-analysis will serve, and to pursue that without solipsism is the continuing challenge. Roth gets as close as anyone ever has to being clinically detached about spreading his own brains all over the operating table. But hold it there. We were going to start again.

And we have to start with the absorbent pads stuffed down the shorts. Zuckerman is leaking yellow water. Doing so, he has run for harbour. To change the metaphor, he has run for cover. He is somewhere up in the Berkshires near Tanglewood, not far from where none other than E. I. Lonoff once holed up to keep the inquisitive literary world at bay. (The possibility that Amy Bellette might really have been Anne Frank would have made the literary world's investigators no less curious, but in this volume Roth has given up on that one.) When Zuckerman comes downtown to see the doctor, he avoids Ground Zero. He no longer wants to keep up with the news, even that news. ('I've served my tour.') But he's still not done with Lonoff.

At the Strand bookshop, Zuckerman puts together, for depressingly few dollars, a complete spare set of Lonoff's first editions. (There was my chance to meet Zuckerman. I could well have been in the Strand at the same time, adding to my row of Philip Roth hardbacks. If they had been first editions, they would have cost me thousands. Was that Zuckerman, the tall, grizzled patriarch in the Rare Book section on the fourth floor who was going through that stack of *New Yorker*s with the original Roger Angell baseball articles? But wait a second: Zuckerman is a ghost.)

In Saul Bellow's first post-Nobel novel, *The Dean's December*, mortal fear centred on the colon: the item of anatomy, not the punctuation mark. ('It's serious enough for me to be wearing the bag.') In Roth's *Exit Ghost*, it centres on the prostate, or anyway on where the prostate used to be. The bearer of the wound can reach no accommodation with his loss. If I can speak for the outside world, which is where I come from, this is the thematic area where the current generation of magisterial American male writers who are now making the last preparations for their immortality – Roth, Vidal, Mailer, Updike – come closest to evincing a common national characteristic.

This glittering crew, a Team America that not even Henry James and Edith Wharton put together could possibly have foreseen, are the most commanding bunch of representatives American literary culture has yet had, but there is something about American culture which doesn't want to accept death as a fitting end to life. They are so incorrigibly energetic that the white light of their expectations bleaches even their pessimism. In that respect, they could all take a tip from, say, Joan Didion, who at least has never imagined that the Grim Reaper gets into the tournament only on a wild card.

But this isn't even a quibble. It's just an observation from someone standing awed and stunned on the sidelines. In my own country, Australia, *Portnoy's Complaint*, first published in 1969, was a banned book for the first five years of its career. Having exiled myself to London, I was able to read it, but even in London there was no mistaking that the Americans were leaving the old British Empire looking not just superseded but mealy-mouthed.

American English had become the dominant language of modern reality. There was still a lot to be said for a version of English that wasn't dominant (the British and ex-colonial writers would go on to prove that post-imperial confusion was at least as fruitful as the imperial success had ever been) but you couldn't mistake the shift of cultural power. Even today, decades later, a British professor of American Studies at a provincial university is in the position of someone with the free run of the PX at the local US Air Force base: he has access to goods whose quality is hard to match locally. As for the home-grown literati, listen to Martin Amis talking about Bellow, and Ian McEwan talking about Updike. Try to imagine the same mentor-prentice relationship in reverse. It might happen one day, but not quite yet. For my own part, I can only say this much: of the two funniest books I have ever read in my life, *Lucky Jim* made me laugh loudest, but *Portnoy's Complaint* set me free.

But in culture as in military strength, preponderance has its drawbacks. The big guns get a sense of mission, and their very confidence invites questions about their vision, even about their ability to gaze within. Just as Bellow, in his factual writings, never asked himself the awkward question about divisions within Israel, so in his fictional writings he stifled a question that would have multiplied his range: he never made a subject out of his succession of discarded wives, when you would have thought – must have thought – that for a writer otherwise so brilliantly introspective, there lay the essence of his subject. Similarly, Mailer, unceasingly writing advertisements for himself, never delved far enough into his own psyche to make a subject out of his complicity in the death of Jack Abbott's victim: the great writer could face every embarrassment except the one that pierced to the centre of his responsibility as a public writer.

Vidal has never admitted, let alone explored, the question of whether his criticisms of the American power elite might not be compromised by his membership of it. Does he really think, when he argues that FDR tricked Japan into World War II, that the Japanese right wing, currently making a come-back, will not take this as an endorsement of its views? And does Updike think we will never ask how his basket-balling Rabbit can have the sensibility of Proust, or whether Bech, the character he created to embody his fame as a writer, was not calculated to increase it?

Finally it is only Roth who takes himself entirely to pieces. Has he been cruel to leave recognizable the outlines of discarded loved ones? Yes. Has he made a subject of that? Yes again. That's why his father keeps on coming back. Even less inclined to be shaken off than the awful Kliman, the fathers of Roth's leading men walk the platform by dead of night. But does even Roth complete the peeling of the artichoke? To look for the answer, we must go back again to the beginning of this new novel, and try, this time, to finish up somewhere beyond the start. For Zuckerman, if not for Roth, potency is gone. Has desire gone with it? You bet your life it hasn't. Listen to this.

> And so I set out to minimize the loss by struggling to pretend that desire had naturally abated, and I came in contact for barely an hour with a beautiful, privileged, intelligent, self-possessed, languid-looking thirty-year-old made enticingly vulnerable by

her fears and I experienced the bitter helplessness of a taunted
old man dying to be whole again.

But she's been there since *Goodbye Columbus*, and as long as he
can imagine her, he *is* whole again. The wholeness is in the style,
which even now, as he (wait a second: as Zuckerman) prays for the
collagen injection to take effect on his slack urethra, proceeds with
the delicious complexity of dream baseball. 'I write a sentence and
then I turn it around,' Lonoff once said in *The Ghost Writer*. 'Then I
look at it and turn it around again. Then I have lunch.' Roth can still
do that. It's still all there. Only the big jokes are gone. He doesn't
laugh that way much any more. The style that sprang from sexual
energy has moved up too far into the head to permit any more gut-
busting inventions like Thereal McCoy. She's still lurking in the
bathroom in *Portnoy's Complaint*, waiting to blow the minds of the
next generation of horny male adolescents: but the man who thought
of her has moved on. A long way from the entrance now, he is near
the exit: or he says he is.

When the Ghost exits, he leaves us asking whether he is real. But
he is real as long as Hamlet thinks so. Lonoff was the ghost of
Zuckerman's father the way that Portnoy's father was the ghost
of Roth's father, who, we may deduce, was pained by the way his
brilliant son won fame. But we deduce it from one of his novels.
In *Zuckerman Unbound*, Zuckerman emerged as the author of
Carnovsky, a book as scandalous to the older generation of Jews as
Portnoy's Complaint. Zuckerman went on to became further established as a writer with a career path very much like Roth's, except of
course, it isn't. Or what if 'isn't' isn't the word? Only the stage
directions confirm that the speaker was ever there.

Exit Ghost. Great title. The book of a great writer. A great book?
Maybe it's just another piece of a puzzle. A great puzzle, and true to
life in being so. In these strange and wonderful books that he writes
under or about another name than his, Roth has been mapping the
geography in an area of life where only his literary heroes – Kafka, of
course, is one of them – have ever gone. The labyrinth of conscious-
ness is actually constructed from the only means by which we can
find a way out of it. It's a web that Ariadne spins from her own
thread. You don't get to figure it out. You only get to watch it being
spun. And if you are Nathan Dedalus (it was Zuckerman's name for

himself in the running heads to the second chapter of *The Ghost Writer*) you are in love with her for life, even if it kills you.

New York Times, October 7, 2007

Postscript

Some of my fellow critics thought I had been far too soft on *Exit Ghost*. But I wasn't just making up for having had to be so hard on *The Plot Against America*, which I reviewed for the *Atlantic Monthly*. (The review is collected in my book *The Meaning of Recognition*, and I hope it shows that I found Roth's book weak only in the context of a strength that I had always revered.) I really do think that Roth's later follow-up novels, the ones that pick up on themes he treated earlier, are valuable even when the action seems thin. They give us his later views on earlier conclusions, and show that they were never concluded. They project the author into time. When the day comes that he is projected into time all the way, even his merest after-thoughts will be seen to enrich a picture which he, after all, was solely responsible for having brought into being. And if Roth's voice seemed less vigorous as time ran out, well, wasn't that part of the story too? As with Kingsley Amis and *Lucky Jim*, Philip Roth, the inventor of *Portnoy's Complaint*, was fated to spend his career on a long march through his own shadow, because that single, early, violently funny book had changed the sensibility of the generation who would read everything he subsequently wrote, and they could never go back to a state in which he seemed so new. But the penalty for knowing only the formative book (what Martin Amis calls 'the talent novel') is to miss the full spiritual development of the author, and, as Martin Amis said again, we don't read books, we read authors.

CULTURE

THE FLIGHT FROM THE DESTROYER

Artists in Exile: How Refugees from Twentieth-Century
War and Revolution Transformed the American Performing Arts,
by Joseph Horowitz

Imagine Balanchine watching a bunch of cheerleaders and you've got this book in a flash. Vignettes are its basic strength, as was bound to be true. The subject of the twentieth-century European artists in exile is too big for one book. Jean-Michel Palmier proved it by publishing his pioneering compendium *Weimar en Exil* as two books, one of them called *Exil en Europe* and the other *Exil en Amérique*. Since there could easily have been others – *Exil en Australie* would have been interesting – it will be appreciated that Palmier himself felt obliged to limit his purview.

Joseph Horowitz gets the story into a single volume by concentrating on a single destination, America, and even then he trims the field. His subtitle 'How Refugees from Twentieth-Century War and Revolution Transformed the American Performing Arts' leaves out the writers, painters, photographers and architects, which means we aren't going to hear much about any of the Mann clan, and nothing at all about Mondrian, Ernst, Leger, Moholy-Nagy, Mies, Gropius, Andreas Feininger, Lyonel Feininger ... but let's stop. Horowitz gives us mainly those exiles who worked in music, theatre and film. Even then, there are more than enough names to be going on with: Balanchine, Stravinsky, Koussevitsky, Toscanini, Stokowski, Kurt Weill and Rouben Mamoulian are only the most prominent.

Horowitz provides biographical sketches for them all, each sketch studded with quotable illustrations. (Otto Preminger, hearing a group of his fellow émigrés speaking Hungarian, said, 'Don't you people know you're in Hollywood? Speak German.') The result is a rich assembly, an unmasked ball teeming with famous names, but you always have to remember – and our author, to his credit, never forgets – that in too many cases their attendance was compulsory, a fact which can lend a sad note to the glamour.

There was a trend towards America anyway. Market forces did their stuff, and even if there had been no wars and revolutions there would have been a transfer of creative power. Horowitz is right to feature Dvorak prominently at the beginning of his line-up of the musicians. In the late nineteenth century, Europe wasn't trying all that hard to drive Dvorak out, but he could see how America was trying to pull him in. The 'New World Symphony' was written not just out of appreciation for America's plantation melodies and rolling landscapes, but out of gratitude for America's readiness to employ him. Mahler, too, went to America for the job opportunities. Caruso could have stayed in Europe but he wanted to sing at the Met, correctly estimating that it was the centre of his world.

In the twentieth century not even the Nazis could send Picasso transatlantic, but after his 1939 MOMA retrospective exhibition New York became the centre of Picasso's financial empire. If Horowitz had been following the money, Picasso would have got a mention. But our author can be excused for following only the physical freedom, which was the thing that the combined totalitarian assault from Soviet Russia and Nazi Germany made obviously crucial. There had always been a flight from Eastern Europe. The flight increased after the Russian Revolution in 1917. Even before the Nazis came to power in 1933, the flight had turned into an exodus. Between 1931 and 1945, fifteen hundred European musicians arrived in America. Most of them would have been superfluous to requirements if there had not been a demand to match the supply.

There was, on the whole, but what America most wanted was the performers, not the composers, who would always be up against it unless, like Korngold, they went to Hollywood because they already had Hollywood in their souls. Stravinsky is famous now mainly for what he composed before he got to America in 1939. Horowitz can make such judgments boldly, out of deep knowledge. The quondam *New York Times* music critic and executive director of the Brooklyn Philharmonic knows the American classical music scene inside out, which is a good thing because that's largely what the European influence did to it, although part of his central point is that the switch had already been worked before the main influx arrived.

Horowitz has a paradox to deal with here, and out of it he makes his most useful general argument. According to him, the American home-grown composers were up against it too. The pressure was always on them to produce a uniquely American equivalent of the European serious musical tradition. This being so, they tended to ignore the implications of the American popular music tradition that had already burgeoned in the jazz joints, in Tin Pan Alley and on Broadway. George Gershwin and Leonard Bernstein, both of Russian parentage, would be exceptions in seeing a way ahead in the Broadway musical show. Copland, also of Russian parentage, was more typical in finding no time at all for jazz: he sought a more elevated way of sounding American. Most of the immigrant composers, however, were impressed by the native vernacular energy, just as Dvorak had been, although he was in America for only two years and wrote the Negro Spiritual themes in the 'New World Symphony' well before he had ever travelled far enough outside New York to hear them being sung in their locations of origin.

For the new arrivals in the twentieth century, most of whom made landfall with nothing but their luggage to call their own, the upsurge of American popular music was so clamorous that they had to be theorists to miss it. Adorno ran true to form by dismissing jazz out of hand, but he was only an intellectual. Kurt Weill, Adorno's *bête noire* (the feeling was mutual), immersed himself in the new vitality. It had already reached him at long range when he was still in Weimar Germany, composing the music for Bertolt Brecht's words. Closer now to the source of the theatrical exuberance he felt himself cut out for, Weill embraced Broadway with an intensity that most of the American native big names – they included Sessions and Ives as well as Copland – never dreamed of.

George Gershwin, the most gifted of all the home-grown American composers, was similarly open to the demotic allure of his birthplace, but he died young. Weill himself was dead when he was fifty, but in his time alive in America he exemplified how a newcomer was more likely to be impressed by his new country than anyone who was born and raised there. Weill built up an achievement with his Broadway show music but after the war the achievement was put in the shade by the arrival in New York of a *Threepenny Opera* production, starring Lotte Lenya, that enabled his critics to say he had expressed his real strength in the old country and had been dissipating it ever since he arrived on the Great White Way.

Horowitz rather agrees with them, saying that Brecht's lyrics had given Weill's music the 'distance' it needed not to sound compromised by the desire to please. Horowitz doesn't say what Lotte Lenya once said on television in her old age. (She said, 'What was Brecht without Kurt?') Most of us rate the *Mahagonny* music above, say, *Lost in the Stars*, but surely we should avoid the kind of determinism that would blame America for restricting Weill's range. Weill himself thought his range had been increased, and only a snob would call him materialist for viewing the cash-flow that rolled in from a hit show like *One Touch of Venus* as hard evidence that it had.

Bartok wrote some of his best music in America. In 1945 he died broke, but only after a wave of artistic success that included the Sonata for Unaccompanied Violin, the Concerto for Orchestra, and the Third Piano Concerto. If he had accepted either of the posts offered to him by the Curtis Institute and Tanglewood he might even have had some money in the bank. Krenek, Eisler, Dessau and Zerlinsky all flopped in America but they would have cared less about that if they had really thought that the odds were stacked against art. The odds were stacked against a free ride. When Krenek, who had made his name in Europe as the composer of *Jonny Spielt Auf*, denounced the American requirement of 'comprehensibility' as an automatic diluent, he was really saying that there was nobody to pay him for incomprehensibility. By the time he died, at ninety-one, the day had already arrived when American cultural foundations were ready to pay for anything, down to and including John Cage composing passages of modified silence, but for Krenek that final expansion of American hospitality had come too late. Even when the last door was still shut, however, all the other doors were open. Schoenberg, Hindemith and Bartok couldn't make a living like Stravinsky, but at least they had the chance. Sometimes it must have seemed tantalisingly close. In Hollywood, Schoenberg played ping-pong with a neighbour. It was George Gershwin.

The case of Schoenberg raises the character issue: he actually had to concentrate quite hard to stay unpopular, cursing himself whenever he lapsed from the atonal back into something that a non-expert audience might have liked. Not even the basket cases could honestly say that they had fallen among Philistines. They had fallen into a larger competitive market than the one that they had been driven out of, and even if they failed in it they would have liked to succeed. Korngold's success might have seemed silly and Weill's meretricious, but the possibilities were there: more possibilities than most of them could handle. Weill welcomed the chance to work without subsidy in a country where he had to make his luck. Weill phrased these opinions in press releases that now sound like publicity material for a right-wing think-tank, thereby handing his latter-day critics large sticks with which to beat him. But none of those critics could have written 'September Song'.

All six of Martinu's symphonies came from his time in the US, between 1941 and 1953. In sum, even when they failed, the non-American composers did a more thorough job than the home-grown Americans of being turned on by America. Some of them felt limited by the indifference of the audience to anything labelled as art, but there was always a minority audience for that. There was a minority audience even for Schoenberg. On a world scale, Schoenberg's audience, for his atonal music that came after *Verklärte Nacht*, is still a minority today, but most of the minority is in America, where the minorities are larger. As for the American majority audience, they wanted music they could enjoy on the night. They wanted to go home whistling the tune. (Horowitz could have made a lot more of this point. There was a crisis going on in serious music, not just in world politics.) They wanted a show.

They so much wanted a show that they rated performers over composers. Performers stood out from the orchestra and could be admired for their virtuosity. The financial rewards for virtuosity were so huge that they needed satirical apology: Heifitz had a cash register standing on the bar of his apartment. The conductors stood out more than anybody and could inspire cults. Horowitz is particularly good on the conductors. Koussevitsky and Toscanini come out of the book as towering figures, as we might have expected. But Horowitz, always with his fine ear turned towards the quality of the music, generously lets Stokowski do a bit of towering too. The Stokowski paragraphs add up to a box of chocolate-dusted truffles.

As opposed to some of the other European con-men, Stokowski was fake to the roots. Erich von Stroheim at least knew how to pronounce the word 'von' before he stole it. 'Leopold Antoni Stanis-law Boleslawowicz Stokowski' undoubtedly had a Polish background back there somewhere, but his real name was Leopold Anthony Stokowski and he was born in England. His first wife, Olga Samaroff, was really Lucy Hickenlooper. She had met the right man. Stokowski made up the whole thing. Even his accent was made up.

Yet Stokowski, where it counted, was the real McCoy. Arriving in Philadelphia in 1912, he built up its orchestra into a sensationally effective musical instrument all on its own. Rachmaninov thought it was the finest orchestra he had ever heard. And whether or not Stokowski ever slept with Greta Garbo – his personal testimony on the subject might be comparable to the Hollywood restaurateur Mike 'Prince' Romanoff's personal testimony that he was a Russian noble-man who shot Rasputin – there can be no doubt that the conductor could read the dots. Admirers of Furtwängler must always deal with accusations that too much rubato alters the score. Stokowski practi-cally rewrote the score. (After every performance, all the parts had to be returned to his safekeeping, as if they were atomic secrets.) But the results were stunning.

Stokowski conducted the first performance in America of Mahler's 8th Symphony. Brought up on the Solti rendition, I had never got around to seeking out a recording of Stokowski's later live concert performance of the work. Now I will. Similarly, Horowitz recommends the recording of Stokowski with the Boston Symphony on the night of January 13, 1968. The way Horowitz raves learnedly about the great Eurofraud's treatment of Tchaikovsky's *Hamlet* Fantasy Overture ('such lightning velocity, hair-trigger intensity, and opulent upholstery ... the plush but tensile string choir') should send any reader diving into Amazon like Lara Croft into a tomb. I couldn't find the recording listed, but now I know it exists. eBay next stop.

Horowitz's book, always interesting, starts looking essential when it lights up like that, evoking a specific subject of his enthusiasm with sufficient vividness to make the reader want to get in for a share of the delight. I would still recommend the Los Angeles County Museum of Art's 1997 catalogue album *Exiles + Emigres* (published in conjunction with Abrams and edited by Stephanie Barron) as the indispensable first book on the subject, but it is narrated by many voices, and there is always room for a single voice that knows how to register informed excitement. After all, any big picture we might have is bound to have started among those small responses, none of which seemed small at the time – each of them, in fact, was so all-consuming that it drove any question of a big picture clean out of our heads.

Individual works of art can make it hard to get a big picture even of the single mind that produced them. Forty years into its life and still the epitome of international American chic, the iced refinement of Balanchine's 'Jewels' for the New York City Ballet began with the raunch of his 'Slaughter on Tenth Avenue' routine for the Broadway show *On Your Toes* in 1936. Balanchine didn't create music directly but he had a means of interpreting it that made his influence profound. He could remake American ballet in his own manner because America didn't have much ballet in the first place. Once again, a sophisticated American elite's fondness for Europe was a big help. Balanchine's impresario, Lincoln Kirstein, didn't want a Martha Graham-style company. He wanted New York to have a European-style ballet corps. Balanchine, always mad for the girls, was glad to oblige. Crucially, however, Balanchine himself was no longer European. He loved Jack Benny, he had seen the Western movies, he had driven across the country. And he had seen the cheerleaders. The embodiment of high aims yet uninhibited by hierarchy, he could lend style even to the vulgar: his tribute to its energy. It wasn't Walt Disney, it was Balanchine, who first put elephants in tutus so that they might dance to music by Stravinsky. The commission came from Ringling Brothers Circus.

Horowitz sensibly leaves the question open of whether Balanchine brought Europe to America or else helped America develop something it already had. Our author would have been wise to show similar openness when talking about the movies. He tries to, but can't help suggesting that such eminent Europeans as Murnau and Fritz Lang had a hard time adapting to the new populist idiom. He fudges the question of whether the new populist idiom might not have had a narrative power far in advance of expressionism, symbolism or any other ism that the refugees had been forced to leave behind. One gets the sense that Horowitz, worthily brought up in the concert hall, missed the chance to waste his early years in the movie house, and has only recently been catching up with the filmed masterpieces.

But there were plenty of second-rate Hollywood movies that would have told him how the studio moguls often had first-rate tastes. (They were continually spatchcocking operatic arias into musical comedies otherwise uniformly dire.) Stuck with nothing except quality, Horowitz can appreciate the achievements of Wilder and Lubitsch. He appreciates Lubitsch so well that he crosses his own wires when he calls Lubitsch 'a clever middlebrow craftsman mistaken for a highbrow genius.' After spending a whole book usefully arguing that the refugee highbrows seldom got the point about democratic art, it seems Quixotic to belittle Lubitsch for not having been one of them.

Still, Horowitz can see that *Ninotchka* is an extraordinary example of America projecting a liberal vision of Europe back into its own ruins. He just might have made more of the possibility that it wasn't only a case of the refugees changing the American arts, it was a case of the American arts changing the world, refugees included. Through the movies, a single refugee, Rouben Mamoulian – the star of the book's useful chapters on theatre – opened the way for the most globally influential trend of the lot: the Broadway show expanded for the screen. One could only wish that Horowitz had seen *Luxury Liner* the year it came out, and had therefore seen Lauritz Melchior singing from *Aida* for Jane Powell. But he has seen and remembered every frame of a much earlier movie, *Love Me Tonight*, in which Mamoulian created, almost in its entirety, the cinematic language for the Hollywood musical, at a time when, many critics will tell you, the sound-proofed camera was still confined to its booth. Mamoulian made it fly.

The result was a marvel. How Horowitz says so will set his younger readers clamouring to see it. The book thus once again fulfils an aim that it didn't know it had. Meanwhile the principal aim, to give the big picture, retreats further into the distance, as was inevitable. European and American culture have always been a two-way interchange and to talk about either of them exclusively is like trying to cut water in half with a knife. Horowitz says that Stokowski's dream of a democratic high culture never arrived. But it couldn't, because such a thing can exist, as an aim, only in theory. In practice, a successful artistic event deals with the anomaly by removing it. On radio, Stokowski conducted the Mahler 8th Symphony for an audience bigger than the population of old Vienna. On screen he shook hands with Mickey Mouse. Yet there was talk of a movie about Wagner with Stokowski in the leading role. You can bet that he worked on the accent, waiting for the green light. Stokowski, like Gatsby, believed in the green light. So did they all, even when their ambitions came to nothing. A least they were free to try.

TLS, July 9, 2008

Postscript

The critic with aspirations to scope should always be aware that a sideswipe might dismiss a life, but I must try to forgive myself when it comes to the case of Adorno. He has enough champions, especially in the academy, but there are too few independent voices ready to admit how tremendously wrong he was about popular music. A pianist good enough to play Bach at concert level, he had solid qualifications for promoting serious music as the only kind that counted. But as a sociologist, he had no business peddling the idea that the American popular music industry imposed bad taste on the public as a matter of deliberate engineering. The tastes of the public shape the industry, and not vice versa. Only a sociologist could believe anything different. Hit songs, no matter how bad, come from inspiration, not calculation. Luckily it was only a tiny minority of refugee artists and intellectuals who managed to convince themselves that they had fled one tyranny only to end up in another. Adorno, however, was that minority's key man, and his vision of capitalism's infinite powers of repressive calculation infects the academy to this day, making its views on how popular culture actually works almost useless. Adorno, by and large, was a chump. But I still would like to have written *Minima Moralia*.

SAYING FAMOUS THINGS

Nobody knows who said it, but it was no accident, as the more pompous academics say, that the magnificent cod-Latin joke *Sic transit Gloria Swanson* was cracked somewhere in the vicinity of Billy Wilder. The professionally witty Viennese master had the blessed gift of making amateurs funny too. He heightened the atmosphere; everybody wanted his respect; people wanted to be remembered the next day for having said something funny the previous night, with Wilder listening.

According to legend – i.e. the facts are almost certainly otherwise – the line was delivered in the foyer after the premiere of *Sunset Boulevard*. According to likelihood, it was probably first delivered in a Paramount screening room at an early stage of assembling the rough cut, and might even have been said by Wilder himself. Not all of Wilder's best ideas were hatched in tandem with I. A. L. Diamond: only most of them. Wilder's wit benefited from collaboration, which graces you with the presence of an editor.

Judging from his interviews, Wilder noticed everything, but rarely narrowed the focus of his observation to the point where an epigram flared into independent life. It was because English was not his first language. When hearing it, he was sensitive to every nuance, but when speaking it he was only as quick as he spoke, and to construct a striking remark as you go you have to be ahead of the game. Working with Diamond, Wilder could realize his potential. In their best lines, nobody will ever puzzle out which of them did what: they were like songwriters. In one of their minor comedies, there is a whole scene which they probably dreamed up just for one line. The pretty girl is given a knee injury just so that the hero can examine it and say: 'What's a joint like this doing in a girl like you?'

It doesn't really matter which movie it is. Ideally, Walter Matthau should have said it to Kim Novak in *Kiss Me Stupid*. But Walter Matthau got sick and couldn't play the lead in that one. He played the lead in *The Fortune Cookie*, but I can't remember a pretty girl with a bad knee. (Since you can't yet Google on that deep level, I will have to go right though both DVDs to track down the line: but one day I'll nail it.) Still, you don't have to imagine Matthau saying the line. It's enough to imagine Wilder saying it: perhaps saying it just after Diamond whispered it in his ear. Nobody ever heard Diamond say much. It seems safe to conclude that he spent most of his time listening. In Hollywood, there was always a lot to listen to.

In Hollywood, 'The son-in-law also rises' is a remark that was already part of the culture before World War Two. Like the original author of 'Sic transit Gloria Swanson', the original author of 'The son-in-law also rises' has never been tracked down, possibly because the joke was first made before David O. Selznick ever met Louis B. Mayer's daughter, after which it was on everybody's lips, the name players being on everybody's mind. But although the prospect of their marriage might possibly have inspired the remark, it is much more likely that the marriage simply made an already circulating witticism current.

The same remark about the son-in-law became current all over again when Count Ciano married Mussolini's daughter Edda, and was rewarded with an exalted portfolio as Foreign Minister for Italy. In other words – or, rather, in exactly those words – everybody was saying it. All we can be reasonably sure of is that nobody said it before Hemingway first published a book called *The Sun Also Rises*. Like all of Hemingway's book titles, this one continues to be a sure-fire draw in the book shops. Part of its charm, however, is in its indeterminacy, as with a beautiful woman who might be smiling specifically at you or just happen to be smiling in your direction.

When correctly emphasized – on the word 'rises' – Hemingway's title tells us that the sun does one of two things. The joke, therefore, depends on a misreading. In the joke, there is no suggestion that sinking is the other thing that the son-in-law does. The joke means that the son-in-law rises like the son. It could have been the lurking ambiguity in the title, incidentally, that encouraged Hemingway's English publishers to insist on a change, to *Fiesta*: clean and neat, but nothing like as haunting. The American title worked so insidiously on the memory that it was widely recognizable even to people who had never read the book. Having attained such currency, it attracted variations: hence the success of the joke.

After World War Two, Edward Albee's title *Who's Afraid of Virginia Woolf?* attained a similar currency. Albee's title was already a joke, depending on the neat substitution of 'Virginia' for 'the big bad'. But in several thousand titles for magazine articles – it still happens today – that point, which was the only point, is blithely ignored, and little is kept except the 'Who's afraid' and the concluding question mark. In 'Who's Afraid of Virginia Wade?' the joke was still there, if only at two removes, but a title like 'Who's Afraid of Varicose Veins?' tells you nothing except the name of the subject. Who's afraid of a clapped-out trick? No magazine editor. The wittiest variation on the standard line was a title by Alan Bennett – 'Me: I'm Afraid of Virginia Woolf' – but it was a crucial one word too long to catch on.

Every smart remark has to be made for the first time, but we should be suspicious when a famous person gets the credit, unless the famous person is also a famous wit. An obvious example is Marilyn Monroe's reply to the set-up question about what she wore in bed. 'Chanel No. 5,' she is reputed to have said, but even at the time there was a wide-spread assumption that a publicity man had both prompted the question and supplied the answer. The chances are good, however, that Noel Coward actually did make up on the spot his famous remark about the very large Queen of Tonga and the very small man who was in the open carriage with her at the Coronation of Queen Elizabeth II: 'That's her lunch.' Nowadays the joke needs a health warning on grounds of its flagrant political incorrectness, but at the time it was thought hilarious, and not least because the fastidious Coward had said it.

Though Coward was not, at that time, generally known to be homosexual – the acknowledgment came only after his death – he was universally recognized as being dainty in his ways, so the brutalism was all the more delightful. (Robert Helpmann got the same reaction for his reputed reply to a New York cop who called him a fairy: apparently Helpmann took to the air, touched the cop with an imaginary magic wand, and squealed 'Disappear!') The best reasons for thinking that Coward made up the line about Queen Salote's lunch was that he had a reputation to protect, and would not have wanted to be caught borrowing. But there is also the possibility that, even if he thought of it on his own, he might not have been the first to do so. White imperialists visiting Tonga might long before have noticed the discrepancy in size between Queen Salote and any attendant male. Most people who recount the story now – usually as part of a roster of Noel Coward anecdotes –supply the information that the small man in the carriage with her was the king.

If somebody else made the remark first, the remark still didn't come into its own – into its life – until it was heard from Noel Coward, because at last it had found someone famous enough to be its author, even if, as it were, he wasn't. The same might apply to Liberace's supposed authorship of a classic response by an artist to his hostile critics: 'I cried all the way to the bank.' Prey to the delusion that a candelabra on the piano would add something to Tchaikovsky, Liberace over-delivered his signature wisecrack as he over-delivered everything, and that should have been a tip-off, because the phrasing belongs to someone who understands under-statement. It sounds, in fact, like New York humour (i.e. Jewish humour) and was almost certainly already old in the nineteenth century, let alone the twentieth. All it needed for immortality was a sufficiently famous mouth to say it. Liberace's mouth got the job, and took the credit.

A full sixty years after his suicide, every article written about the unspeakable Hermann Goering still gives him respectful acknowledg-ment for the crack about reaching for his gun when he heard the word 'culture'. (The respect comes from the fact that the journalists themselves secretly rather fancy the idea of armed philistinism.) Though Goering reached for the cyanide when he heard the word 'rope', his lasting reputation as a wit was already secure. The real author of the remark was the official Nazi writer Hanns Johst, but he was never remembered for saying it, mainly because he was an official Nazi writer, and therefore never remembered for saying anything, even at the time.

The dim bulb Johst's solitary flash of inspiration – far more successful than any of his plays and poems – refused to stick with him. A smart saying is usually as anonymous as a sucker fish in search of a shark. When it finds one, it begins its long ride in a tunnel of reflected glory, while the source of the glory gets the credit for powers of invention equal to its prominence. By now more than forty years have gone by since Lyndon Johnson added to his fame for an acutely foul mouth by giving the press an exclusive on why he hadn't fired J. Edgar Hoover. 'I'd rather have him inside the tent pissing out than outside the tent pissing in.' It's the perfect smart remark, but that's exactly the reason to suspect that LBJ didn't think of it first. No amount of harping on the point, however, will ever again get such a saying separated from the celebrity who is reputed to have said it. Does this anomaly matter? Only as a reminder that even the written record consists almost entirely of distortions. One of the basic things a young writer about any branch of history needs to learn is that if a quote sounds good, the person quoted is saying something that somebody else said first.

The Monthly, March 2007

Postscript

The treasuring and propagation of smart remarks is a tribute we pay to an ideal. We would all like to take part in conversations where things that neat are said. In reality, they seldom are. Most conversations are babble. A tape-recording of all the conversations at a book launch, with all the cleverest authors in town duly present and striving to impress, would sound not much better than Christmas Eve in a mental hospital. Every year, some aspiring young television producer gets the idea of shooting a dinner party. It never works, not because the dinner party in a studio doesn't sound like a real dinner party, but because it does.

INSULT TO THE LANGUAGE

In which English-speaking country is the English language falling apart fastest? Britain. Are things as bad in Australia? I hope not. In Britain, in 2006, the Labour government is still trying to fix Britain's education system, but surely one of the reasons it's so hard to fix is that most of the people who should know how are themselves the system's victims, and often don't even seem to realise it. They need less confidence. Even when they are ready to admit there might be a problem, few of them realise that they lack the language to describe it.

An appropriate sense of desperation has been insufficiently quick to set in. As recently as 2001, one of Britain's higher educational journals carried a letter signed by more than five hundred university professors, lecturers and teachers of English. They all concurred in a single opinion. 'The teaching of grammar and spelling is not all that important.' But every signatory of that letter must have been well aware that a depressing number of his or her students and pupils would have written the sentence another way: 'The teaching of grammar and spelling are not all that important.' We can only hope that the number has since decreased. The government would like us to think it has. But the evidence from the media and everyday life suggest that most people would be at a loss to find anything wrong with the first clause of the sentence I am writing now, except, perhaps, the whining irascibility of its tone.

Unless taught better, even a quite bright student will not realise that 'the evidence' is the subject, and takes the singular. The 'and' linking 'media' and 'everyday life' makes the noun phrase look like a plural, and so, by attraction, the plural verb is put in automatically. People who have learned English as a second language rarely make the error, because they were taught some grammar along with the vocabulary. But people who have learned English as a first language are increasingly likely to be driven to a plural verb by a plural-sounding singular subject, and precisely because they have learned the language by ear, instead of by prescription. In an infinite variety of forms, the same mistake can be seen in the feature pages of the British quality press every week. (The trash papers, oddly enough, are still relatively immune: perhaps because some of the old union-ised subeditors are still on the case.)

Even the most intellectually upmarket publications are not exempt. Before Fleet Street's necessary but regrettable disintegration, the editors and subeditors of the quality broadsheets knew how to fix the solecisms of ambitious young journalists who had some-how dodged the school system. But at the very time when the school system itself became a potent incubator for the semi-literate scribbler, the sudden multiplication of culture-page outlets meant that there were no longer enough cultivated editors and subeditors to go round, and by now some of the editors and subeditors are themselves products of the anti-educational orthodoxy by which expressiveness counts above precision. It would, if the two terms were separable. But they aren't. Beyond a certain point – and the point is reached early – precision is what expressiveness depends on.

Startled by the high-level declaration in 2001 that grammar and spelling were not very important, I began keeping a record, for the first time, of the blunders as they flooded by. I expected the flood to abate. But by now I am sitting on top of the house, and my notes for that crucial year are in my trembling hand. Things had gone haywire a long time before that, of course, but that was the year when the people in charge had the hide to tell us that it didn't matter. They could hardly have picked up even the most posh of newspapers without encountering evidence that it mattered like mad. On 12 May 2001, someone on the *Guardian*'s literary page asked, 'What would Philip Larkin make of a new collection of his work, *Further Requirements*?' Reasonably all right so far, although the unspecific 'a' would have been better as a 'the' or a 'this'. But then the literary someone answered his own question. 'Having selected all the material for *Required Writing*, in 1983, and then died a mere two years later, one might regard a second volume as *de trop* . . .'

The French tag is a claim to clerical expertise that the dangling participle scarcely supports. In 2001, the literary someone has failed to notice that he has composed a sentence in which he dies in 1985.

It would be asking too much to expect the literary someone to realise that he is not qualified to read Beatrix Potter, let alone Philip Larkin: but he might at least read his own stuff with his ears open. Evelyn Waugh occasionally dangled a modifier, and Anthony Powell dangled them like a boat fishing for tuna; but a less gifted writer would do best to avoid the practice. All too often, such blunders of mismatched apposition drive the reader to re-work the sentence himself before he can figure out what the writer must mean. When the writer is getting all of the fee, and the reader is doing at least half of the labour, the discrepancy can cause resentment.

In the *Observer* of 13 May 2001 the aviation correspondent drew on his reserves of metaphor to recreate the Concorde crash near Paris the previous year. The historical present is a bad tense in which to evoke anything, but worse than that is on offer. 'Already mortally wounded, flame bleeds uncontrollably from beneath the left wing.' The bleeding flame has everything wrong with it apart from the mixed metaphor: for the aircraft to bleed flame, it would have had to have flame in its veins and arteries, whereas what it had was aviation gasoline. But what really screws the sentence is the dangler, which makes the bleeding flame mortally wounded. He means that the aircraft was mortally wounded. Luckily you know he must mean that, because he has been talking about the aircraft in the previous sentence. So this sentence counts as a mild case. In thousands of more severe cases, from hundreds of other writers, mismatched apposition introduces genuine confusion. 'At the age of eight, his father died in an accident' can be construed on its own, after a brief pause for thought. 'At the age of eighteen, his father died in an accident' gets you into the area of needing to look elsewhere in the piece to find out what's going on.

In its best years, *Private Eye* was written by privately educated junior mandarins who could make a stylistic analysis of yob-speak in order to score satirical points. But in June 2001, issue No. 1029 carried the following sentence as straight reportage. 'Unheard of before the Tories plucked them from obscurity, cynics suggested that Smith Square couldn't afford a more established agency . . .' After looking back, you can deduce that an advertising agency called Yellow M was plucked from obscurity, and not the cynics. A thousand issues before, you would never have had to bother. For a long time, *Private Eye*'s literary page was free of illiteracy, but now the disease is rampant even there. In No. 1042, for 30 November 2001, Andrew Morton's catchpenny biography of Madonna was given what was obviously meant to be an exemplary wigging, but the reviewer calamitously proved that his grip on the language was no more firm than that of his lumbering victim. 'With countless newspaper serialisations and the most fortuitously timed royal death in the history of publishing behind him, any celebrity bum-chum knows that the phone call from Morton is akin to Judas's 30 pieces of silver.' In whatever way something is timed, it can't be timed fortuitously: the reviewer means 'fortunately'. But the real damage is done by the muffed apposition. It can't be the celebrity bum-chum that has all that stuff behind him, so it must be Morton. Or so we presume, if we are still reading. But why would we be doing that?

The Internet magazines are a rich source of tangled connections. Their contributors are computer literate but that doesn't make them literate, and indeed seems to ensure the opposite. Here is a sentence from the July 2001 issue of one of the glossiest Internet magazines, *the net*. (The preference for lower case, incidentally, is already a bad sign about the standard of literacy in the wired world: the illustrative use of upper case amounts to an information system, and to abandon it means being less communicative, not more.) But let's try again: here is the sentence. 'Once up and running the guardians of copyright are really going to have their work cut out to close it down.'

Sad experience has already taught the reader that 'it' is more likely than 'the guardians of copyright' to be the noun element that will soon be 'up and running'. Previous sentences reveal that 'it' is the Freenet file-sharing system for pirated feature movies; and that the Freenet system is still in development, and is therefore a likely candidate for being described as not yet up and running. Armed with that information, you can put the meaning of the sentence together. But the saddest thing about the sad experience is your hard-won knowledge that if the author had meant the guardians of copyright to be the subject of description, he would have put the adjectival element in the wrong place by about the same distance: 'The guardians of copyright are really going to have their work cut out to close it down, once up and running.'

On the Web itself, the standard of English is even worse than in the magazines. The characteristic sentence on the Web is transmitted in a nano-second across the world and then slows to a crawl within

the reader's brain, almost always because the grammar is out of
whack: vocabulary is abundant, but its analytical deployment is an
approximate mess. Efficiency of expression is in inverse proportion
to the precision of the machines. It is sadly possible to predict a
future in which anybody will be able to transmit any message at any
speed but nobody will be able to say anything intelligible.

Especially in those American glossy magazines with pretensions
to being investigative, there is a brand of lumpen prose that perpe-
trates no real howlers but still weighs like lead because the reader
continually has to join in the writing. In *Vanity Fair* for May 2001,
an informative article about Bill Clinton's abandoned colleague
Webb Hubbell evoked the scene when Hubbell was taken back to
Little Rock to testify. 'He arrived in the city where he had once been
mayor handcuffed and shackled.' Unless he was handcuffed and
shackled while he was mayor, this sentence is just a mass of raw
material waiting for the reader to make something of it. Ostensibly
there is nothing much wrong with the grammar, but the word order
is out of control; and in English composition, because the language
is relatively uninflected, word order and grammar are seldom without
connection. The sentence could be mended at the price of one
comma: 'Handcuffed and shackled, he arrived in the city where he
had once been mayor.' The *New Yorker*'s style police would probably
want two commas ('He arrived, handcuffed and shackled, in the city
where he had once been mayor') because the *New Yorker* likes the
noun stated in front of any qualification, in case the reader cancels
his subscription while being kept in suspense.

But faulty word order, when it does not introduce confusion, is a
secondary issue compared with faulty grammar when it does. You
can write charmlessly without insulting the reader. But to write
ungrammatically, and not realise it, is to insult the English language.
It also removes the possibility of being ungrammatical on purpose:
a real impoverishment when it comes to special effects. And in this
respect the British are a long way ahead of the Americans: a long way
ahead, that is, on the road to perdition.

'Even as Congress was voting,' wrote Anthony Holden in his New
York Diary for the *Observer*, 18 November 2001, 'one rogue security-
dodger in Atlanta was enough to grind the world's busiest airport to
a prolonged halt . . .' Anthony Holden once gave me some crucial
help on a Washington assignment, so to quote one of his less polished

sentences might seem a harsh way to reward him, but I like to think he would do the same for me. The language, as Keats said after being repelled by Milton, should be kept up. Holden is a long-serving professional whose prose is normally as well calculated as his poker playing, and the *Observer* section editors were once the best in Fleet Street. But on this occasion both the writer and his editor must have nodded off at once. The original metaphor depends for its effect on evoking the sound of some mechanism grinding to a halt. The metaphor is fatally diluted when something grinds something else to a halt: for one thing, it would be a slow way of stopping an airport.

Usually, when a metaphor slithers into imprecision, it is because the activity from which it was drawn is no longer current practice. Nobody gets the picture, because there is no longer a picture to be got. The expression 'loose cannon', for example, grew from the actuality of an untethered cannon, through its enormous weight, working havoc on the gun-deck of a wooden warship rolling and pitching in heavy weather. For a long time there have been no wooden warships, but the metaphor stayed accurate while everybody who could read was still reading C. S. Forester. Finally some journalist who hadn't, but who liked the ring of the expression, falsely deduced that the loose cannon caused damage because its barrel was too big for the shot, and so we started hearing about the damage the loose cannon might do when fired.

Similarly, 'he shot himself in the foot' originally referred to a soldier in the Great War who hoped that a self-inflicted wound would buy him a ticket out of the trenches. Perhaps because of the irresistible mental image of a Western gunslinger pulling the trigger while getting his revolver out of its holster, the metaphor is nowadays almost universally used to evoke clumsiness rather than cowardice. Sometimes the words within the metaphor change. 'Home in' is now often written as 'hone in' because the writer thinks 'hone' sounds rather grand without knowing what it means: the age has passed when knives needed to be re-ground. Now they can just be replaced.

Examples of deteriorating metaphors could be multiplied. There is seldom any stopping the process after it begins to affect good writers. Bad writers can be mocked, but good writers inexorably spread the word: and if the word is the wrong one, the language changes. As I put the finishing touches to this piece in May 2006, A. A. Gill, the excellent television critic on the *Sunday Times*, has just used the word 'solipsisms' where he obviously meant 'solecisms'. Gill is dyslexic, so he had a good excuse. But his editor had no excuse at all. The chances are that he simply didn't know the difference, and that on the *Sunday Times* the number of solecisms will inexorably increase, and that they will be called solipsisms if they are noticed at all.

The language has always changed, so to protest looks reactionary. If there were no reactionaries, however, deterioration would become galloping decay. In reality, decay does not gallop, but we all know what a horse is even if we have not ridden one, so everyone realises, so far, that 'galloping' is being used metaphorically. When all the horses have gone, 'galloping' will just mean 'rapid'. After a galloping shave that spattered the bathroom mirror like a loose cannon, he honed in on his car, but when he could not find his keys he was ground to a halt by the awful realisation that he had shot himself in the foot. You know what I mean, even though every component of that sentence has lost touch with its own history. The typical prose of the present has no past. Whether it has a future remains to be seen.

The Monthly, May 2006

Postscript

I owe it to A. A. Gill, a must-read journalist of fluent originality, to admit the possibility that he phoned in his copy on this occasion, and the copytaker misheard a word. Copytakers rarely do, but they are only human, although when they are at their best you would swear that they had powers of telepathy. The wrong word having been written in, the section editor might have thought that Gill was aiming for an extra shade of meaning, and let it stand. On the whole it is better if the section editor trusts the writer's wording, but a writer caught out in this way will often go up in flames because the system has betrayed him with excessive respect. During my own career in Fleet Street I oscillated between anger at mistakes made on my behalf and mistakes that I had made myself but had been left in. The resulting picture of choleric schizophrenia might have looked less disarming than I thought.

THE PERFECTLY BAD SENTENCE

In writing, to reach the depths of badness, it isn't enough to be banal. One must strive for lower things. Almost five years have gone by since I cut out from a British newspaper the article containing the following passage, and I think I am finally ready to examine the subtleties of its perfection. But first, let the reader judge its initial impact.

> Now, the onus is on Henman to come out firing at Ivanisevic, the wild card who has torn through this event on a wave of emotion . . .
>
> Neil Harman, *Sunday Telegraph*
> sports section, front page, July 8th, 2001

Time has elapsed, Tim Henman has dropped out of tennis altogether after never sticking long in the top five, the original clipping has gone a mellow colour at the edges, and the featured sentence is at last ready to be analysed, as a fine wine slowly makes itself ready to be tasted. Ivanisevic aside, there are two men involved here: Henman and Harman. One is a tennis player, and one writes about tennis. It is Mr Harman, I think, who is better equipped for his career. Tim Henman was always a bit too lightly built in the chest and shoulders. Mr Harman has what it takes to go on serving his clichés and solecisms with undiminished strength for ever.

But let's take a look at how he does it – or how he did it, on the day that no spectator of bad writing will ever forget. At this point the reader should scan the sentence once again, slowly, as with an action replay.

An 'onus' is a weight, but the word has been so long in the language that its derivation can safely be left for dead: Shakespeare himself would have no quarrel there. For Henman 'to come out firing', however, is borderline at best. We can leave it neutral, but would prefer to know why the metaphor is military. Baudelaire, in *Mon Cœur mis à nu*, warned us that journalists with a fondness for military metaphors were proving their un-warlike nature. For all we know, Baudelaire's stricture fails to fit Mr Harman, who might have been in the SAS before he turned journalist. We can't help suspecting, though, that Mr Harman has no accurate picture in his mind of what sort of weapons Tim Henman might be firing at Ivanisevic. The writer simply means that the British tennis player is behaving aggressively. But then we find that the British tennis player is behaving aggressively towards a wild card. The wild card, again, is metaphor that can be left for dead: it was brought in from gambling for use in tennis, but we court pedantry if we ask for it to be brought alive. All we can ask for is that it be not too grotesquely transfigured in its death: the corpse should not be mutilated. If a wild card tears through something, it should not be on a wave of emotion. Suddenly, in the face of a British tennis player weighed down with unnamed weapons, the wild card has become a surfer. And the sentence isn't even over.

But neither is its impact, which has only just begun. Speaking as one whose flabber is hard to gast, I'm bound to say I was floored. Not bound in the sense of being tied up with ropes by a burglar, or floored in the sense of having tipped my chair over while trying to reach the telephone with my teeth: I mean floored in the sense of having my wings clipped. One of my convictions about the art of composing a prose sentence in English is that for some of its potential metaphorical content to be realised, the rest must be left dormant. You can't cash in on the possibilities of every word. In poetry you can do more of that than in prose, but even in poetry, *pace* Baudelaire, you must concentrate your forces to fight your battles, and there is no concentrating your forces in one place without weakening them in another – a fact that Field Marshal von Manstein vainly tried to point out to Hitler.

To achieve conscious strength in one area, we must will a degree of inattention in other areas: such has been my conclusion from long experience. But here, from out of the blue, *per media* the genius of Mr Harman, is a sentence that demonstrates how the whole construction can be inattentive, and achieve an explosive integrity through its having not been pondered at all. Imagine the power of being that free! Imagine being able to use a well-worn epithet like 'out of the blue' without checking up on whether its implied clear sky comes into conflict with a storm later in the sentence, or whether it chimes too well, but in the wrong way, with a revelation in the previous sentence that the person being talked about once rowed for Oxford or Cambridge! Imagine not having to worry about 'explosive integrity'! Imagine, just imagine, what it would be like to get on with the writing and leave all the reading to the reader!

Too late. I missed the wave, perhaps because I was carrying too many weapons. A kind of wild card myself, I might have ridden my potato-chip surf-board more easily if I had not been burdened with all my onerous ordnance. The mine detector, especially, was the straw that broke the camel's back – or, as Mr Harman might have put it, was the bridge too far. At high school in Sydney I was taught not just to parse a sentence but to make sure than any pictures it evoked matched up. Our teacher, Mr Aked, was not a professional philologist, but like all people with an ear for language he was a philologist at heart. He taught us enough Latin roots to make us realise that etymology was a force in the language, and the more likely to be a confusing force the less it was recognised. He didn't make it all fun. Some of it was hard work. But he made the hard work satisfactory, which is the beginning of good teaching, and I suppose that period was my one and only beginning of good learning: that I began to become the student I would be in later years, long after I had proved that formal study was not my gift.

It was also, alas, the beginning of my suffering. My antennae for linguistic anomaly were extended and I could never afterwards draw them in. Even today, half a century later, I can't use a word like 'antennae' without first picturing in my mind what kind of antennae I mean. Are they metal antennae, like the basket-work arrays of a radar station, or are they organic antennae, as on a bug? Having decided, I try to make something else in the sentence match up, so as not to leave the word lying inert, because it is too fancy a word to be left alone, while not fancy enough to claim its own space. Having finished the piece, I comb through it (what kind of comb?) to look for what I overlooked: almost always it will be a stretch of too-particular writing, where the urge to make everything vivid gets out of hand. But I will still question what kind of urge gets out of hand, and I might even have to look up the origin of 'out of hand', to make sure it has nothing to do with wild cards.

Purple patches call attention to themselves and are easily dealt with by the knife. The freckle-sized blotches of lifeless epithet, unintended repetition and clueless tautology are what do the damage. In the first rough draft of this piece, in the first paragraph after the quotation from Mr Harman, I had a clause, which I later struck out, that ran thus: 'with the bonus of its proud owner's barely suppressed grief.' But 'barely suppressed' is the kind of grief that any journalist thinks a subtle stroke; and, even less defensibly, 'bonus' echoes 'onus', one of the key words of the fragment under discussion. All that could be said for my use of 'bonus' was that I used it without tautology. In journalism, the expression 'added bonus' is by now almost as common as it is in common speech. (My repetition of 'common' is intentional, and the reason you know is that you know I must know, because the repeated word comes so soon.)

Too many times, on the way to Australia by air, the helpless passenger will be informed over the public address system that his Qantas flight is 'co-shared' with British Airways. The tautology is a mere hint of how the Australian version of English is rapidly accumulating new tautologies as if they were coinages: as an Australian police officer might say, it is a prior warning. Already the spoken term 'co-shared' is appearing as 'code-shared' when written down: I saw it this year at a Qantas desk in Terminal 4 at Heathrow, and Terminal 5 isn't even built yet. If the language goes on decaying at this rate, an essay consisting entirely of errors is on the cards. In the television studio it is already on autocue. (In America I could have said 'cue-cards' for 'autocue' and got a nice intentional echo to make 'on the cards' sound less uninspired, but it would have been unfair: American English is the version of the language least prone to error at present – or, as the Americans would say, at this time.) But when all the nits are picked, and the piece is in shape and ready to be printed, one can't help feeling that to be virtuous is a hard fate. Most of the new errors I couldn't make if I tried. In the Melbourne *Age* for August 27th, 2001, an article that it took two women to write included the sentence 'The size of the financial discrepancies were eventually discovered.' I couldn't match the joyous freedom of that just by relaxing.

What I would like to do, however, is relax my habitual attention to the sub-current of metaphorical content. Most of the really hard work is done down there, deep under the surface, where the river runs in secret. (Watch out for the sub-current and the river! Do they match?) No doubt it would be a sin just to let things go, but what a sweet sin it would be. It is sometimes true of poetry, and often true of prose, that there are intensities of effect which can be produced only by bad writing. Good writing has to lay out an argument for the collapse of a culture. Bad writing can demonstrate it: the scintillating clangour of confusion, the iridescent splendour of decay. A box of hoarded fireworks set off at random will sacrifice its planned sequential order, but gain through its fizzing, snaking, interweaving unpredictability.

The handcart of culture has to go a long way downhill before the hubs wobbling on its worn axles can produce a shriek like Mr Harman's prose. You will have noticed how, in my previous paragraph, I have switched my area of metaphor from chaos to decay, and then from pyrotechnics back to chaos. I would like to think that this process was deliberate, although there is always a chance that I undertook it in response to a reflex: the irrepressible urge to turn an elementary point into a play of fancy. If it is a reflex, however, I hope it lurks in a deeper chamber than my compositional centre, and so leaves room for conscious reflection – a word from the same root, but suggesting a very different tempo.

Mr Harman's reflex occupies his whole mind. But he should worry: look at what he can do without pausing for thought. In his classic sentence, Mr Harman does not commit a single technical error. It is on a sound grammatical structure that he builds his writhing, *art nouveau* edifice of tangled imagery, as if Gaudi, in Barcelona, had coated his magic church of the Sagrada Familia with scrambled eggs, and made them stick. Mr Harman has made a masterpiece in miniature. There is an exuberant magnificence to it. As Luciano Pavarotti once said, I salute him from the heart of my bottom.

The Monthly, January 2008

Postscript

After the turn of the millennium, when I finally began the actual writing, so long put off, of the book that was eventually called *Cultural Amnesia*, I spent about a year collecting examples of misused language in the newspapers and the periodicals. A year was more than enough and I had to abandon the practice, lest I give way to that weird cocktail of depression and self-loathing that comes from irritability too often driven to its limit. I also abandoned my plans of incorporating into the book a long section that would demonstrate how our beloved tongue had gone to the dogs. For one thing, a few pages would be enough to prove it, and for another, the theme looked petty beside the twentieth-century political tragedies which provided the book's fulcrum – if a fulcrum can be something spread out over almost a thousand pages. Outside the world of my book, however, in the real world which persisted in maintaining its separate course, the written language continued to fall to bits, so that the once glitteringly busy traffic of the up-market British newspapers on the weekends began to look like a demolition derby. It therefore seemed only like duty, over the course of the next few years, to take some of my annotated examples out of their low-tech cardboard file and work them up into separate essays, in the hope that I might deploy them as weapons in a counter-campaign against (and here I employ the kind of mixed metaphor that was becoming increasingly prevalent) the tsunami of decay.

For anyone who volunteers to fight in this doomed battle it is important, I think, to distinguish between mere bad grammar and more elevated bad writing. The question of bad grammar I tried to cover, or at any rate make a start on, in the first of the two preceding essays. But bad writing often doesn't need bad grammar to make it awful. It can be awful even while keeping all the formal rules. A perfectly bad sentence, indeed, can be an intricate miracle of ostensibly correct construction. Often, indeed, it's the mandarin elevation of the approach that leads to the disaster, as a new ambassador bowing himself elaborately backwards out of the monarch's presence might end up in a broom cupboard. There are reasons to think that the urge to accident-prone highfalutin' is an aspect of personality.

As I know from my own time in broadcasting, it takes a degree of egocentricity to feel that one has a natural affinity with a microphone. People eager to get on air are often bent on impressing you with their superiority, and the rule applies all the way down to those whose only access to broadcasting is a public address system associated with some means of transport. Many an announcer on a British train is as stilted in his diction as a minor Victorian novelist, and there must be something about the atmosphere of an airport that drives would-be broadcasters to the heights of rhetorical bravura. At Stansted one afternoon I heard a strident female voice warn all of us under the terminal's elegant metal roof that any car left incorrectly parked outside would be 'subject to a towing procedure'. You couldn't say that the announcement was grammatically incorrect. Semantically, however, you yourself would never have thought of saying it at all. It's a whole new language, closely based on ours yet infinitely foreign, like a penthouse hotel suite in Dubai.

HAPPINESS WRITES WHITE

Usually attributed to that prolific aphorist Anonymous, the sadly true notion that 'Happiness writes white' probably emerged from Tin Pan Alley or Broadway, when somebody finally realised why most of the good love songs were about love lost. The idea might seem to conform to the standard Romantic conception of poetry, but it is important to remember that the Romantic conception was a real discovery of something that had always been true: art is an outward integration inspired by the artist's inner disintegration.

The converse holds. Contentment has either no need of artistic expression, or few resources for it. Even when we doubt this is so, we think it ought to be so, and apply the concept to other arts as well as to poetry. One of the reasons we speak so slightingly of Mendelssohn when we put him beside Beethoven is that we can hear Mendelssohn's music smiling – or anyway we believe we can, which is enough to make us patronise him, reserving our unmixed approval for Beethoven, even when the personality revealed in his life story strikes us as actively unpleasant. With a less glaring discrepancy, but in the same way, our opinion of Renoir will always be lower than our opinion of Monet, because Renoir suffered less. Renoir might have suffered more had he not been so reasonable, but he gets no points for that. Renoir correctly found Monet irresponsible and loathed the way he spread misery among his women, but the more that the truth of their lives came out, the more that Monet looked serious vis-à-vis Renoir, until, by now, Renoir's reputation carries an indelible question mark. Instead of putting himself to the anxieties of developing his *manière aigre*, he might have done better studying to be more miserable.

Unhappy artists are to be pitied, but often not for the apparent cause of their unhappiness, which they might have arranged. If they had become artists in order to deal with a psychic imbalance that was implanted early, the urge to remain productive might well entail a deliberate avoidance of ordinary happiness, especially in its domestic branch. When Philip Larkin said 'Deprivation is for me what daffodils were for Wordsworth' he was giving a powerful hint that he would stay deprived if he could. Eliot showed the cost of settling for bliss: it produced exactly one late, pale lyric, whereas the opposite had produced *The Waste Land*.

Yeats probably knew he was a fool for love. Knowing it, he was no fool at all, but perhaps something even more pitiable, an artist so dedicated that he would hoodwink reality if it threatened to make him content. His instruction to himself – 'Never give all the heart' – would have killed his work had he obeyed it. He always gave all the heart, over and over: but only to those women who shared the useful characteristic of incomprehension. His wife, George, paid the penalty for understanding him: she inspired him often to gratitude, but seldom to a rhapsody.

Yeats's muse, on the other hand, whoever she might happen currently to be, fled forever out of reach, like a Daphne just a touch faster on her feet than Apollo. In Norman Jeffares' excellent *Commentary on the Collected Poems of W. B. Yeats*, we find Yeats expressing himself thus: 'How much of the best I have done and still do is but the attempt to explain myself to her? If she understood I should lack a reason for writing, and one can never have too many reasons for doing what is so laborious.' He means that he wouldn't write poetry unless he had to, and implies that nothing must be allowed to remove the reason. Chateaubriand, in the preface to *Atala*, said that when the Muses cry, it is only to look more beautiful. The immediate implication was that the poet might not be beyond courting some high-quality misery in order to make the Muses tearful.

There is a deeper implication: the poet will exploit grief when it comes. Peter Porter, with characteristic frankness, laid bare this truth in the sequence of monumentally beautiful poems he wrote in commemoration of his first wife. But true artists don't need love trouble to stave off happiness: all they have to do is look at the world. In that regard, all the great art we know of carries within its compass a guarantee that its creator is not content. Shakespeare's sonnets are the most powerful possible assertion that love is not only a fine thing but that we have scarcely lived if we are shut out of it, yet all the ecstasy in the sonnets would amount to nothing if it were not threatened by time and death, which he evokes with at least the invention that he lavishes on the erotic. Similarly Dante's *Inferno* might be hard to take if we didn't know that he would later write the *Paradiso*, but the *Paradiso* would be unbearable without the *Inferno*.

We don't allow our master artists to be merely twee, but neither, on the whole, do they themselves; and they, as we, will always put Boucher and Fragonard in the second rank merely for suggesting that Arcadia can be an unmixed pleasure and go on forever; although it could be said that the melancholy of monarchical absolutism impos- ing its requirements somehow seeps through to give even manufac- tured bliss an undertone of menace. Besides, Fragonard's pretty girl reading her book will grow old and die: we know that, and we know he knows that, or he would not have been so seized with the beauty of her concentration. French painting and music are copious with what we would call the merely lovely but we can be confident about bringing our own unhappiness to the picture or the composition even when they are careful to avoid any of their own. We can be equally confident that their makers would never have shown that care if they themselves had been truly untroubled. To be undisturbed and yet still creative would be impossible. When playing Vermeer in *Girl with a Pearl Earring*, Colin Firth looked grief-stricken but probably underplayed it. To *want* to produce that degree of serenity is a sign (for once the semiotic vocabulary becomes appropriate) of a sensitivity to turbulence that can't, as it were, be brushed away. If the world's horror had not been eating at the artist's soul, we would never have seen the girl. The instinct, on the part of those who project utopia, to leave the artists out of it is politically deplorable but aesthetically sound: they would produce anodyne art.

The Monthly, December 2006 – January 2007

Postscript

Coughing apologetically as I run, let me hasten to add that I don't put Fragonard in the second rank when I am actually looking at one of his pictures. I put him first and everybody else nowhere. Any successful work of art drives all the other works of art out of your head while you are in its grip. In the Oval Room at the Wallace Collection hangs the great Fragonard picture in which the love-sick young swain is forever looking up the skirt of the girl in the swing. If Hieronymus Bosch had painted the same scene, the stricken youth might have been looking into the pit. But if that idea occurred to me while I was looking at the Fragonard, it would only mean that my attention was wandering. The insidious fault of all criticism that ranks artists is to convey the impression that we can do that while we are occupied with the works of art. But a work of art is successful precisely to the extent that it stops us doing any such thing. Hence the folly of asking whether Bob Dylan is as good as Keats: the mere question means that we aren't listening properly to Bob Dylan.

ALL STALKERS KILL

There are few passages of poetry that I have ever underlined, put a mark beside or made notes on, because any real poem or body of poetry is not susceptible to having fragments snapped from context without the fragments losing colour. In the Selfridge's Shakespeare I carry with me on long trips I put dots in the margin, but they are not admonitions as to what I should remember, merely guides back to what has already been remembered, so that I can check up on whether distortions have crept in. Otherwise, in less copious reservoirs, if poetry makes me remember it, I remember it all: *omnia mea mecum porto*. I carry it all with me. But here are two lines I marked in the margin of a newspaper. 'Nicole, your eyes are like the stars / I think of them in various bars.' As far as I know, these two lines constitute the complete poetic works of Elmer O. Noone as they have come down to us, and perhaps repay study on the clinical level, if not the critical and aesthetic. To cease being coy for a minute, I should grasp the nettle, or poisonous coral fragment: Elmer O. Noone is a stalker, and his poem was addressed to my talented compatriot Nicole Kidman.

When you know that much for background, his seemingly slight poem gains weight, in the same way that a cockroach would gain weight on the surface of Jupiter. In 2001 Nicole Kidman applied for a restraining order against Elmer O. Noone: an action which automatically ranked him high in her swarm of stalkers. Any female celebrity of her eminence attracts dozens of them, but we assume that most of them can be seen off by private action. Since to go public inevitably generates an atmosphere of vulnerability that excites a fresh supply of heavily breathing candidates to try their hand, Elmer O. Noone must have been unusually persistent even in a field where persistence is one of the chief qualifications. By what we know of him, he had a romantic sensibility to temper his determination, although it is fair to assume that his unsolicited tenderness made her feel even worse. He must have been horrifying enough when he rang her doorbell a few hundred times, but he also brought flowers. He invited her to the ballet. He offered to tutor her children, pointing out that such an arrangement 'would give us the chance to know each other better'. Possibly it was his avuncular concern with her children that sent her to the cops, but his protestations of courtly love would have been enough.

The most depressing aspect – depressing because it concerns us all – is that it *was* love, and probably still is. I have talked of him in the past tense so far because time has gone by and he has not yet been given his own talk show. He has submerged, down to where the forgotten stalkers slowly swim. The three-year restraining order might have made him give up. (It sometimes happens, although I personally know two female television presenters and one actress whose stalkers regarded their restraining orders as a mere bachelor's degree on the academic ladder towards a doctorate.) After the court found against him, he concentrated his efforts on suing Nicole Kidman for 300,000 US dollars on the grounds that she had defamed him, and on persuading the next court to find for him, on the grounds that his human rights had been abused. I had expected him to take his case all the way to the Hague by now. Whether he is out of action or not, however, he will never get over his relationship with Nicole Kidman. For him, the fact that the relationship never existed will be the least of his considerations. He believed it did exist. He felt it. But something went slightly wrong. He could have fixed it, if only he could have explained it to her: if only she had given him a chance. If only she had *listened*. And here is the connection with the rest of us. When we are given the elbow, there is always a terrible, sleepless period when we believe that one more phone call will set things right. The phone call doesn't work out. She tells us we are making too many phone calls. No, it can't end like this. She hasn't understood. Better call her again. She's not picking up. How can she do that? Luckily, in all this turmoil, the moment arrives when we realise that if we really love her, her welfare comes before ours, and that we owe it to her, for the love we have had, not to punish her for the love we have lost. Better call her and tell her that. No, better not. Put the phone down. The moment of sanity.

For the stalkers, the moment of sanity never comes. Love can unbalance anyone for a time, but Elmer O. Noone was unbalanced all the time. His feelings of love were so powerful that they drove him to poetry. But he was a solipsist. He believed that Nicole Kidman would reciprocate his feelings if she were allowed to, because he couldn't imagine that she might not. It wasn't that her welfare meant nothing to him: he thought that to love him *was* her welfare, and all she needed to do was admit the fact. Most men spend a good part of their lives learning that other people are alive too, but in a democratic society all normal men learn it to some degree. Elmer O. Noone never learned it, because Elmer O. Noone was a psychopath. (I have changed his name in this piece, because on past evidence he is perfectly capable of bringing a court case that he is bound to lose, simply for the satisfaction of tying up a sane person's life for years on end.) In him, solipsism and egomania were compounded into a one-man universe. The woman destined to be his bride turned out to be Nicole Kidman, not that nice-looking girl at the check-out counter in his local Wal-Mart. Apart from his eminence in the field of sexual allure, he was equally exalted in his worldly ambitions. He announced that he had plans to become 'a trillionaire'. Being a mere billionaire obviously wouldn't do. He wanted to be elected President. No Vice-Presidency for him, and don't even mention Secretary of State. Where have we heard this sort of stuff before?

We've heard it from adepts of the occult: from people whose current earthly existence is a mere episode in their miraculous ability to be born and re-born in all the most resplendent epochs of history. Frequently to be seen on television – in America they have their own cable channels – they tell us who they used to be. The lady with the bangles, the purple bouffant and the asymmetrically lifted face used to be Mary, Queen of Scots. The man with the mascara and the comb-over used to be Tutankhamun. He is one of the many currently practising occult adepts who once held the rank of Pharaoh, supreme ruler of Upper and Lower Egypt. It is notable that none of them, during their ancient Egyptian incarnations, used to be the 157th slave from the left at the raising of the obelisk. What they used to have was a world in which their will was law, and that is what the stalkers have now: unrestricted individual significance.

When we are in love, we all have a touch of that. We get a taste

of what it feels like to be deranged. It feels as if all uncertainties have
been expunged. It feels, that is, like the very opposite of derangement.
Luckily, if we are normal, we remain sane enough to realise that we
have gone crazy. There is a way back to a pluralistic world, in which
the possibility exists that the adored woman was born not to fulfil
our lives but to fulfil hers. We can argue with ourselves, and make
ourselves see reason. But the stalker brooks no argument: not from
his victim, who is not really protesting, merely failing to accept the
inevitable; and least of all does he brook argument from himself.
He has a perfectly integrated personality.

Should women fear us? Only for what we might do. If they feared
us for what we might think, there would be no end to it, and no
continuing with human life. Female beauty projects a male into a
realm of fantasy, and does so because it is meant to. Sanity is not to
be without fantasy, but to know reality, and remember the difference.
When I was much younger, I might have felt about Nicole Kidman
the same way Elmer O. Noone did, and might well have written a
poem, which might well have been even worse. (When I was still in
short pants I certainly felt that way about Audrey Dalton, the ingénue
in the best ever movie about the *Titanic*. A Google search reveals that
she is still alive, in her early seventies. Does she remember what I
said to her, as I lifted her into the lifeboat and kissed her goodbye?
She should: I said it every night for months on end.) But even when
young and stupid I would have turned away from Nicole Kidman's
door when my first bunch of flowers was rebuffed. Similarly with
regard to my current fantasy about Nicole Kidman, in which I
arrange a cheap date with Elmer O. Noone, stick the muzzle of my
.44 Magnum in his mouth, and blow his diseased brains all over the
back wall of Burger King. I don't even tell her I've done it. I require
no reward: not from her or from any other woman whose little
problem I have been glad to solve. All over the world, the stalkers –
they call me the Vigilante – are thinking twice before they order
those flowers, book that ballet ticket, write that poem. I wish it could
be true. But what can one man do? Well, one thing he can do is
realise that when Nicole Kidman looks straight at him out of the
screen, she is almost certainly in love with someone else, even if it
seems to defy all reason that it should be so.

Weekend Australian, April 15–16, 2006

Postscript

Sometimes not even the UN can get it wrong. Nicole Kidman was the ideal appointee as the UN Goodwill Ambassador for the Development Fund for Women, and that benighted organization is lucky she said yes, just as the ambassador herself is lucky to be alive. Injustice against women is something she knows all about. Her principal stalker had murder written all over him and so does every other stalker in the world. I suppose journalists have to be forgiven for their concern with the irritation Nicole Kidman supposedly suffered from Tom Cruise's bared teeth, hyperactivity and loopy religious beliefs, but all of that was notional at worst. Stalking is the actual thing: psychological rape by a psycho who won't give up. It's like having the Terminator on your case. The superstar bore up bravely but it took deep stupidity on the part of the press not to realise that she was in deadly danger. Stalking is not just a problem in law, it's a problem for the media, because it lays bare the media's incapacity to tell any story whose plot-points are not obvious. If a thirteen-year-old girl gets raped in Somalia and then stoned to death because she confesses her 'crime' – this actually happened in 2008 – there will be press coverage on the grand scale. But a Western woman, a citizen of a free society, whose sanity is steadily threatened by a well-organized whack-job is at the centre of a story too uneventful to tell. Not to realize that both of these terrible acts of injustice spring from the same violent impulse, however, is sheer sentimentality. All men are allowed to fall in love with Nicole Kidman, and the more intelligent they are, the more likely they are to do so. (David Thomson, a valuable critic of the movies, wrote a book about her which is nothing short of a glorified mash note.) But we are not allowed to hang around outside her house.

IN PRAISE OF TOMMY COOPER

'Through the generosity of my grandmother in her will,' mumbled Tommy Cooper, 'I am holding in my hands a Rembrandt and a Stradivarius. Unfortunately the violin is by Rembrandt ... and the painting is by Stradivarius.' His trademark red fez still firmly in place, Cooper climaxed this front-of-curtain routine by shoving the violin through the painting.

Even with a full measure of his long, Pinteresque pausing, the whole number took about thirty seconds. I may have misremembered the bit about his grandmother, through having laughed so hard that I caused lesions to my memory. Superficially, Cooper was a throw-back. He rigged the TV studio to look like a theatre, which was the exact opposite of what was going on in the theatres. But he was out ahead of everybody in the way he combined daring of concept with economy of execution. A typical Cooper brainwave was so good that even his fellow professionals would laugh just to be told about it, but the way he carried the idea out would make them whistle as well. Everything was set up and timed so that he barely had to roll his eyes to clinch the effect.

In one of Harold Lloyd's movies, Lloyd is running wild on a motorcycle that won't stop. We see the bike descend at full throttle into a trench beside the road. Behind his glassless spectacle frames Lloyd's eyes pop at what he can see in the trench that we can't. In the next shot, the camera is panning at high speed beside the trench while workers come jumping out of it one after the other. Lloyd and the motorcycle aren't on the screen, and he might not even have turned up for work that day. Cooper's stage routines affected me like that: he was present, but often he wasn't doing anything. He established the conditions for the gag and you could feel the collective psyche of the helpless audience rushing towards him to do the rest. The audience was already hysterical at the idea of the Rembrandt violin and the Stradivarius painting before he did the sight-gag. He could have done it later in the show. He could have done it out in the street afterwards, while the audience was waiting for the bus. These displacements of cause and effect were so much a part of his act that when he actually died on stage – one of the few headline performers ever to do so, although Houdini and Caruso both came close – the audience was slow to catch on. It could have been a number.

I met Cooper only once, in a canteen queue at London Weekend Television on the South Bank. I introduced myself, overdid the effusive gratitude, and spilled my newly purchased cup of tea, luckily not all over him. He was very good at pretending that I had staged a comic number for his benefit. Eric Morecambe was another idol of mine among the comedians. When I met him for the first time at the BAFTA awards in Grosvenor House, he had already suffered the first version of the heart attack that eventually killed him. He was working again by then, but he was very frail. His enjoyment seemed unimpaired, however, when he told me that the first thing he heard when he woke up on the stretcher was one of the ambulance men asking him for an autograph, 'for my daughter'. Even the best-behaved citizens will usually find a reason for expressing their admiration if it is sufficiently intense, and that was certainly the way I felt about Tommy Cooper. In retrospect, however, I'm very glad that it was my tea I spilled and not his, and not over his shoes but over mine. Otherwise he might have found it harder to make a joke of it, and I might have remembered the moment in a different way.

I might even have remembered him in a different way, which is always the risk, and the best reason never to inflict your personal enthusiasm on celebrities, no matter how much you admire them. It is a form of conceit, after all, to think that their lives will be improved by hearing from you that yours was improved by them; and you might not catch them in the right mood. Some of them are never in the right mood. Just as, in war, there are men who can go on being brave for battle after battle and then suddenly find that they can do no more, there are performing artists who can be miracles of amiability for years on end and then suddenly find that one more unsolicited conversation will break their nerve. You don't want to be the next punter who comes along. It is better to adore from afar.

It helps, of course, to have had some experience of being in the public eye yourself, because the experience will tell you that the capacity for reciprocating an outburst of familiarity from a stranger is essentially artificial. There is no natural well of fellow feeling to draw upon. Our normal instinct, when accosted by strangers, is at least as protective as welcoming; few performers in any field are even as normal as that; and among comic performers paranoia is not only endemic, it is almost always justified, because the natural impulse of the nervous fan is to entertain the entertainer, invariably with dire results. Tommy Cooper might well have believed, for the first few seconds, that my tea-spilling act was rehearsed, until I dropped the saucer while catching the cup. No amount of rehearsal could have made me look as ridiculous as that: it was overdone.

On stage, he himself never overdid anything. What W. C. Fields had to learn from years in vaudeville, Cooper had from the jump: the gift of making the audience come to him. He never tried to astonish them. He made them astonish themselves. His elliptical mastery made his work very hard to analyse, and thus almost impossible to copy. Most exponents of the bad conjuring routine can conjure quite well. That was how they got into comedy, when they realised that there were too many good conjurers. But what most of the intentionally bad conjurers can't manage is the audience contact while things are going wrong. In the re-runs of Cooper's television specials, you can watch him watching you: his eyes are the focal point of his act. In the magic numbers, there is no mistake he can't make. In the juggling numbers there will be stuff bouncing all over the stage. But don't study the way he hasn't caught it. Study the way he has caught your eye.

Cooper had perfect pitch for what the audience needed to know so that they could congratulate themselves for guessing how much he wasn't telling them. He judged exactly, for example, that any audience he met, no matter how unsophisticated, would know that Rembrandt was a painter and Stradivarius made violins. If he had said Botticelli and Guanieri it wouldn't have worked. Today it probably wouldn't work even with Rembrandt and Stradivarius. But today he would think of something different. I can still see him, laughing at the way I caught the cup. I had got into his act, which is something the fan always wants to do for the hero. But the wise fan will remember that the last thing his hero needs is to be burdened with an unsolicited audition from some klutz he has never met, in the private time that he has so little of.

Previously unpublished

A MICROPHONE FOR THE AUDIENCE

In the broadcast media, technical considerations can often shape events, and sometimes create them. To illustrate this awkward truth, let me begin with a quotation.

'It was said that I was facing political oblivion, my career in tatters, apparently never to be part of political life again. Well, they underestimated Hartlepool and they underestimated me, because I am a fighter and not a quitter.'

When Peter Mandelson made this brief, improvised and personally damaging speech at the count in Hartlepool in 2001, all those watching him on television, including the Prime Minister, Tony Blair, thought that it must mean the end of Mandelson's career. Mandelson sounded shrill and petulant. When he saw himself on screen later, he would have agreed that his performance was of an unsettling stridency. I myself, after a working lifetime in television, didn't guess immediately what had really damaged him.

It was the sound balance. The audience at the announcement had been very noisy. Mandelson had been shouting against the noise. The microphones on the podium were all pointed his way, so they had left the audience out. The next night, after seeing the moment replayed a few times, I belatedly figured out what had happened, and sympathised with the victim. It had happened hundreds of times to me, with a cumulatively disheartening effect which finally got to the point where I trusted studio production no longer. For years I had been knocking myself out in studios with an invited audience, only to view the show and hear no convincing evidence that the audience had been present. On the night, their reaction had been a tide of friendly enthusiasm that I had to raise my voice against if I was to keep the momentum. In the transmission, I was just a man unnecessarily raising his voice. On countless occasions I protested to my own producers. All repeated the sound engineer's opinion that the audience's reaction had been faithfully captured, and that the optimum balance between performer and audience had been attained. In other words, accept the professional opinion of the technicians, or else get out of the studio altogether.

Eventually I chose the second course, and one of the reasons – there were several, but this was the one that had been nagging longest – was that the problem of performing on two levels had proved insuperable. To entertain the audience in the studio, the performer must project, as on a stage. To entertain the audience at home, projecting is the very last thing a television performer should do. All the evidence of my time in British television studios suggested that there was no remedy. The evidence presented by American television we had better leave aside. American talk shows are rowdy, scruffy events, but one thing you can never complain of is any sense of the performer slaving away on his own. The audience is at least as generously amplified as he is. Also there are always plenty of cutaway shots of the audience to prove that there are real people sitting there.

I could rarely persuade the directors on my shows to include shots of the audience, perhaps because the directors didn't much care for the adverse sartorial effect that might be created by old ladies wearing knitted hats who had been brought in by bus. British television directors all want to be film directors one day, and they care about the look of the thing. As a result of this misplaced visual fastidiousness, I regularly had to read newspaper reviews in which it was stated that I had been mugging away to an empty studio. This opinion was usually given by some young wit who would have been able to swear in a libel court that the evidence of his eyes and ears led him to no other conclusion. After a few decades of that, I had plenty of experience behind me in order to assess how Peter Mandelson must have felt when he saw himself on screen and realised that he had caught himself out. But I still didn't spot it while it was happening. That's how tricky a game television can be. Unless you can lay down conditions in which you can be both performing and watching yourself perform, you will eventually be caught looking like a dunce, and usually at the moment when it matters most.

Previously unpublished

Postscript

Each of the above two pieces was on my desk for years, always demanding to be tinkered with. It sometimes happens like that, especially when the subject is someone's personality, more than his work. You can judge work, but a soul is a lot harder to pin down. Tommy Cooper was an incredible hulk with an even more incredible spirit inside him, like some angelic child pleading for release from a rubber clown costume. He had made me laugh as hard as I ever laughed in my life, and I felt I owed him. Debt can be paralysing. I also felt indebted to Peter Mandelson, who gave me an interview, when I was on assignment for the *Independent*, that could have been a lot more difficult. The future Lord Mandelson's taste for the high life would probably have ensured his eventual emergence as the media's ideal political villain even if he had not compounded his faults with personal charm, a quality which always sets journalists looking for the hidden story. Since there was plenty of hidden story to uncover – a sense of entitlement that outsoars one's income is bound to cause trouble – he soon found himself with no competition for the role of Dracula. But the mistake that could never be recovered wasn't his. At the Hartlepool count, in the moment of victory, the faulty sound balance made him sound petulant. A politician can survive being savaged in Alastair Campbell's diary, but the wrong few minutes on screen can rarely be expunged. There could be no clearer instance of how television, at least in Britain, has become a city of nets. In America the politicians are better protected, by a team of people with no other task except to ward off danger from technical errors. Sarah Palin was caught out on air, but at least the fault was all hers.

BEST EATEN COLD

Alain Finkielkraut needs a new name. Al Falco? If the most interesting of the recent French philosophers is ever to make an international impact, he can't be called Alain Finkielkraut. For one thing, 'Finkielkraut' doesn't even sound French. For another, he has a one-part, unhyphenated first name. As things are, the distinctly less original Bernard-Henri Lévy appears in open-necked splendour on American talk shows. Not only is Lévy's latest book displayed in the *vitrine* of Sonia Rykiel's boutique in the Boulevard Saint-Germain, it is read on the lawn at Berkeley by beautiful female students dreaming enviously of his luxuriant hair-style.

None of this ever happens to Finkielkraut. Though he runs a nifty multimedia website and has published his fair share of books and pamphlets about love and sex, he has never shown any sign of rivalling Levy's skill with the hairdryer. But Finkielkraut is the one who can write. Listen to this, from his *La sagesse de l'amour*. I will do my best to catch its rhythm, but the tartness of the thought should come through anyway.

> The more the other man distinguishes himself, the more I dislike him for the admiration that his exploits oblige me to bring him: one day he will have to reimburse me for the laurel wreaths with which I crown his successes and capacities. My praise demands revenge.

Not that Finkielkraut was first with the general idea. 'It is not enough to succeed', said Gore Vidal, 'friends must be seen to have failed.' In thus echoing Rochefoucauld, Vidal knew he was being mean. By identifying an impulse within himself he was guarding himself against any inclination to follow it up. Finkielkraut is probably doing the same here. Hence we can trace the parentage of the aphorism only half-way back to Rochefoucauld. When Rochefoucauld said that we always take a certain amount of pleasure in the pain of others, he wasn't pointing out a danger to be avoided: he was calling it a principle that always applies. Finkielkraut has merely pointed out a danger. We would be glad to think that it didn't exist.

Inexorably, one is forced back to one's own case, for good or ill. I would like to think that my own record is fairly good, or anyway became so with time. I can't remember ever praising someone's work and then taking revenge later. I can remember plenty of cases in which I dispraised someone's work and then did the opposite later. Usually it was because I thought he had improved. Sometimes it was because I had finally realised that I had been simply wrong in the first place, and needed to make amends. The question arises of how, or why, I was initially wrong, and gave a false account of something worthy. Resentment and revenge might have come in there. Young writers don't much like to see other young writers suddenly getting attention, and often they feel that older writers are blocking the sunlight.

As a perpetrator, I had a bad history in my youth of writing what the Germans call a *Verisse* – the knife job, the review that carves up the victim. At Sydney University one of my fellow students, a Polish immigrant, wrote a play and put it on, with himself in the lead. Reviewing the production for the student newspaper, I stamped him into the earth. Almost straight away I regretted the tone I took, but I should have regretted more than that. I had envied him his burst of publicity and his blonde girlfriend. I should have realised –a decade later, I did realise – that as a young writer still learning his second language, he had achieved something interesting in itself, even if it was not a very coherent play. It was he, after all, and not I, who had a right to comport himself as the incarnation of an historical saga of disaster and dislocation. When we met again in Europe, he praised me and my own achievements: the Chinese revenge. I learned a lesson. But I had learned it at his expense. I made it a rule for the future to be harsh only with the mighty.

It took me a long while to realise that the mighty have feelings too. A critic's language should respect the creator's sensitivity, which is always there even if he appears to have suppressed it in the interests of ambition. After I became an established writer myself, I found that contemporaries who had once praised me changed their tone. This reversal took time to get used to. In the interests of sanity, I tried to keep in mind that they might be right: perhaps my work was getting worse, or at any rate had failed to develop in ways that they expected. Occasionally I had to admit to myself that I had written something feeble, and I tried to be grateful that the fact had been pointed out. (Here I was following Karl Popper's celebrated advice that we should welcome disagreement as a contribution to our process of reasoning: I was as yet unaware that Popper himself never welcomed it, and reacted to the slightest criticism like a cornered wildcat.) Gratitude strained the resources of humility, but it seemed right to try. More often, however, I was asked by my apparently neutral friends to entertain the possibility that my critics might be annoyed at the attention I was getting.

Rather than question the motives of the friends, it seemed better to question the motives of the critics: but not much better. Usually their arguments seemed coherent and even well informed. A critic who tells the world that your latest novel was not written by Tolstoy is bound to seem substantial if he proves that he has read Tolstoy, even if he fails to prove that he has read you. Some critics make a point of never delivering any praise at all. Aiming never to be quoted on a book jacket, they achieve their aim. Most books will not survive, so a reviewer who writes as if none of them will is sure to look good in the end. A wise writer will learn to live without accolades, although it is tough on the publisher, and eventually that will be tough on the writer. But outright abuse is a different matter. Where does it come from?

Well, one of the places it once came from was within you: a sad fact that needs to be remembered. The sad fact also hints at the answer. The abusive critic often *is* envious. But he is not necessarily envious of what you have achieved. He is envious of the noise you have made in achieving it. Safe in the limelight, you can afford to sound dedicated. You might even mean it when you borrow Tocqueville's remark and say you prefer glory to success. But your critic would like the same luxury of choice for himself. Watching publicity work for you, he can't help being annoyed that it hasn't worked for him. After all, you are both living the literary life. So where is the justice? If, early on, in his own mind if not on paper, he acknowledged you as a colleague, his resentment will be all the more acute. So he takes revenge.

He will probably keep taking it. Almost any established writer will pick up a persistent tormentor the way a beautiful woman picks up a stalker. On the grand scale, Thomas Mann could never quite understand why the literary journalist Alfred Kerr – a comparatively minor figure but equipped with the sting and the turning circle of a wasp – kept coming back to the attack. Down here at my end of the rankings, I have acquired one young critic (not quite as young as he was, which seems to be making things worse) who goes out of his way to give it to me in the neck twice each time, once under his own name and once anonymously. His anonymous incarnation actually works my way, because the hatred is expressed in such extreme terms that anyone who reads it will probably pick up my book in the bookshop and leaf through it, just to see if I could possibly be that bad. But I can't help looking on my tormentor's expenditure of energy as a flaw in nature. What does he stand to gain?

If trapped at gunpoint, the mugger is quite likely to announce that he liked your early work. As far as you can remember, he wasn't around to say this when your early work was coming out, but it is probably true: otherwise why would he have followed up on what you did next? He could have ignored it. That is what he wants the world to do now, and he could have done the same then. But he loved you once, and now he can't let you go. One can only sympathise. Sympathy comes hard, however, when insult is added to injury. I was once abused personally for a full thousand words in the *Sunday Times* by a young television critic to whom I had refused an interview. He was off his beat, doubling as a reviewer of novels, and clearly thought that I, by having written a novel, was off my beat too. He might have been right. But in his use of language he sounded as if he was indicting Heinrich Himmler.

A year later he introduced himself at a party and apologised. He said my early writings had been an influence on his life. They had inspired him to become a journalist. I accepted the apology. (In those circumstances you should always accept the apology, because the apologist is swallowing a toad, and might regurgitate it all over you if thwarted.) But I couldn't help thinking that a better order of events would have been to put the acknowledgment of my inspiring influence in print, so that the public could see it, and then call me a war criminal at the party, where it would have been a private matter.

Perhaps I should have told him that, but it would have been too late. Once upon a time he had praised me, and the day came when the praise demanded its revenge. For me, the object of this sequence of mistimed emotions, the most uncomfortable aspect was the consideration that if he had been so wrong the second time he might have been wrong the first time too. But one's aim as a writer should go beyond preserving one's self-esteem. Nothing can be done without it, but as an end in itself it always causes damage even to the writer of poetry, let alone to the writer of fiction; and to the writer of criticism it is quite ruinous. Rebecca West once argued that bad poems and bad novels can be counted on to get rid of themselves but bad criticism is a true calamity, breaking the chain of a long conversation by which sound opinion is transmitted through the generations. She might have added that the motor of bad criticism is almost always conceit, readily detectable by its interest in revenge.

Australian Literary Review, June 2007

Postscript

My 'Al Falco' joke was just another attempt to focus attention on the name of Alain Finkielkraut, one of the modern-day French philosophers that serious English-speaking readers really should know more about. Since Raymond Aron, following on from Albert Camus, successfully completed the first stage in the long task of discrediting Sartre's wilful political cretinism, French philosophy, despite the noise kicked up by the academically popular hoopla of the cultural theorists, has been steadily restoring itself to the centre of intelligent discussion. Jean-François Revel and François Furet between them were enough to make the French discussion essential listening. Unfortunately not many of the key books were translated. Today, Bernard-Henri Lévy is the most thoroughly publicized of the newer men. I, too, am impressed by the way he looks with the top buttons of his shirt undone, and I would sincerely like to have hair like his. (Would I also like to see multiple copies of my latest book displayed in the *vitrine* of Sonia Rykiel's shop in the Boulevard Saint-Germain? You bet your life I would.) Just as Carla Bruni looks the way a songwriter should, so does Bernard-Henri Lévy look the part of the philosopher. But amid all the media coverage for his international chic, it is seldom mentioned that his final arrival at a liberal position was preceded by a history of the very stamp of bizarrerie that a writer like Revel was dedicated to taking apart. In the Sixties, Lévy, following the example of Althusser, seriously proclaimed that the only way forward from Stalinism was through Maoism. Thus the cool sage began his career as a preening enthusiast. At his best, he can examine his own past aberrations, but only on the assumption that they were historically inevitable: i.e. that to have been wrong was a mark of seriousness. There are tougher French thinkers who would be ashamed to perpetrate such a confidence trick. Finkielkraut is one of them, and we also ought to hear far more than we do of Michel Onfray. But the truly essential man right now is undoubtedly Pascal Bruckner. The central argument of his *La tyrannie de la pénitence* should be at the fingertips of every serious political commentator in English. I have to admit, however, that I myself would have been slow to discover him if Jonathan Meades, who lives in France, hadn't tipped me off. If you really want to keep up, you have to be there. But it's a counsel of despair to say that if we can't be there, we needn't try to find out what's going on. One of the wonders of the modern world is how the British universities continue to turn out whole generations of ambitious literary critics who seem to have given up on learning to read French. One can understand their giving up on learning to speak French – I give up every two weeks – but if they have not made a decent beginning on learning to read it, you can't help wondering what they were up to at university. And then they tell you: they were reading Derrida in English.

THE VELVET SHACKLES OF A REPUTATION

In Dr Johnson's little novel *Rasselas*, the Poet tells the Prince about the psychological requirements of a poetic career. The poet, says the Poet, must 'content himself with the slow progress of his name'. On the other hand he should learn to 'contemn the applause of his own time.' We would have liked to hear more, but the Prince has more boring things to do and cuts the Poet short.

My own view is that the second requirement sounds a bit hard: I would like to have a lot more of the applause of my own time before I contemn it. I don't think that the whole idea of a 'reputation' for poets has done much for poetry in modern times, but while reputations are thought to matter it would be nice to have one. Leaving that second requirement aside, however, the first requirement is one I recognize by necessity. Speaking as one whose name, for a long time, was all too recognizable from every activity except the one that mattered to me most, I can only wonder, looking back, if my name as a poet might not have made quicker progress had I been less notorious for the other things.

Even today, when I have been absent from the screen for more than five years, interviewers take it as self-evident that I have a question to answer: didn't television fame rule out any possible reputation as a serious writer? A variation on this, if the interviewer is ready to concede that I might be some kind of serious writer after all, goes thus: didn't my reputation as a prose writer rule out any possible reputation as a poet? These questions are really based on two different levels of the same assumption: that poetry should be pursued as a single, dedicated vocation. Proper poets really don't do anything else. If any of them ever do, it can only be as a way of making the poetry possible.

Well, of course there's a lot to that argument. If poetry is a dedicated activity like brain surgery, we don't want the poet dreaming of being a TV presenter any more than we want the brain surgeon dreaming of being Eric Clapton. Just as the brain surgeon might start playing air guitar at the critical moment, the poet might imagine himself jumping into the hot tub at Playboy Mansion West with three gatefold girls, thus inevitably coarsening the texture of his latest tender love lyric. (Yes, that's what I did. There were reasons, which I don't have time to explain now.) But the argument is based on a conception of poetry that I don't happen to share. I have always admired the priesthood of the profession, but was cut out by nature for the limelight, not the pulpit, and what really screwed my reputation was when I took my poetry into show business in the 1970s. Some of the details of how I did it are in my latest volume of memoirs, *North Face of Soho*, and I won't repeat them here. But I can summarize them by saying that after my first mock epic *Peregrine Prykke's Pilgrimage* made its scurrilous mark, I became typecast in the literary world as a kind of performance poet, like all those American visitors who turned up at the Albert Hall in their overalls. I was an Australian visitor (cue artwork of man in bush hat with corks around the brim) making the same sort of flagrant assault on local reticence.

From then on, my fate was sealed, and anything I wrote in verse form was regarded as a would-be entertainment. The literary gossip column coverage that accrued to such poems as 'The Book of My Enemy Has Been Remaindered' and 'Bring Me the Sweat of Gabriela Sabatini' confirmed that view. It became a given. What made it hard for me to fight this invisible but all too palpable straitjacket was that I actually did believe a poem ought to be something that could be recited and performed: something entertaining in the first instance. I wrote lyric poems that were meant to be as deep and intricate as anybody else's, but I still wanted them to be able to pass that first test in front of a live audience. For all poets, critics and literary journalists wedded to the belief that poetry was a private matter meant only to be overheard, this attitude was anathema.

I was ready to live with that assessment, but it undoubtedly had some uncomfortable consequences, and continues to do so. A few years ago one of my poems about my dead parents – a particularly serious theme in my recent work, I would have thought – was up for consideration by a British literary tribunal known as the Forward Prize committee. I heard privately that one of the judges threatened to resign from the panel if my poem was even mentioned. If I had ever depended on prizes I would have been dead by then, but the news was still disturbing.

My volume of collected poems, *The Book of My Enemy* (Picador, 2003), received a Poetry Book Society special commendation, ran through five printings in its first year, and was widely, and often favourably, reviewed. Some of the most generously thoughtful notices, I'm glad to say, were in Australian publications: I think particularly of Peter Craven in the *Adelaide Advertiser*, and Peter Goldsworthy in the *Australian Book Review*. But the two serious British literary papers in which most of the book's constituent poems first appeared still haven't reviewed it, three years later. Neither periodical is known for being quick off the mark, and one of them is famous for delaying a review until the author can be proved to have entered the nursing home, but you would have thought that having been actually published so often in their pages would have been a qualification for the acknowledgment of one's existence.

It could be said, even by me, that my existence as a poet gets acknowledged quite enough. I suppose that being blessed, or cursed, with a showbiz name did something to save me from the usual crepuscular stretch in the specialist magazines. But it gave me no automatic entry to such outlets as the *Spectator*, the *Guardian*, the *TLS*, the *LRB*, the *Australian*, the *Australian Book Review*, *Meanjin*, the *New Yorker* and *Poetry* (Chicago). Almost all of those publications, in my case, continue, as they should, to do at least as much rejecting as accepting. I have no reason to believe that the interior editorial voice saying, 'He's a well-known media name, let's print his poem,' does much to quell the other interior editorial voice saying, 'He's playing at poetry, let's leave his poem out.' All too often, indeed, I am the victim of the strange medical condition which its victims call Death by Acceptance, whereby a poem is accepted and then not printed for months that stretch into years. The only way I can explain this is that the editor, having temporarily convinced himself that my reputation for frivolity can be ignored for once, starts realizing that he might run the risk of acquiring the same reputation for himself. So he just parks the thing. Or she does. One of my London editors proved incapable of responding in any way during the two full years that I intermittently quizzed her on the fate of one of my poems that she had accepted. She smiled at me very nicely at parties, but the smile got broader after I finally let somebody else print it.

Luckily I don't have to hold my breath. I get enough attention to be going on with, and most of it is the best kind. I wrote a poem called 'When We Were Kids' about my memories of childhood in Australia. Now I can't sit down to read and write at Rossini's on Circular Quay without people coming up to me and telling me what I left out of it. My website www.clivejames.com is a vanity press the size of a space station. So far, on the Web, I have published only those poems which have already found a first home in print, but if the site got famous enough I could easily contemplate forgetting about print publication altogether, and just send the stuff in through the Earth's atmosphere from cyberspace, like cosmic rays. If I went on the road with a show based on reading out nothing except my verse – with, of course, a suitably subversive commentary damning all editors to hell – I would probably even make a living, in the way that Robert Frost pioneered. He got paid thousands of dollars a pop, not just because he was correctly perceived to be a great man but because he could put on a show.

Most poets can't do that, because they are steeped in the private ways of being merely overheard. Good luck to them, but I prefer to take stage centre. I'm used to it, and nobody has asked for their money back yet. Also it's the sort of applause I care about most. But there's no denying that I could use a bit more of the other kind of applause as well. Still hankering for that, I would be hypocritical to contemn it, not to say unwise. A good reason for being at least sceptical about the approval of the poetic establishment of the day is that is has never been very good at separating the poet from his publicity. Unfortunately any poet who complains about his publicity is likely to be reminded, by fellow poets who don't get enough of it, that he sounds like Jennifer Lopez complaining about the size of her trailer.

The Monthly, August 2007

Postscript

This piece was a clear case of blowing my own trumpet, but I still felt, at the time, that I had nobody else to blow it; and poetry needs pushing, because the poet is facing something far more unyielding than sales resistance. Poetry has a restricted market even for Seamus Heaney, so he has to go on the road. In the popular music industry they call it Touring the Album. With poetry you have to tour the book or it's as good as dead. Later on, in 2008, my book of selected poems *Opal Sunset* came out in America, and it was followed in Britain by *Angels over Elsinore*, a collection of poems written since 2003. Though there was quite a lot of press coverage for both books, in Britain I still had to work the festivals. A festival appearance really means going on stage without a fee, but it's worth it if you can sign the crucial few extra copies that will make your publisher feel he hasn't just set fire to a wad of his own money.

DON'T HOLD YOUR BREATH, ARGENTINA

To have a selection of my essays published in Buenos Aires is more than flattering. It seems fitting, because the city has not only touched my heart, through the tango, but has helped to form my mind. Though I love to dance the tango, I will never be much good at it beyond a certain point. I found that out in Buenos Aires, when my teachers, the great tango couple Jorge and Aurora Firpo, would demonstrate what I had to do next. Even when I learned to do it, I knew that I would never look as graceful as they did. But I can live with that knowledge because there is something else I do better: the essay. Even with the essay, however, it helps to have a supply of role models if you want to find out how good you can get. I found many of my role models in Latin America.

When I started learning to read Spanish, about twenty years ago, the essayists were my way in. I would recommend that priority to any student who is making a beginning with a foreign literature: start with the essays. Especially if they are about politics or the arts, they are likely to have an international vocabulary that will help you keep the main thread while you are reaching for the dictionary to clarify a subsidiary point. My first great exemplar was Octavio Paz. I accumulated a row of his essay collections and read everything in them. I never did learn enough about Mexico, but his opinions on international subjects all got into my head, to reinforce my own opinions when they were similar, and make them more subtle when they were different. The same could be said for Mario Vargas Llosa, who emanated from the other end of the continent but talked about a world you recognized even if you had never been that far south. In fact he talked incomparably about Europe: nobody has ever described better the process of evolution by which the young intellectual gets out from underneath the influence of Jean-Paul Sartre, and starts to recognize the lasting humanist significance of Albert Camus. I had already been through that process myself when I read Vargas Llosa on the subject and realized, to my discomfort, that he could express it better. I resolved to try for the same clarity, and the same flexibility. (Young readers who doubt that latter quality in Vargas Llosa, and think he has moved irretrievably to the right, should read one of his recent essays on illegal immigration, and take in the implications of his being for it, not against it.) With both those essayists, I was always taking notes, always arguing.

The arguing grew heated when it came to the essayists from Argentina. Borges I already admired as a poet and a writer of short fiction. There was no alternative to admiration: trying not to admire him would have been a protest against the weather. But his essays and dialogues brought politics in, especially when he tried to leave politics out. Some of his Argentinian critics taught me a lesson there. They pointed out what I would not have seen: that Borges's early silence on the subject of the Junta has been eloquent. His critics admired him too, but he had disappointed them. I tried not to get into a position where he could disappoint me, but there can be no question that my view of Borges was made much more nuanced by what he wrote, or failed to write, in his essays, and what his critics, in their essays, wrote about him.

The essay was the revealing form: even more so than the dialogue, which I soon found was practically a speciality of Argentina, if only because it was so often practised by Borges and Sábato, both separately and together. Borges has a way of retreating into the dialogue in order to avoid saying what he would have had to advance in an essay. Sábato, in both forms, was, it seemed to me, more likely to say what was really on his mind. I enjoyed the transcripts of his dialogues but his essays I more than enjoyed. I know that this opinion might seem strange to many literary people in Argentina who remember that Sábato, too, just like Borges, sat down to break bread with demons. Those people, brought up in the Spanish language as I am not, are apt to regard his style as a back-number. But eventually he saw the point about the men who wore dark glasses at night – to the extent of editing a book about their crimes – and the clarity of his prose is a gift to the foreign student. At this point I hasten to admit that what I hear as the simplicity of his style might be exactly what's wrong with it: we characteristically over-praise, when reading in a second language, those writers that we can wolf down.

With all that said, however, Sábato, more than anyone else, is, for me, the most fascinating essayist of the recent Spanish world: the modern Unamuno, the Ortega of our time. One of the many reasons he qualified for those titles is that he so thoroughly took in the lesson of the philologist Pedro Henríquez Ureña. (It was literally a lesson, because they were master and pupil.) Ureña said that the one-time colonial countries were not on the edge of the Spanish world, but at the centre – the centre of its future. From the literary angle, Sábato was the living expression of everything that Ruben Darío had ever dreamed of, and for a younger would-be critic from an outpost of a different vanished empire, Australia, his style was a constant lesson in how to pack a complex argument into a natural-sounding sentence. 'Mankind is conservative,' said Sábato. 'When this tendency weakens, however, revolutions devote themselves to its renewal.' A mature and tragic historical view could scarcely be put better. (When young Spanish-speakers tell me that Sábato sounds no more natural than a cranky old man abusing the passing traffic, it makes me wonder: how bad is my Spanish?) One by one and two by two, I bought all of Sábato's slim volumes of essays, and finally the big compendium called *Ensayos*, and over the years I made a point of reading them in the coffee-shop of the book-store where I first bought them, Gandhi in the Avenida Corrientes. I also read Bioy Casares there, and Cortazar, and wondered, as I read her memoirs, how Victoria Ocampo could ever have climbed into bed with Drieu la Rochelle. Even more thoroughly than when I tried to steer Aurora Firpo through a *media luna* while Jorge, with folded arms, frowned at me in despair, it was when I was reading in the Buenos Aires cafes that I felt tied to the city, to the country, to the continent, and beyond that to the miraculous unfolding new reality of an intellectual *reconquista* – the restoration of the Spanish world to the world itself, to the culture of the liberal, democratic, humanistic universe that Vargas Llosa, when praising Darío, hailed as *cosmopolitanismo vital*. We haven't really got, in English, a term as unblushingly exultant as that. Reason enough, all on its own, to learn a language.

I hope some of the readers of this book might get the urge to start learning English, if only to find out what I really sound like. But finally I sound like the mentality underneath the prose. I hope that sounds like a liberal democratic mentality, of the type which, in the twentieth century, each of the two most virulent totalitarian forces thought was a worse threat than the other. The ideas constituting that mentality were hard won by people who paid a higher price to hold them than I ever did. All I ever did was learn to write them down. I'm proud of having worked hard at the intricacies of the English language, my means of expression, but the effort was wasted if the things I have expressed don't translate into other languages as well. A language matters but it isn't everything, whereas the liberal democratic idea very nearly is everything.

Let me end this short introduction – I can feel it already threatening to grow as long as the book – by mentioning another writer from Buenos Aires who affected the course of my life almost as much as the writers I have mentioned above. But he didn't write in Spanish. He was the Polish exile Witold Gombrowicz, and most of his marvellous journals I read in French. Suspicious of all art forms, he nevertheless treated his journals – really they amount to a vast collection of essays – as an art form, and his ability to charge the merest paragraph with meaning was the final evidence I needed that my seemingly incidental prose might be at the heart of what I could hope to achieve. There was a Polish bookshop in the Boulevard Saint-Germain and I used to buy the latest volume of Gombrowicz every year and sit reading it at my unknown but welcoming cafe in the Rue de l'Université. Paris, like Buenos Aires, is a magic city, but only if the magic is in you. And finally, for me, the books are where the magic comes from. They don't need a city. They are a universal city in themselves. In Dante's time, the writers blessed their new book when it set off on its travels. If this book should be fortunate enough to travel through the Spanish world – if it should travel all the way to Spain – I hope it will bring its readers just a touch of the excitement that their beautiful language brought me when I began to learn it, when I was still a stranger among strangers.

Previously unpublished

Postscript

The biggest publishing house in Buenos Aires flatteringly sent me a message announcing that they wished to publish a comprehensive selection of my essays, and asked me to write an introduction for it, which they would translate into Spanish. I wrote the above piece with some care and sent it off. I heard nothing for a year. Then they sent me a message announcing that they wished to publish a comprehensive selection of my essays, and asked me to write an introduction for it. I sent off the same piece again, and again heard nothing. Two more years have gone by and I have begun to understand why the potholes in the sidewalks of that beautiful city are never filled in, and why the missing tiles in the floor of the *Ideal* tango salon are never replaced. Last year the biggest publishing house in Shanghai sent a message announcing that they planned to publish a translation of *Cultural Amnesia*. I was relieved to note that they did not ask me to write an introduction.

WHITE SHORTS OF LENI RIEFENSTAHL

A brazen shout from long trumpets held high at the angle of a Hitler salute. Cut to medium close-up of young Aryan faces with puffed cheeks. Dolly back as two new biographies of Leni Riefenstahl appear virtually at once. Jürgen Trimborn's book has the better pictures, Steven Bach's the better text. Though neither is precisely adulatory, put them together and they add up to an awful lot of attention. She might be dead, but she won't lie down.

The same was true for much of the time she was still alive. Born in 1902, she lived for a hundred years. In less than half that time, she acquired a brilliant reputation. But she had to spend the rest of her life mounting a posthumous defence of it. She might have made a more convincing job of exploiting her victim status if she had ever shown a single sign of caring about millions of other victims whose relationship with the regime she helped to glorify had been rather less privileged.

Already nationally famous in the pre-Nazi period German cinema as an actress and director, in the Nazi period she grew world famous by giving the new, globally ambitious political movement a screen image of overwhelming authority, glamorous even to those who sensed its evil. A duly grateful Hitler indulged her whims, granted her total access, and financed her from his personal funds.

Some spectators thought even at the time that her cinematic gift had served to legitimise a murderous ideology, but almost nobody belittled her artistic talent. She was thus able, when the Nazis lost, to invoke the principle that art trumps politics. Photographed too often with her raised hand pointed in Hitler's direction, quoted too often on the subject of his transformative vision, she was unable to deny that she had held her mentor in high regard, but she nevertheless did deny — spent more than another half century denying, and never stopped denying until her last gasp — that she had ever known much about what the Nazis were really up to. She had been too busy being a great artist.

To make this line stick, she had the help of her two big movies from the Nazi-dominated 1930s, *The Triumph of the Will* and *Olympia*. Though the first now stands revealed as a gruesomely choreographed hymn to naked power and the second spends too much of its time weighing sport down with a neoclassic gravitas that feels like being hit over the head with the Parthenon, there were, even after the end of the Thousand Year Reich's twelve-year run, plenty of knowledgeable critics in the victorious democracies who called her portentous epics masterpieces. For her cineaste admirers, the aesthetics left the ethics nowhere. It seemed a fair guess that anyone so wrapped up in creating an imaginary world would be bound to miss the odd detail about what was going on in the real one. The Holocaust? Forget about it.

To assist in the forgetting, she also had the help of her histrionic abilities, which might never have been subtle, but were always in a good state of training, because there had rarely been a moment of her conscious life when she had not shown her emotions as the only way of having them. (In her early phase as a film star, she hammed it up even in the stills.) Leni would act indignant when she was asked an awkward question. If you asked it again, she would storm out, fall down, shriek, weep. The effect, fully as bogus as a child's tantrum, was just as unnerving to any surrounding adults.

Above all, however, she had the help of time. After the trap-door stopped rattling and banging at Nuremberg, it got harder and harder to find a Nazi with a famous name. The ones in Argentina had unlisted telephone numbers. But Leni Riefenstahl's new shyness was all a pose. She had a way of hiding only where she could be found, and she never ceased to assure the world that although she and Hitler had spent a lot of time talking in private the Jews had never got a mention.

More than half a century went by and she was still there, popping up at film festivals to keep her cinematic legend in trim, conspicuously disappearing into Africa to build a new career as a photographer, steadily acquiring the validation that comes automatically with endurance. 'Of what am I guilty?' The martyred look that went with that refrain made it seem as if the suffering had all happened to her. She showed no remorse, saying that she had no reason to. Those who were all too well aware that she did have reason to died off faster than she did, so finally there were whole new generations to take her genius for granted.

We might as well do the same, because over the question of her talent it isn't worth fighting a battle. Finally every geriatric artist is a genius, and especially if the artist is a woman. Among the people who run the movie business anywhere in the world, women are a minority even today, and still under pressure to exercise feminine wiles. When the lowly born Leni was starting out, the minority, even in go-ahead Weimar Germany, was the merest handful. Luckily for her, she had feminine wiles to burn: until she was old and grey, she met few men who didn't fall for her on the spot. It could be said that she had looks and energy but no real brain. The evidence was overwhelming that she didn't need one. What marked her out was her ambition, which was always boundless.

As a young actress, she was so beautiful that other women could find nothing bad to say about her except that her eyes were too close together. But her acting on screen was strictly frown, laugh, bubble and jump. She made it as a star because she was good at climbing rocks. There was a whole genre of German movies about clambering around daringly at high altitude. In a string of mountain pictures culminating in *The White Hell of Pitz Palu*, Leni proved that she could do that stuff without a double. There was no peak, however vertiginous, that she could not sprint to the top of wearing very few clothes. On the other hand there was no director, however illustrious, whom she could not hurl herself beneath wearing no clothes at all. Or at least she gave him the illusion that she might: a power of suggestion that we can usefully regard as her most persuasive thespian gift.

Fixed on becoming a director herself, she applied the same gift when bending producers and studio bigwigs to her triumphant will. Her real originality was in setting her sights high, up there where the men were making the decisions. All the right potentates duly succumbed to her allure. 'I must meet that man' was an exhortation often on her lips. Before the Nazis came to power, some of the men she felt compelled to meet were Jews. Afterwards, none of them were. It could be said that she never came out as an anti-Semite, but it could also be said that there is a green cheese moon.

Made on the eve of the Weimar Republic's final agony, her film

The Blue Light – she was producer, director, writer, editor and star – was a critical dud. She blamed the Jewish critics. She might have had a case. After the Nazis came to power, her co-writer on the movie, Bela Balazs, was too insistent about getting paid. Balazs was a Jew. Eventually she got him off her back by turning his name over to Julius Streicher. For that, she had no case at all. Everybody knew what Streicher stood for. Gauleiter of Nuremberg, editor of the lethally scurrilous *Der Stürmer*, he was the most famous Jew-baiter in Germany.

But she had a bigger buddy than Streicher. Hitler had liked *The Blue Light*, so when she once again said, 'I must meet that man,' her wish was easily answered. Coy for the rest of her endless life on the subject of whether she threw him one, she always wanted it to be thought that only his total dedication to the cause held him back. Given her track record with men, the mere fact that she spent time alone with him was enough to confer on her all the power of the Führer's public darling. (Hardly anybody knew about Eva Braun. Everybody knew about Leni.) She was given full access to film the 1934 party rally. After a year of editing – possessing almost no sense of story, she invariably overshot by a hundred miles – the film appeared in 1935 as *The Triumph of the Will*.

Hitler loved the movie. Critics who still feel the same way are apt to underrate the part played by Albert Speer, whose lighting and décor were all his own idea. The camera had to look up at Hitler because Speer put him there. But Leni undoubtedly did a thorough job of making what was already frighteningly impressive look more frighteningly impressive still. If ten thousand men marching in lock-step are what turns you on, Leni could make them look like twenty thousand. Her style was computer-generated imagery *avant la lettre*.

The top Nazis were delighted. They included Goebbels, whom Leni, after the war, found it expedient to characterise as a danger-ous enemy jealous of his bailiwick as the supreme studio executive nominally in charge of Nazi movies. In fact Goebbels, generously overlooking her refusal to put out for him, thought highly of her artistic prowess, blowing his top only when she went mad with the money. (Stephen Bach, who wrote *Final Cut*, the best-ever book about a film director on the rampage, is especially good on the subject of how Leni treated a budget as the merest letter of intent.)

After *The Triumph of the Will*, the road was open for Leni to do what she wanted. What she wanted was to turn the 1936 Berlin Olympics into a celluloid masterpiece. By far her most palatable cinematic achievement, *Olympia* was, and remains, crucial to her later reputation. Even more crucial is that the film is not notably a Nazi one. Hitler the arch-nationalist didn't enjoy being stuck with staging an international event, but while he was at it he had enough sense to go light on the ideology. The Jews are, of course, absent, but there are blacks present, notably Jesse Owens, whom Leni didn't hesitate to caress with her lenses as if he were a god-like presence.

She wasn't having a thing with Owens. She was having that with another American, the decathlete Glen Morris, whom she obliged to add an eleventh discipline to his event. But she filmed Owens with loving appreciation. It's a shameful consideration that no Hollywood director would have been encouraged to do the same, at the time. Owens in repose looked lovely anyway, and on the move he was poetic, but it took a fine eye and a lot of knowledge to get the poetry on film, and Leni knew how to do that with him and with many another athlete. It was only logical for the camera to climb the tower with the diver, for example, but she figured out how to do it.

Knocking herself out to catch the unforgettable moment, this was the hard-driving, indomitable, manpower-manipulating Leni at her best, and Susan Sontag later made a serious mistake in arguing that *Olympia* was entirely steeped in fascist worship of the beautiful body. It's nature that worships the beautiful body. Fascism is natural. That's what's wrong with it: it's nothing else. Much of *Olympia*'s reputation for beauty can thus safely be endorsed, but always with the proviso that a lot of the athletic events were beautiful anyway, and that her technical inventions for capturing them would eventually suffer the fate of all technical inventions, and be superseded: everything she did in Berlin in 1936 was topped by what Kon Ichikawa did in Tokyo in 1964. Nevertheless, Leni, with her material handed to her on a plate, and unhampered by those requirements of invented narrative that she could never manage, had made quite a movie for its time. It was a huge hit all over Europe.

In November 1938, Leni, who had probably always had one eye on Hollywood, flew the Nazi flag to America. In Los Angeles she was scheduled to walk the red carpet at the premiere of an entirely de-Hitlerised copy of *Olympia*. She had every reason to expect that she was heading for a big welcome, and she might still have had one, even though *Kristallnacht* happened only five days after her ship docked in New York. But she blew the scene with what she said. She said that nothing had happened, and that to suggest such a thing was a slander.

Hollywood gave her the freeze. Almost nobody in America except Henry Ford even invited her for drinks. Back in Germany, she reported to Goebbels, who was suitably indignant on behalf of his thwarted artist. 'The Jews,' he told his diary, 'rule by terror and bribery.' When the Nazi counter-terror against the Jews went rolling into the East, Leni, in sole command of her own film unit, was along for the ride, but she saw something in Poland that stopped her in her tracks, even if it didn't stop the Nazis. Accidentally present at a mass shooting in the town square of Konskie, she was photographed looking distraught.

As a general rule, any expression on Leni's face when a camera was pointing in her direction was adopted at her own command, but in this case it might have been possible that her distress was genuine. Whatever the truth of this permanently controversial moment, however, it seems probable that Leni, when she next saw Hitler, asked permission to be excused from the war. She didn't opt out of the Nazi party's inexorable conquest of the world – she was there to film Hitler's victory parade in Warsaw, the only time he lent his presence to such an event – but she never again went near a battle. Instead, she asked and received permission to resume filming *Tiefland*, the dramatic blockbuster which she had abandoned when the Nazis came to power. Here was the chance for her to prove, to the full satisfaction of her post-war admirers, that she was indeed an artist who had no knowledge of what the Nazis were really doing.

Once again, however, she blew it. Personally financed out of Hitler's deep pocket (he got a royalty for every postage stamp with his face on it), *Tiefland* had unlimited resources, but it needed some Spanish-looking child extras, and all the children readily available looked too Aryan. So Leni shipped in some gypsy children from a holding camp where they were waiting for a train to Auschwitz. Long after the war, the tirelessly litigious Leni won a law-suit against a documentary maker who suggested that she, Leni, had known about Auschwitz. She might just possibly not have known. But she certainly did know that she was employing forced labour; and her claim that she met some of the children after the war was a flat lie.

She lied about everything. She just went on lying until people got tired, or old, or died. One of her most telling lies was the one she told about Streicher. She said that she had loathed him. But there is preserved correspondence to prove that she invited his company and treated him as a close friend until quite late in the war. The idea that Streicher would never mention to her what was happening to the Jews is preposterous. He was proud of it, and was eventually hanged for it.

Leni, although she never managed regret, had enough sense to feign ignorance. Playing dumb, she was de-Nazified in the second least noxious category, which meant that she could continue her career, if she could pick up the pieces. High-ranking Allied officers of various nationalities were eager that the process of de-Nazifying Leni should be continued in private. But one of her closer questioners got the admission out of her that really mattered. He was Budd Schulberg. His famous days as a screenwriter were still ahead of him, but he would never dream up a neater scene than the one he played out with Leni. After unrolling her usual impatient rigmarole about having known nothing about any Nazi atrocities, Leni made the mistake of saying that she sometimes, against her will, had to do what Goebbels wanted, because she was afraid of being sent to a concentration camp. Schulberg asked why she should have been afraid of that, if she didn't know that concentration camps existed.

So there was the whole story. For anyone with a memory for recent events, the question of Leni's moral status was settled. What came next, stretching on to the end of the millennium and now beyond, was the question of her artistic stature, supposedly a different thing. She built another career photographing tribesmen in Africa, and then yet another one, filming life below the waves in yet another new role as the oldest diver in the world. And as the people with a memory for the real world grew fewer, those who knew about nothing except the movies gradually redefined the issue.

At the end of the first *Star Wars* movie, George Lucas copied the ambience of *The Triumph of the Will* with no apparent sense of how he was really proving that the cause in which Luke Skywalker and his friends had just triumphed could not have been worth fighting for. Mick Jagger, Andy Warhol, and Madonna all enrolled themselves on the growing list of Leni's fans. So did Siegfried and Roy. Francis Ford Coppola said he admired her. Steven Spielberg said he wanted to meet her. If he had made *Schindler's List* ten times, he could not have undone the portent of such a wish, because he was really saying that there can be art without a human framework, and that a movie can be made out of nothing but impressive images. Some of Leni's images were indeed impressive. But the question is never about whether or not you are impressed. The question is about whether you can keep your head when you are. Leni Riefenstahl was impressed by the Nazis, and look what happened.

New York Times, March 25, 2007

Postscript

Walter Benjamin, who said so much that was deliberately incomprehensible, spoke the simple truth when he said that all aesthetic politics lead to fascism. The connection is made especially clear in our memories of the top Nazis. Civilized people with a yen for Leni Riefenstahl are flirting with horror. She looked good in shorts, but her mind was a madhouse. Is there any stopping this tendency to sentimentalize the unspeakable? Probably not: and certainly not where the movies are involved. Even the best movies about the Nazi era, if we can bear to look at them at all, are performing cosmetic surgery on the past. Admirers of *Downfall* are right to be impressed by its narrative drive, but they ought to be aware that the glamour principle has done its debilitating work. The actor playing Albert Speer does a fine job of modelling a full-length leather coat, but his fastidious, concerned expression is the exact face that the post-war Speer so successfully presented to the world. Wouldn't that have been us? we ask. No it wouldn't, because there was no such man. Speer, one of the best-informed men in Germany, knew all about what was going on. 'I should have known', his post-war mantra suitable for all media, was just a classy way of saying, 'I never knew.' It was a lie, but people went along with it because they could imagine themselves sitting down with him to dinner. The beautiful young secretary who was stunned to learn that Hitler hated Jews is another fairytale. Interviewed in her old age, she regretfully said that she should have found out. But she had more to regret than that. She already knew when she applied for the job. Up on the screen, however, her lovely young worried eyes are pools for our doubts to drown in. Throughout the movie, our imagination rushes in to fill the gaps. But our imagination is benevolent. The Nazi imagination wasn't. Similarly, when we look at Riefenstahl's movies we imagine that such glamour must have had a brain behind it that was something like ours. But it was nothing like ours.

MADE IN BRITAIN, MORE OR LESS

Even as Ingmar Bergman and Michelangelo Antonioni came to the end of their lives, the BBC, to accompany a long summer season of British films, gave birth to a multi-part documentary round-up called *British Film Forever*. The first part was called 'Gangsters Guns and Getaways': no comma, no apologies for brashness. 'Us British love films,' the commentary began, grammatically daring from the first word. Had Bergman ever spoken like that in Swedish, or Antonioni in Italian?

But the slapdash exuberance of language, one hoped, might still leave room for a less approximate underlying idea. Perhaps us British – I was keen to include myself in this possibility, having once, while still in short pants, seen *The Sound Barrier* two nights running at the Rockdale Odeon in Sydney – did love films. On the level of handing out addictive free samples, the series had to be counted a success from the jump. Clips from much-loved British films abounded: *Brief Encounter*, *In Which We Serve*, *Gone With the Wind* . . .

Wait a second: *Gone With the Wind* was made in Hollywood. So why were we looking at Clark Gable? Well, he was holding on to Vivien Leigh, a star born and raised in Britain. And why were we looking at *Wuthering Heights*, which was also made in Hollywood? Well, Laurence Olivier was in it, holding on to Olivia de Havilland. Follow the British stars and you could often get to a great big film that us British loved, although it might not always be a British film. In Britain, Leigh and Olivier, the nation's second most regal married couple, starred together in very few films, most notably *That Hamilton Woman*, an Alexander Korda misfire which not even us British love any longer.

In Britain, Olivier on his own made *Henry V*, *Hamlet* and *Richard III*, each of them as home-grown as his kipper breakfast on the *Brighton Belle*: taken together, they put him at the apex of achievement in world cinema both as actor and director. But on the scale of international box office, which effectively meant Hollywood, Olivier never became established as a film star. He could say it didn't matter to him, but it still matters to everyone who writes about him. It certainly mattered to Matthew Sweet, who wrote the commentary for *British Film Forever*, and might have done better to subtitle it *Despite the Yanks* before going on to face the subject of the Special Relationship squarely, instead of finding a dozen different self-deceiving ways of leaving it out.

The most glaring self-deception was a persistent failure to follow the money. The director John Boorman once said that film turns money into light. In cinema, money might not be everything, but it is always the first thing. In the chapter devoted to Romance ('Longing Loving and Leg-overs' was the exciting title), the commentary, when it dealt with *Dr Zhivago*, followed Julie Christie (British star) into the arms of Omar Sharif (not British star) without noting that David Lean (British director) was bankrolled, for his big international films, by Sam Spiegel (not British producer), the erstwhile S. P. Eagle of Hollywood. If Spiegel, in his role as Lean's bagman, had needed to rely on British money, his yacht would have been propelled by a pair of oars.

Spiegel put the dough together on the assurance that the finished product would be readily intelligible to an American audience. There was never then, and still isn't, a reservoir of finance within Britain to sustain a film industry without a pipeline to the American market. Korda's productive heyday lasted for a while, and Michael Balcon's for a while longer, but without one eye on America nobody can last indefinitely: the true wording of *British Film Forever* should have been *British Film Sporadically*. This was the biggest theme demanding to be treated by a documentary survey of the history of British Film. Its almost complete absence guaranteed that the commentary could not be serious. So we got sprightliness instead.

It pains me to say that the results were seldom tolerable and all too often deadly. But Jessica Hynes, the actress who was given the task of speaking the words of Mr Sweet, is yet young, and it wasn't her fault that she had to say, when evoking the directorial rigour of David Lean, 'And if it meant getting the shot he wanted, Lean could *lean*.' It probably wasn't even Mr Sweet's fault that he had to write such stuff. It's a tone, the tone of British documentary television in its last speeding inches of terminal decline before it hits the concrete, and the tone was almost certainly imposed on him by producers who no longer know any better.

Leaden verve used to be the occasional mistake made by documentary production teams who, when the task dictated, thought that they could achieve humour just by fiddling with their diction. (Cue archive close-up of Kenneth Williams with mouth forming a small circle.) They had seriousness to depart from, and could always get back to it. But the *British Film Forever* bunch think that an unswerving facetiousness is the only way to talk.

Would-be liveliness came stumbling from the screen. Every few minutes the stream of semi-consciousness unintentionally revealed that Hollywood was being held as the measure of true success. Who was the author of some of 'the greatest thrillers in the history of Hollywood'? Alfred Hitchcock. 'Where else could he come from but good old Blighty?' Alas, the voice-over narrative was not alone in its capacity to irritate. Too large a number of the numberless guest experts talked the same way.

Among those that didn't, some weighty people had been interviewed for the usual half a day so that the occasional single short utterance could be extracted. From the top of the heap, Harold Pinter was intermittently present, and one doesn't doubt that his complete interview would make an excellent programme about British film on a serious channel in a serious world: for one thing, his jokes, even when bitter, would be funny. The same could be said of Frederic Raphael, who was called upon to say exactly one line. Sir Richard Attenborough, who has never talked for less than a whole day about anything, was cut to a few paragraphs. Anna Massey was briefly there too, and many another established actor, although one doubts that Mischa Barton falls into that category quite yet. She was there because she was a real live American.

After a clip showing a fragment of the tremendous performance by Diana Dors in *Yield to the Night*, Pauline Collins spoke with authority when she said she couldn't help wondering why Dors was never rewarded with 'a really big Hollywood career.' Thus was the game given away completely, or would have been if it hadn't already been given away ten times in every episode.

Canvas-chair veterans from Jack Cardiff through to Bryan Forbes were on hand for a few seconds each. Cardiff, if asked, could have told them that the only thing that might have stopped him from being lighting cameraman on a Spiegel-global international block-buster like *The African Queen* was a few more all-British projects like *Black Narcissus* and *The Red Shoes*, but they were in short supply, because not even Powell and Pressburger put together added up to a British Film Industry. Forbes, if asked, could have told them what he once told me, that if his popular thriller *The League of Gentlemen* had featured even one American big name, it would have cleaned up.

These and many other formidable people of the British film world deserved better than to be given equal time, or even less, with some standard television face-workers whose specific qualifications weren't always obvious. Daisy Goodwin might conceivably know something about poetry, a subject she had previously been deputed to make approachable for audiences who presumably knew nothing about poetry at all. But speaking about British Film, she deployed an even less analytical vocabulary. About the famous scene in *Tom Jones* when Albert Finney and his next female target eat themselves into bed, Daisy had this to say. 'It's all very kind of, you know, phwoar!' I couldn't remember her speaking the same way about John Donne.

To remind us that she was not just a hot number but a highbrow as well, Daisy managed to squeeze the word 'quintessentially' into her lightning discussion of *Far From the Madding Crowd*. In the new low language of the higher journalism gone wrong, 'quintessentially' is the only way to say 'essentially', just as 'implode' is the only way to say 'explode'. Ever more grandiose and less accurate, this detestable meta-language is always in the process of – to use one of its favourite words – 'reinvention', as in 'reinvention very much the name of the game.'

Very much characteristic of a self-generating patois like this is its levelling effect, by which nobody can think but everybody can have an opinion. Speaking of *The Long Good Friday*, someone billed as a broadcaster said that 'Thatcherism, the IRA and the Mafia' gave the film its edge. He might have at least considered that Thatcherism gave the film some of its finance. Haunted all over again by the film's savage visual imagery, I wondered if he would have spoken more to the point, as it were, if he had been hanging upside down from a hook with Bob Hoskins breathing the aftermath of a hot curry into his face.

What nobody said was that this deservedly celebrated nail-biter, for all its crackling plot and stellar performances from Hoskins and Helen Mirren, was yet another British film that gave the game away: the Mafia were in it because the local gangland scene was thought to need beefing up a bit for international distribution. From just the same perennial impulse, *Yield to the Night* had featured a Ford Thunderbird in the streets of Soho.

But *Get Carter* stuck manfully to a Sunbeam Alpine, not to mention a G Reg. Cortina. Against all odds, there have been British gangland films that have managed to snare a world audience while remaining socially realistic. It might have had something to do with the unexpected success of Social Realism itself. After half a century, the chapter on Social Realism ('Hardship Humour and Heroes') was still getting over the shock inflicted by the unexpected interest shown by a respectable number of British people in films concerned with their own unadorned lives.

As the commentary told us in a rare moment of pertinence, the directors, most conspicuously Lindsay Anderson, were, in the main, distinctly upstairs. Whether their view of downstairs was in service to a political programme was not questioned here, but their daring was made plain: realism should have been a formula for bankruptcy. (The culminating example was Ken Loach's *Kes*, which, though it looked good, sounded as if designed to go broke, with dialogue that would have benefited from being subtitled even in Britain.) My own memories, however, tell me that *Saturday Night and Sunday Morning*, one of the movement's first international hits, worked not so much because of its cutaway view of the decaying class system as because of its view of Albert Finney's face.

Out there in Sydney I copied Finney's libidinous smirk the same way that I had previously copied Marlon Brando's sneer. It was a portent: there was as much glamour in the muck as in the brass. But unless they employed star power, the consciously subversive British films nearly always tanked: whatever the commentary to these programmes thought, *A Taste of Honey* will remain obdurately un-forever, and *Scum*, which the BBC refused to transmit in its original form as a television drama, survives as a film now only because Ray Winstone became well known later. (See him in the wonderful *Sexy Beast*, featuring Sir Ben Kingsley as a psychopath with an unsettling resemblance to Gandhi.)

But with the right cast, British Social Realist films could, and did, give the makers of gangland and action movies the idea that the whole thing could stay British and still interest the world. If the story was good enough, even the Americans would sit still for the preposterous idea that there might be another country that spoke their language but looked different, with tiny cars and plates with hardly any food on them. Somewhere out of that idea came *Get Carter*, whose permanent status was only momentarily compromised when it was remade with Sylvester Stallone in the leading role.

That role, as we all know, belongs always (British Film Forever!) to our (all right, your) very own Michael Caine, lips pursed with contempt over teeth bared in anger – the greatest thespian feat of his life, and a living demonstration of the eternal truth that all a star has to do is be. (An actor has to do more, but even Olivier, with thousands of lines of Shakespeare in his head, would have given a lot for even one role in which he only had to stand there in a smart blue raincoat while the surrounding action made a hero of him.)

When *Get Carter* came out, I saw it several times on the trot, dazzled by the neatness with which it was put together. In *The Ipcress File*, which I had also memorised shot by shot, Michael Caine had worn glasses. In *Get Carter* he didn't. What a range! And once again, the leading man had a superbly suave, impeccably British heavy to outwit. In *The Ipcress File* it had been the great Nigel Greene, he who had murmured 'Look to your front' in *Zulu* and died too young. In *Get Carter* it was none other than John Osborne, unforgettably proving that he could have had an authoritative screen career had he wished, although he might have needed a fully functioning British film industry to hold his magnetically petulant face aloft, up there where the money turns to light.

There for a triumphant moment and then gone again, exultant at the black-tie awards ceremony and then back scrambling for a pittance, the British Film Industry has always been a creature in oscillating transit, somewhere between a phoenix and a dead duck. Even in the glory years of J. Arthur Rank, the man beating the gong was the only reliable element in the picture. As the Americans discovered in the earliest days of their studio system, a film industry must have two tiers, in which the second-rate output is good enough to pay the overheads: rely on the first-rate and you're dead. But who would be allowed to say so? At one of the serialised commentary's many moments of concentrated fatuousness – Ruth Ellis was being described as having been 'hung for a crime of passion' when, unless I have always been misinformed about her gender, 'hanged' must have been the word they meant – I started to concoct my own ideal version of the script in my mind.

Pinter would say more than just a few words about how he and Joseph Losey and Dirk Bogarde put *The Servant* together, and then, after the clip of Muriel Pavlow saying that in *Doctor in the House* she and Bogarde were just having 'innocent fun', there would be someone else to say that Dirk Bogarde was a brilliantly complex one-off whose idea of innocent fun was to don full leather and rev his motorbike in the attic, and then Sir David Puttnam would give a twenty-minute lecture on just why, in *Chariots of Fire*, the two lovers had to look out of the window of their hotel in Paris and discuss an Olympic stadium that the audience couldn't see. (The budget barely ran to three pairs of long white shorts.)

And then there would have been selected readings, perhaps by Sir Ian McKellen and Dame Judi Dench, from the best book ever written about the British Film Industry, *My Indecision is Final*, by Jake Eberts and Terry Llott, wherein it is explained how Goldcrest, even after *Gandhi* became a sacred cash-cow world wide, still managed to go bust because there was nothing else on the production slate that made money except Paul Knight's television serial about Robin Hood. And then . . .

I noticed, however, that my ideal script was leaving less and less room for the clips. The far from ideal script on the screen still had the only right idea, which was to introduce the history of British movies to an audience that knew little about the movies and nothing at all about history. That, you had to remind yourself, was the purpose. For a few lucky young people out there, half a minute of Celia Johnson and Trevor Howard struggling to make their clipped accents heard above Rachmaninov's Second Piano Concerto ('You know what's heppening, don't you?') would introduce them to *Brief Encounter*, not to mention Rachmaninov.

They might even be introduced to the bewildering concept that there was once an almighty war in which the Americans, when they finally came to the aid of us British, saved us from tyranny, but the salvation led to the dissolution of our empire, and then to slowly dying dreams of power, and then, finally, to a new assessment of reality – a process in which British film has played a vital part, if only by providing us with a store of visual and verbal markers we can exchange when we meet. In that regard, even the pitiable epigrams supplied to James Bond come in handy, to remind us that Felix Leiter and all the other Americans really do regard Britain as a source of sophistication.

And they're right. One of the clueless viewers who needed informing was myself, because I hadn't yet got round to seeing Steve Coogan in *A Cock and Bull Story*, the film based on *Tristram Shandy*. The quoted clip made me determined to tune in when the complete film took its allotted place in the season. I did so, and I was bowled over. Coogan is so adventurous that other people catch originality from him: when I realised that the voice his sidekick Rob Brydon was using to impress Gillian Anderson had been borrowed from Roger Moore, I fell out of the couch.

The Americans can do some weird and wonderful stuff, but they can't do anything as bent as that. Us British have got Laurence Sterne in the background. Us British have got Jane Austen in the background. Let's face it: us British have got background in the background. Administrative talent – the talent to handle talent – might always be hard to find, but creative talent has been omnipresent since Shakespeare wrote his first Oscar-winning original screenplays for Larry. Some of it has even been creative enough to do the whole thing in Britain, with no concessions to the Americans at all.

That's what Coogan says he wants to do, although the British press, incurably servile in this respect, finds it impossible to accept that a British filmmaker has dreams of anything except Hollywood. Joe Wright, the director of *Atonement*, has announced that he wants to make more films in this country. The press will no doubt remind him that his wife, Rosamund Pike, wants to make films in America. She is too lovely and gifted not to. Half a century ago, the equally lovely Patricia Roc was lashed by her contract to a small island, waiting for the British Film Industry to materialise and save her. It never did.

By now, though, the penny has irretrievably dropped. Rosamund Pike will appear in American films, in that strange land where men make love with their clothes on, even to someone as beautiful as her. If she appeared only in British films, she would hardly ever appear. The duality is the reality. But at least we can now see the reality for what it is. What makes the post-imperial era so much more interesting than the imperial era is that it nurses fewer delusions. When I first saw *The Sound Barrier* I fell so hard for Ann Todd that I believed the script, and concluded that the British really had been the first to go supersonic. But it was the Americans.

Even then, they had the financial power. Luckily they have not always used it as crassly as it suits the rest of us to suppose. For a miracle, the final script of *British Film Forever* didn't end with a phone-in quiz. My ideal script does. Who insisted that *The Third Man*, perhaps the greatest film us British ever made, should have a scene to convince the audience about the hideous effects of Harry Lime's dud penicillin – the scene that gives the story its moral core? Was it (a) Carol Reed, (b) Graham Greene, or (c) the clumsily interfering American producer David O. Selznick? But you already knew.

TLS, September 28, 2007

Postscript

Out there in the remains of the old Empire, we were brought up on British war films. They were invariably less silly than the American equivalent. But they were fighting a losing battle. John Mills was boring as the ordinary chap doing his bit, Richard Attenborough was boring as the apprehensive chap below decks, Richard Todd was boring as the heroic chap with his hands on his hips delivering an inspiring address to all the other chaps. It helped that Richard Todd really had been a war hero, whereas John Wayne in *The Sands of Iwo Jima* had never left Hollywood. But in the long run the American war movies had the excitement, and the British war movie finally reached its imploding apotheosis when David Puttnam made *Memphis Belle*, which was all about how the Americans bombed Germany. In the long run, the money talked. British television, however, is better protected against global market forces. It can go to hell on its own tab. I should add that my remarks about the decline of British television's documentary style, though I think they have general validity, are subject to conspicuous exceptions. Under the guidance of Laurence Rees, historical programmes about the wartime period have never been better, and just because most of the TV producers can't tell the difference between good writing and rubbish doesn't mean that a one-off writer-performer like Jonathan Meades isn't turning out work comparable with Betjeman's at his height. But the general trend is downwards, and not because visual techniques are inadequate. On the contrary, they get better all the time. But the language is in decline. No British television company could produce a series like *Californication* even if it wanted to. The imbalance might be redressed, however: predictions about creativity are often confounded. Nobody ever expected that American network TV, in all its mediocrity, would be rivalled in power by the output of the cable channels whose competitive energy revitalized the networks before going on to conquer the world. In Spain, Pedro Almodóvar became a film industry all by himself. It depends on the people. But when art is an industry, there are a lot of people to organize, and the shortage is always in the number of people who can do the organizing. That's where the money should be spent, if there is any.

MOVIE CRITICISM IN AMERICA

American Movie Critics: An Anthology From the Silents Until Now,
edited by Phillip Lopate

Since all of us are deeply learned experts on the movies even when
we don't know much about anything else, people wishing to make
their mark as movie critics must either be able to express opinions
like ours better than we can, or else they must be in charge of a big
idea, preferably one that can be dignified by being called a theory.

In *American Movie Critics*, a Library of America collection drawn
from the work of almost 70 high-profile professional critics active
at various times since their preferred medium was invented the day
before yesterday, most of the practitioners fall neatly into one category or the other.

It quickly becomes obvious that those without theories write
better. You already knew that your friend who's so funny about the
Star Wars tradition of frightful hairstyles for women (in the corrected
sequence of sequel and prequel, Natalie Portman must have passed
the bad-hair gene down to Carrie Fisher) is much less boring than
your other friend who can tell you how science-fiction movies mirror
the dynamics of American imperialism. This book proves that history
is with you: perceptions aren't just more entertaining than formal
schemes of explanation, they're also more explanatory.

The editor, Phillip Lopate, an essayist and film critic, has a
catholic scope, and might not agree that the nontheorists clearly win
out. They do, though, and one of the subsidiary functions that this
hefty compilation might perform – subsidiary, that is, to its being
sheerly entertaining on a high level – is to help settle a nagging question.

In our appreciation of the arts, does a theory give us more to think about, or less? To me, the answer looks like less, but it could be that I just don't like it when a critic's hulking voice gets in the way of the projector beam and tries to convince me that what I am looking at makes its real sense only as part of a bigger pattern of thought, that pattern being available from the critic's mind at the price of decoding his prose.

For as long as the sonar-riddled soundtrack of *The Hunt for Red October* has me mouthing the word 'ping' while I keep reaching for the popcorn, I don't want to hear that what I'm seeing is an example of anything, or a step to anywhere, or a characteristic statement by anyone. What I'm seeing is a whole thing on its own. The real question is why none of it saps my willingness to be involved, not even Sean Connery's shtrangely shibilant Shcottish ackshent as the commander of a Shoviet shubmarine, not even that spliced-in footage of the same old Grumman F9F Panther that has been crashing into the aircraft carrier's deck since the Korean War.

On the other hand, no prodigies of acting by Tom Cruise in *Eyes Wide Shut*, climaxed by his partial success in acting himself tall, convinced me for a minute that Stanley Kubrick, when he made his bravely investigative capital work about the human sexual imagination, had the slightest clue what he was doing. In my nonhumble ticket purchaser's opinion, the great Stanley K., as Terry Southern called him, was, when he made *Eyes Wide Shut*, finally and irretrievably out to lunch. Does this discrepancy of reaction on my part mean that the frivolous movie was serious, and the serious movie frivolous? Only, you might say, if first impressions are everything.

But in the movies they are. Or, to put it less drastically, in the movies there are no later impressions without a first impression, because you will have stopped watching. Sometimes a critic persuades you to give an unpromising-looking movie a chance, but the movie had better convey the impression pretty quickly that the critic might be right. By and large, it's the movie itself that tells you it means business. It does that by telling a story. No story, no movie. Robert Bresson only did with increasing slowness what other directors had done in a hurry. But when Bresson, somewhere in the vicinity of Camelot, reached the point where almost nothing happening became nothing happening at all, you were gone. A movie has to glue you to your seat even when it's pretending not to.

As the chronological arrangement of this volume reveals, there were good American critics who realized this fact very early on. Several of the post-World War I critics will come as revelations to anybody who assumed, as many of us have long been led to assume, that America was slow to discover the fruitfulness of its own cinema. The usual history runs roughly thus: even in the Hollywood-haunted America of the years between the wars, the best critics concentrated on the work of obviously major artists, most of them foreign. Then, after World War II, generous young French critics armed with the *auteur* theory discovered that a cluster, or pantheon, of directors within the Hollywood system had always been major artists too: Nicholas Ray was up there with Carl Dreyer, and so on. After that, American film criticism grew up to match European maturity.

It took a theory to work the switch, and the essence of the *auteur* theory was that the director, the controlling hand, shaped the movie with his artistic personality even if it was made within a commercial system as businesslike as Hollywood's. This fact having at last been discovered, film criticism in America came of age. It's a neat progression, but this book, simply by its layout, shows it to be bogus.

Among the early critical big names, some were big names in other fields. Vachel Lindsay and Carl Sandburg were bardic poets, Edmund Wilson was a high-flying man of letters, H. L. Mencken was the perennial star reporter-cum-philologist of the American language. None of them had any real trouble figuring out what the commercial filmmakers were up to. Edmund Wilson didn't just praise Chaplin at the level due to him, but dispraised Hollywood 'gag writers' at the level due to them: he didn't, that is, dismiss them out of hand, but pointed out, correctly, that their chief concern was necessarily with storytelling structures that worked cinematically, and that there might be limitations involved in doing that. There were and there still are.

'Go! Go! Go!' 'Five, four, three, two, one!' 'Take care of yourself up there/out there/in there.' It doesn't matter how formulaic the words sound, because at those moments the movies are essentially still silent. The writing all goes into deciding who falls backward through the window, has his head ripped off by the alien, bares his bottom amusingly to get his shots from the pretty nurse, or pouts tensely when the sonar says, 'Ping!'

Mencken fancied himself above it all, but he had a penetrating understanding of star power. Sandburg is unreadable today only because of the way he wrote. His prose was bad poetry, like his poetry. ('The craziest, wildest, shivery movie that has come wriggling across the silversheet of a cinema house,' he wrote of *The Cabinet of Dr. Caligari*, his grammar flapping irrepressibly in the rhetorical wind.) The important consideration here is that everything these superior minds approved of in the foreign art film they also looked for diligently in the American industrial product, and were touchingly glad to find any signs of its flowering.

They were more likely to find those signs, however, if they weren't functioning as general commentators on the arts or as visiting firemen from ritzier boroughs, but had a regular job reviewing the product as it came out. Hence the first critic in the lineup likely to knock the reader sideways is Otis Ferguson, who started reviewing movies for the *New Republic* in 1934 and kept it up until the year before his lamentably early death at the age of thirty-six. Had he lived, none of the later pantheon aberration might have got a purchase, because he was perfectly capable of seeing not only that some of the American movies were terrific, but that even the best of them often took a lot more than a director to put together. This last bit was the key perception that the pantheon's attendant incense burners later managed to obscure with wreaths of perfumed smoke, but before we get to that, let's be sure of just how good Ferguson was.

As a first qualification, Ferguson could see that there was such a thing as a hierarchy of trash. He enjoyed *Lives of a Bengal Lancer* even where it was corny, because the corn ('execrable . . . and I like it') was being dished out with brio. This basic capacity for delight underlay the vigour of his prose when it came to the hierarchy of quality, which he realized had its starting point in the same basement as the trash. A Fred Astaire movie was made on the same bean-counting system as a North-West Frontier epic in which dacoits and dervishes lurked treacherously on the back lot, and Astaire wasn't even a star presence compared with a Bengal lancer like Gary Cooper. 'As an actor he is too much of a dancer, tending toward pantomime; and as a dancer he is occasionally too ballroomy. But as a man who can create figures, intricate, unpredictable, constantly varied and yet simple, seemingly effortless . . . he brings the strange high quality of genius to one of the baser and more common arts.'

Decades later, Arlene Croce wrote about Astaire at greater length, and possibly in greater technical depth, but when she got the snap of his dancing into a sentence, she was following a line that Ferguson had already laid down. Hear how he rounds it out: 'Fred Astaire, whatever he may do in whatever picture he is in, has the beat, the swing, the debonair and damn-your-eyes violence of rhythm, all the gay contradiction and irresponsibility, of the best thing this country can contribute to musical history, which is the best American jazz.' Take out the word 'gay' and it could be something written now, although there aren't many who could write it. Look at the perfect placement of that word 'violence', for example. It's not enough to have the vocabulary. You have to have the sensory equipment. You have to spot the way Astaire, in the full flight of a light-foot routine, could slap the sole of his shoe into the floor as if he were rubbing out a bunch of dust mites.

Ferguson's sensitivity to the standard output made him more adventurous, not less, when it came to the indisputable works of art. Sometimes it made him adventurous enough to dispute them. He wasn't taken in by the original or the re-edit of Eisenstein's movie about Mexico, which he could see was an incorrigible heap of random footage that would have continued to go nowhere indefinitely if it hadn't been forcibly removed from the master's control. 'A way to be a film critic for years was to holler about this rape of great art, though it should have taken no more critical equipment than common sense to see that whatever was cut out, its clumping repetitions and lack of film motion could not have been cut in.'

With a good notion of how hard it is to make ordinary film narrative unnoticeably subtle ('story, story, story – or, How can we do it to them so they don't know beforehand that it's being done?'), Ferguson was properly suspicious of any claims that *Citizen Kane* represented an advance in technique. He admired it, but not as a breakthrough: 'In the line of the narrative film, as developed in all countries but most highly on the West Coast of America, it holds no great place.' A harsh judgment, but Ferguson had put in the groundwork to back it up, and Welles, after the first flush of his apotheosis, might have reached the same conclusion: *The Magnificent Ambersons*, even in its unfinished state, is a clear and admirable attempt by the boy genius to get a grip on the technical heritage he had thought to supersede.

One could go on quoting from Ferguson, and expatiating on the quotations, until hell looked like the set of *Ice Station Zebra*: there is a book buried in every essay. But the same is true of every good critic. The poet Melvin B. Tolson, who wrote about movies for the African-American newspaper *The Washington Tribune*, saw *Gone With the Wind* when it came out and reviewed it in terms that could have been expanded into a handbook for the civil rights movement twenty years before the event. One look at the relevant piece will tell you why a critic has to know about the world as well as the movies: Tolson could see that *Gone With the Wind* was well made. But he could also see that the script was a crass and callous rewriting of history, a Klan pamphlet in sugared form, a racial insult.

If, then, the selection from James Agee shines out of these pages a bit less than you might expect, it isn't because he's lost his lustre; it's because there's so much light from those around him. And Agee, as well as possessing the comprehensive intelligence that the critical heritage had already made a requirement, also possessed an extra quality that we later on, and perhaps dangerously, came to expect from everybody: he had the wit. At the time, it was a first when he wrote this punch line to his review of Billy Wilder's sodden saga about dipsomania, *The Lost Weekend*: 'I undershtand that liquor interesh: innerish: intereshtsh are rather worried about thish film. Thash tough.' Today, you can easily imagine Anthony Lane of the *New Yorker* doing that. Lane, being British, isn't in the book, which is a bit like not letting Tiger Woods play at St Andrews. And Peter Bogdanovich – surely a key figure, and not just as an archivist, in the appreciation of American movies – is another conspicuous absentee. But it's a sign of a good anthology when you start bitching about Who Isn't In It – not a bad title for a book by Bogdanovich, come to think of it.

And Stanley Kauffmann isn't in it enough. A film critic still in action after more than half a century (most of that time spent at the *New Republic*), he was the one who took Ferguson's approach, the only approach that really matters, and developed it to its full potential. He knew a lot about every department of the business, but especially acting. He was kind but firm about Marilyn Monroe in *The Misfits*: 'Her hysterical scene near the end will seem virtuoso acting to those who are overwhelmed by the fact that she has been induced to shout.' He could see what was wonderful about Antonioni's *L'Avventura*. So could I, at the time; but later, after suffering through *Blowup* and *Zabriskie Point*, I started to forget what had once thrilled me. Here is the reminder: 'Obviously it is not real time or we would all have to bring along sandwiches and blankets; but a difference of 10 seconds in a scene is a tremendous step toward veristic reproduction rather than theatrical abstraction.' (And, he forgot to add, it gives you 10 more seconds to look at a veristic close-up of Monica Vitti, who did to us in those days what Monica Bellucci is doing to a new generation of horny male intellectuals right now.)

Kauffmann had an acute sensitivity to the story behind the technique. It meant that he didn't fail to spot real quality, and it also meant that he was rarely fooled by empty virtuosity. His classic review of Max Ophuls's supposed masterpiece, *Lola Montes*, a review mercifully included here as the finale to his oddly meagre selection, tells you in advance everything that would be wrong about the *auteur* theory. Kauffmann could see that *Lola Montes* was indeed the supreme example of Ophuls's characteristic style of the travelling shot that went on forever. But Kauffmann could also see that even if the title role of the bewitching courtesan had been incarnated by a bewitching actress – and Martine Carol, through no fault of her own, was no more bewitching than a bus driver in Communist Kiev – the movie would still have been ruined by its dumb happy-hooker script. In other words, no story.

In Hollywood, for a true masterpiece like *Letter From an Unknown Woman*, Ophuls had had the writers, the actors and the right kind of head office breathing down his neck. On *Lola Montes* he was out on his own. The *auteur* theory depended on the idea that any pantheon director had an artistic personality so strong that it was bound to express itself whatever the compromising circumstances. But all too often, the compromising circumstances helped to make the movie good. That, however, was a tale too complicated to tell for those commentators who wanted to get into business as deep thinkers.

The likelihood that to think deep meant to think less didn't strike any of them until their critical mass movement had worn itself out. Some useful work was done – movies by a cigar-chomping, hard-swearing maverick like Samuel Fuller were resurrected long enough for us all to find out why they had been forgotten – but the absurdities were all too obvious. John Ford's late clunker *7 Women* was praised because it was 'Fordian'. The adjective they should have been looking for was 'unwatchable'. Howard Hawks's *Hatari!*, in which the same old Hawks plot about John Wayne and the drunken friend and the no-bull broad and the young hotshot and the cackling old-timer was eked out with footage of rhinos and buffaloes, turned out to be quintessentially 'Hawksian'. And so it went, but it couldn't go on for long, because unless the undiscovered Fordian–Hawksian masterpiece was actually any good, it never got any further than the film societies. As for the articles and the anthologies and the monographs, they never could outweigh the aggregate of *ad hoc* judgments coming from individual critics. Those judgments might have been right or wrong, but they were seldom crazy, unless the critic had a theory of his or her own.

Some did. Robert Warshow, yet another cultural commentator who died young, wrote a famous long article (which Lopate includes) called 'The Gangster as Tragic Hero'. Citing but not evoking scores of movies to prove that the American gangster is doomed by the pressures of a society that worships success, it says little in a long space, thereby reversing the desirable relationship of form and content, which, as we have seen, had already been established by critics with fewer pretensions to a sociological overview.

The same could be said, and said twice, for Parker Tyler's equally celebrated long article purporting to show that *Double Indemnity* was always psychologically much more complex than was ever thought possible by those who made it or us who watched. You might have deduced that the claims adjuster Keyes (Edward G. Robinson) was secretly hot for the insurance salesman Neff (Fred MacMurray), but could you ever have guessed that Neff was driven to crime because he had *failed* sexually with Phyllis (Barbara Stanwyck)? And there we all were thinking he'd succeeded. But stay! For Tyler has some wordplay yet to deploy. 'Neff, let us assume, wants permanent insurance against Keyes's subtle inquisition into the ostensible claims of his sexual life.' Oh, come on, let's not assume it.

But we don't have to fight for justice very hard, because the fight has already been won by the sanity brigade. The late Vincent Canby could have won it by himself. There might have been even more here from such informed yet readable solo acts – David Denby, Kenneth Turan, David Thomson and A. O. Scott are only a few of the many recent exponents on the bill – if the worthy bores had not been given their democratic chance, but hey, that's America. Nevertheless, Lopate would have done better to stick to the principle that brevity, up to the point where compression collapses, invariably carries more implication than expansiveness ever can. But he might not have recognized the principle, even while dealing with the best of its consequences. There have been plenty of editors who didn't get it. The legendary William Shawn of the *New Yorker* never grasped that he was giving Pauline Kael too much room for her own good.

Although Kael knew comparatively little about how movies got made, she was unbeatable at taking off from what she had seen. But beyond that, she would take off from what she had written, and there was a new theory every two weeks. A lot of her theories had to do with loves and hates. She thought Robert Altman was a genius. He can certainly make a movie, but if it hasn't got a script, then he makes *Prêt-à-Porter*. That's one of the most salutary lessons of this book: what makes the movie isn't just who directed it, or who's in it, it's how it relates to the real world.

That principle really starts to matter when it comes to movies that profess to understand history, and thus to affect the future. Several quite good critics in various parts of the world knew there was something seriously wrong with Steven Spielberg's *Munich*, but they didn't know how to take it down. If they could have put the lessons of this book together, they would have found out how. *Munich* might have survived being directed by someone who knows about nothing except movies. But it was also written by people who don't know half enough about politics. That was why the crucial meeting of Golda Meir's cabinet went for nothing. The movie could have got by with its John Woo-style gunfight face-offs, but without an articulate laying out of the arguments it was a waste of effort.

Similarly, if you know too much about the movies but not enough about the world, you won't be able to see that *Downfall* is dangerously sentimental. Realistic in every observable detail, it is nevertheless a fantasy to the roots, because the pretty girl who plays the secretary looks shocked when Hitler inveighs against the Jews. It comes as a surprise to her.

Well, it couldn't have; but to know why that is so, you have to have read a few books. No matter how many movies you have seen, they won't give you the truth of the matter, because it can't be shown as action. To know what can't be shown by the gag writers, however, you have to know about a world beyond the movies. But the best critics do, as this book proves; because when we say that the nontheorists are the better writers, that's what we mean. That extra edge that a good writer has is a knowledge of the world, transmuted into a style.

New York Times, June 4, 2006

Postscript

Like any other movie by Stanley Kubrick, the dire *Eyes Wide Shut* has its explicators who can tell you why every apparent clumsiness is a piercing insight. But Frederic Raphael, who wrote the screenplay, has since told us the story of how Kubrick encouraged Tom Cruise and Nicole Kidman to improvise 'beyond the script'. Beware the director who thinks that his actors will find, out of their own linguistic resources, a naturalism that is not there on the page. To return to the exemplary case of Robert Altman, there is a wealth of unintended hilarity to be obtained from those commentators who can't see that the crucial difference between *Gosford Park* and *Prêt-à-Porter* is that whereas Julian Fellowes wrote everything in the first movie, nobody wrote anything in the second. Luckily the best American critics, careful writers themselves, have usually been proof against such wilful deafness.

SHOW ME THE HORROR

'There are more bad director's movies than bad producer's movies.'

Anon

A standard piece of Hollywood wisdom would have us believe that there are more bad director's movies than bad producer's movies. I first heard this maxim from Marty Elfand, the producer of *David*, directed by my friend Bruce Beresford. Later on, Beresford became celebrated throughout the film industry because of the Oscar he failed to receive for *Driving Miss Daisy*, which set a strange precedent through being honoured as Best Film while its director was not even invited to the ceremony. The host, Billy Crystal, did something to restore sanity by sardonically referring to *Driving Miss Daisy* as 'the film that directed itself'. Beresford had been through madder moments than that: *David*, for example, which was reviewed as if its director had set out with the intention of destroying Richard Gere's career. Thus launched into a river of acid, the movie sank immediately. I was there while it was still being built. The movie was in the last stages of its studio schedule at Pinewood. Later, on location in southern Italy, which was deputising for the Holy Land, the project was to be fatally compromised by acts of God. In that part of southern Italy, for the first time since the last Ice Age, it snowed in April for weeks on end. The snow formed deep drifts on the pitiless deserts of Palestine, thus restricting complicated action sequences beyond credibility. Taking into consideration that God was practically the hero of the picture, it seems reasonable to conclude that He had visited his wrath on the project for a sound Old Testament reason: human presumption would be conspicuously punished, so that nobody could miss the message.

On the sound stage at Pinewood, however, all seemed workmanlike and under control. So does most of the movie, for those who care to look. *David* still shows up occasionally on television, giving the newspaper preview writers a chance to flex their tiny wits. They know not of what they speak. Apart from the action scenes, which are obviously crippled by lack of coverage – you can see the same army going in opposite directions to do battle with itself – the feeling for the far past is unusually subtle. Beresford when young admired Pasolini's *Gospel According to Saint Matthew*, and some of that admiration rubbed off on *David*. Unlike almost every Hollywood biblical epic ever made, *David* feels like a transposition to another time and somewhere else. At Pinewood a visitor could already sense that something unusual was in the works. The sets, for example, had proper low ceilings, carefully violating the usual Hollywood assumption that in ancient times the ruling classes met to break bread in dining rooms the size of an aeroplane hangar. There was no sense that everybody concerned was participating in a salvage operation with all hands to the bilge pumps. Richard Gere was relaxed and charming. Out of his hearing, I made my standard joke to Beresford: if he wanted a film star with small eyes, why didn't he use me? At lunch, perhaps tactlessly, I offered my favourite aria about movies that had been ruined by the producer's heavy, uncomprehending hand. Beresford, whose knowledge of his medium is encyclopaedic, was hilarious on the subject. Marty Elfand seemed to enjoy the ribbing, but decisively countered with the aforementioned piece of folk wisdom: there are more bad director's movies than bad producer's movies.

I had to admit that he was right. The list of movies ruined by a director's being given a free hand begins with D. W. Griffith, moves on through Stroheim, and can be entertainingly extended far beyond Antonioni's *Zabriskie Point*. The implication, not often enough noted, is that the producer's interference is frequently an important factor in keeping a project within reasonable bounds. Stories about a producer's stupidity or philistinism should always be given a second look from that angle. Orson Welles was appalled when the producer added crass explanatory shots to *Touch of Evil*, but the explanatory shots really do explain things: perhaps Welles should not have left them out in the first place. A key case is David O. Selznick's much-derided interference at the scripting stage of *The Third Man*. Later on, Graham Greene made comic capital out of Selznick's suggestion that it looked 'faggy' for Holly Martins to hang around in Vienna after he had been told that Harry Lime was dead. But if we look at Nicholas Wapshott's hard-headed and useful biography of Carol Reed (*The Man Between*) we find that another piece of interference by Selznick was crucial to the coherence of the movie. Neither Reed nor Greene wanted any scenes dealing with the effects of Lime's penicillin on the children who were treated with it. Selznick insisted, and got his way.

To avoid the obvious, Reed assembled the required scenes entirely out of reaction shots. All we see is Trevor Howard and Joseph Cotten looking at us out of the screen, as if we were the children in the hospital beds. The movie's whole moral structure pivots on that one point. Unless we are convinced that the two men are seeing horrors, there would be no justification for Holly Martins' delivering the *coup de grâce* to his erstwhile friend. No doubt Selznick was a vulgarian compared with Graham Greene, but Selznick was the one who put his unsubtle finger on the point that simply had to be dramatised. It was Reed's job, which he cleverly fulfilled, to find a way of doing it that did not look crass. If Reed had been a greater man, a true *auteur*, he might have written his own scripts and brought out such key points every time. But a working director was all he was, albeit an unusually inventive one. (*Trapeze* was one of the few early Cinemascope movies to fill its format satisfactorily, because Reed spotted that the rehearsing circus acts could fill the yawning background behind the main actors.) Reed was a stylist working within an industry, in conformity with its traditional division of labour. That the division of labour also entailed a division of creative labour was the point missed even by a later generation of critics who knew quite a lot about the technical aspects of film making but not enough about cash flow.

Finally, the money talks. At the time when film criticism first came into its own as a recognised genre, in the 1930s, the critics were still coping with the miracle that the pictures could talk. There was not much that they knew. They could tell that a good movie was different from a bad one, but they didn't know yet quite why. (C. A. Lejeune, a distinguished critic of the post-war period, thought that the tilted pictures of Reed's characteristic manner were obtained in the printing, rather than by tilting the camera.) Nowadays, the critics know about everything, down to and including the money; but unless they have been involved in a collaborative venture themselves, they still tend to heap all the praise, or all the blame, on the head that shows most prominently. Hence the usefulness of the director's movie that turns out to be a mess: when produced by himself, as it often is, it is a powerful hint that in his successful earlier creations there was somebody else behind the scenes, performing the unsung function of the slave in the Roman general's triumphal chariot, but with different dialogue. The Roman slave whispered: 'Remember you are mortal.' The producer, or the money man, or sometimes even the studio boss, whispers something else. He whispers: 'Remember that the audience is mortal.' You can be as subtle as you like, but one way or another you have to spell it out. Why does Harry Lime have to die? Because he is evil. What is the evidence that he is evil? His penicillin. What does the penicillin do? Show us.

None of this means that the money is always right. From the first stage of scripting, Beresford wanted to tie *David* together with a voice-over of David reading the Psalms. The studio vetoed the idea: not because the language was biblical, but because it was poetry. (The King as a *poet*? Too faggy.) From that moment, the film was on the road to ruin. It just took many millions of dollars to get there. If you find, as I do, that the ruin has life in it, there is still no call to believe in the romantic prescription that posterity will decide the issue. The issue has already been decided. Apart from the occasional, very rare exception like *Blade Runner*, lost big movies don't come back, and most of the lost small ones don't come back either. How many people ever saw John Sayles's *Lone Star*? I saw it, and thought it the best movie about racial prejudice that I had seen for a long time. But I find it hard to name, from memory, any of the leading players apart from Chris Cooper. They almost all missed the wave, which is the wave of publicity. Movies are not like poems. They cost too much to be anything except a popular art. If the digital revolution changes all that, it might well be a good thing, but there is always the chance that Dennis Hopper's *Last Movie* will be made a thousand times; and there will never be a cheap way of filming the battle scenes in *David* – the scenes that were never shot because it snowed in Palestine.

The Monthly, December 2005 – January 2006

Postscript

I am aware that I have made the point about Selznick and *The Third Man* twice in this book, but I think it bears repetition: needs grinding in, in fact. Unless a director in full charge of his own project has a producer's instincts as well – unless, that is, he can keep an eye on himself – the chances for a fatal indulgence of his ego are very great. It will always be a good game to list the director's-movie movies that went wrong. My favourites, for their awfulness, include Dennis Hopper's *Last Movie*, Michael Cimino's *Heaven's Gate*, and Francis Ford Coppola's *One from the Heart*. Coppola's *Apocalypse Now* would be on the list too if the whole movie were as terrible as its last act. But nothing could redeem *One from the Heart*: it was a feel-good movie that made you feel bad. It will be noticed that all the people on this list are talented. They made edifyingly bad movies. Directors without talent just make bad movies. Even good directors with their egos well reined in, however, will have failures, because circumstances will conspire against them. A poem can't be stopped even if the poet runs out of ink. A movie can be wrecked by a single actor who flips his lid when it is too late to replace him. I should put in a warning to the reader concerning my opinions about Bruce Beresford's *David*, a film which he himself would rather forget. Beresford has been a close friend of mine since we were students together, so I am vulnerable to the charge that I am apt to overlook the faults in some of his movies because I know too much about the conditions in which they were made. (When I started out as a television critic, I quickly learned to stay ignorant about production problems, having been tipped off to the trap by the number of producers who rushed to tell me about them.) The inventor of *Black Robe*, the best movie I have ever seen about the Red Man, needs no help from a sympathiser who knows something about how hard it was to shoot. *The Getting of Wisdom*, *Don's Party* and *The Club* are all important chapters in the story of the rise to prominence of the post-war Australian film industry, which was itself, in a large part, Beresford's personal creation. I would be free to state that last fact more assertively if I hadn't had a ringside seat for how he did it. One of his secrets was a diligent competence that the money-men always knew they could rely on. Unfortunately they too often exploited the knowledge.

Budgets would dry up in the second last week, leaving Beresford to complete the movie at his own expense. After the box-office success of *Double Jeopardy*, he was in demand for directing Hollywood thrillers. His reputation for getting the job done on schedule left him vulnerable to the kind of producers ready to supplement their own salaries with a share of his. *The Contract* is on a par with *Double Jeopardy* for its gripping narrative, but the production values hit a lower mark because the money ran out. Hence the car that goes over the cliff is not the same car that dives into the gorge. A critic who spots such an anomaly should be slow to assume that the director didn't.

HOMELAND

THE MEASURE OF A. D. HOPE

The first collection of poems by A. D. Hope, *The Wandering Islands*, belatedly appeared in 1955, and consolidated the position he had already established as the leading Australian poet of his time. The book had to appear belatedly (Hope was already 48) because if it had appeared much earlier its author might have been prosecuted. Australia was still a censored country and several of Hope's poems dared to mention the particularities of sexual intercourse. Without his air of authority, Hope might never have got his book into the shops before old age supervened. But an air of authority was what he had. He spoke from on high. His vocabulary was of the present, but it had the past in it, transparent a long way down. And it was all sent forward like a wave by his magisterial sense of rhythm.

> There is the land-locked valley and the river,
> The Western Tiers make distance an emotion,
> The gum trees roar in the gale, the poplars shiver
> At twilight, the church pines imitate an ocean.

The Western Tiers were in his home state, Tasmania: but you didn't have to know that. In fact you didn't have to know that the poems had been written in Australia at all. Most of them sounded as if they could have been written anywhere in the international English-speaking world that had two-way communications with Olympus, which was probably why even those of us in the younger generation who were making a point of not reading much avowedly Australian poetry still felt it permissible to read Hope's. A few people even argued that he had missed a trick by not sounding Australian enough. What nobody argued was that he ever sounded anything less than oracular. His opening stanzas brought his readers to attention like a general walking unannounced into a barracks. I can still remember reading the opening quatrain of 'The Death of the Bird' for the first time.

For every bird there is this last migration:
Once more the cooling year kindles her heart;
With a warm passage to the summer station
Love pricks the course in lights across the chart.

Whatever else you might have conceivably planned to be doing in the next few minutes, going on to the next stanza was what you did, and then to the next, until, in the last stanza, 'the great earth . . . Receives the tiny burden of her death.' The diction was unashamedly grandiloquent – born on the border where the grandiose couples with the eloquent – but the narrative drive made it compulsory to keep reading. And everybody concerned with poetry felt the same imperative. There were other accomplished Australian poets in Hope's generation but they were obliged to acknowledge his primacy even when they weren't glad about it. He was the governor, and after half a century he still is. Though there are questions to be asked about what happened to his poetry after that first amazing volume, nobody worth hearing from has ever seriously tried to attack him. There is an awkward possibility, however, that if he is short of detractors to take him down, he has admirers who might do the same job.

Burdened with the simultaneously vaulting and diffident subtitle 'A Study of the Selected Notebooks of A. D. Hope', Ann McCulloch's *Dance of the Nomad* achieves the rare feat of making you fear for its sleeping subject's repose before the book is even opened. I should hasten to say that much of the fear turns out to be unjustified. Dr McCulloch, although unusually prone to cultstud jargon for the pupil of a man who hated the whole idea of a specialised academic vocabulary, is on the whole a good and faithful servant to her master's memory, and does not deserve to be executed along with her publisher. The publisher is, or are, Pandanus Books, billed as part of the Research School of Pacific and Asian Studies at the Australian National University. For purposes of capital punishment, let us call this organization 'the publishers'. The publishers need to be told, before they are led out to face the firing squad, the following things, lest they rise from the dead and publish something else without ever realising what all the noise was about.

Hope's notebooks are not very extensive anyway, and this selection is quite short. (Why it has to be a selection, embedded thinly in a mass of unnecessary commentary, and can't be a complete transcription with a suitable but more proportionate scholarly apparatus, we are not told – or rather we are, but not in a way that is easy to understand.) No book with so little in it needs to be this big and awkward. You should be able to carry it in a pocket. You couldn't carry it in a saddle-bag. The format is huge. The paper is good enough for a glossy magazine: i.e., needlessly heavy. The bulk of the book is set in a sans serif body type. Nobody outside an advertising agency can read more than a page or two of sans serif type without contracting conjunctivitis. There would be no need to put the word 'page', even if it were capitalised, beside the page number on every page even of a pamphlet, let alone of a book 366 pages long. Hope was a master of economy, and here is his acolyte in charge of a book that uses the word 'page' 366 unnecessary times.

As for the copy editing, the publishers should have been reminded that it is traditional to give the author some help if she can't herself spell or read her own writing, and especially when she can't read the writing of the man she is supposed to be a student of. Just confining ourselves to the mistakes she inadvertently wishes on Hope through not being able to transcribe what he must have written, we are faced with a steady barrage of misplaced creativity. The man who wrote the words for Mozart was Da Ponte, not Da Pente. Apparently not having realised that Hope is referring to Lucretius, Dr McCulloch conveys the impression that her author thought there was a poem written by Alexander Pope called *De Renum Natura*, which sounds like it might have been a versified medical treatise on the proper functioning of the kidneys. What Hope meant was undoubtedly *De Rerum Natura*.

Hope almost certainly did not write the following: 'Teaching university students I have found that if Keats were writing the *Ode to a Nightingale* today he could not rely on his readers knowing what was meant by Bacchus and his bards . . .' Nor could Hope, alas, rely on his star pupil knowing that Keats was talking about Bacchus and his pards. That's pards, not bards: only a little letter, but if it was Dr McCulloch, and not the printer, who mistook it, then one would have thought that her spontaneity of response was in no danger of being inhibited by her erudition.

Dr McCulloch mentions in her introduction the difficulties of Hope's handwriting, but doesn't seem to realise that a guess is inappropriate when it comes to a proper name. Thus she saddles Hope with the responsibility of calling Michael Ayrton Michael Ayston (twice on the one page, making it obvious that she has never heard of him). The authority that Hope quoted on Ariosto was Croce, not Groce. Benedetto Croce was an Italian philosopher. DeJuan Groce is an NFL footballer with the St Louis Rams. Least impressively of all, Dr McCulloch has Hope quoting Horace as saying *Eheu fugaces, Postune, Postune.* Whoever the mysterious friend was that Horace addressed in the vocative, his name was Postumus, not Postunus. Unless Hope himself managed to scramble one of the most famous lines in classical literature, *Postume, Postume* must have been what he wrote down. What made Dr McCulloch think that she could guess at Latin?

Thus proving every few pages that she is a bit light on the general culture her learned subject has in such abundance, Dr McCulloch cracks on with the task of bringing out his profundity as a writer of speculative prose. She does a surprisingly good job of it, which argues well for the potency of his sane influence. He must have been quite a teacher, if he could have transmitted the virtue of general cultivation in the arts to someone who knows so little, and the value of common sense to someone whose whole instinct is to reach for a literary theory as a preliminary to thinking about literature at all. Hope was a great believer in the merits of what Keats (he of the Bacchic bards) called negative capability. Following his example, Dr McCulloch is a great believer in it too, and proves that she is by advancing a theory in its support.

This theory is a theory of something called the rhizome, which, on her account, was first dreamed up by two sparks called Deleuze and Guattari, in their book *A Thousand Plateaus: Capitalism and Schizophrenia.* As far as I can tell from her expounding of it, the rhizome allows a principle of organisation which to the eye of an earthling looks pretty much like a random arrangement of themes. Since Hope's notebook entries amount to a random arrangement (i.e. no arrangement) of themes, the rhizome can be said to fit, and Dr McCulloch is encouraged to proceed with the self-imposed task of bringing, 'in a Deleuzian sense', order out of chaos. The tolerant reader will go with her, perhaps occasionally muttering to himself that a Deleuzian sense sounds as if it could turn delusional after a few drinks, and that the word 'rhizome' has an affinitive similarity to the word 'rissole', the classic Australian term, drawn from the culinary arts, for something being reduced to a wreck. (Used as a noun, the word 'rissole' denotes a kind of proto-hamburger, but used as a verb – as in 'Strewth, we've rissoled the Holden' – the same word means that the machinery has ceased to work.)

But in this case the machinery does work, because the randomness was never chaos. Hope was merely making notes, in his shapely, clear, pregnant prose, and as long as Dr McCulloch contents herself with isolating and highlighting his themes, she is on ground so sure that not even the spectre of the lurking rhizome can rissole her argument. Hope's wide general culture extended to science as well: he had an Empsonian feeling for the poetry of the factual world. Armed with that, he was able to see immediately that Arthur Koestler's attempt to co-opt particle physics as supporting evidence for the paranormal involved a category mistake. Of Koestler's restlessly mutating faddism, Hope, either echoing P. B. Medawar or (more likely) simply arriving at the same conclusion independently, devastatingly said 'once a jour-nalist, always a journalist.' Dr McCulloch might have taken Hope's underlying point further here: Hope was warning against scientism, as if foreseeing a day when pseudo-scientific theory would invade every field, including, disastrously, the humanities. She might have divested herself of her reliance on imported mental snake-oil; but, alas, once a theorist, always a theorist. Still, at least she realises that he was right in that case.

She is commendably ready to concede that he was right, or at least reasonable, in almost every case: a nice instance of negative capability on her part, and a testament to her fundamental generosity, a quality which can't always have been easy to apply to so awkward, and some-times plain provocative, a subject. Hope's celebrated, and eventually notorious, anti-feminism was mainly superficial. You could even say that he conceded women the power, and was always in awe of Eve, as if she carried Delilah's scissors. His 'Advice to Young Ladies' of 1965, celebrating the courage of a vestal virgin who faced the death penalty for being witty, is one of the most effective hymns to female individ-uality ever written by a male. Feminist critics, however, from the late 1960s onward, found Hope's poetry a field rich in opportunities to burn him in effigy. The males in Hope's poems were aroused by the beauty of the females, were they not? Well, then.

Since radical orthodoxies of every kind have established themselves in the Australian academic world's main discussion – or, as the academics themselves would be more likely to say, in its 'discourse' – with a solidity and inflexibility that an outsider would find it hard to credit, Dr McCulloch is actually being quite brave in backing him up. Although she finds some of Hope's more overtly sexy poetry insensitive, she nevertheless thinks that he was always on to something in writing as if the sexual impulse might have a mind of its own, and that women, also, might occasionally be mastered by desire. Her complaint about 'the fact that sexual attraction is often left out of feminist discourse' only sounds trite. In the Australian context it verges on the daring. Similarly, she is going quite a long way towards dangerous independence when she defends Hope's reactionary opinions about modern poetry.

Strangely enough, Dr McCulloch goes further in this direction than she needs to. Hope's reactionary views were attractive when he wanted to warn against pointless innovation and keep faith with the past. (He was dead right, for example, about the cultural impoverishment that would inevitably ensue from Australia's adoption of metrical distance measures. By now it's as if the Australian version of the English language had been taken over by an inspectorate from Brussels: give them 2.54 centimetres and they'll take 1.60934 kilometres.) But he overdid it when he preached against modern poetry, by which he meant anything that wasn't clear in meaning and sustained by an ascertainable structure. According to Hope, there was nothing in English poetry after Yeats, because Yeats, according to him, was the last to write intelligibly, and in forms you could see. This left the way open for Hope himself, who wrote in visible forms too, but it closed off his attention to whole swathes of achievement, including even Eliot, whom Hope managed to find prosaic. By this shared measure of cranky obscurantism, Hope and Robert Graves should have been soulmates. Hope admired Graves's hieratic, muse-wooing attitude to the sacred art they shared. But Hope also found Graves insufficiently respectful of Yeats, lauded in *The Wandering Islands* as the only touchstone in modern times.

> To have found at last that noble, candid speech
> In which all things worth saying may be said . . .

It was a sad joke when Hope boycotted a visit to Australia by Graves, on the grounds that Graves, in his Oxford lectures, had been rude about Yeats: the two eccentrics might have had a fine time agreeing that Auden was overrated. As things happened, nothing happened. Hope demonstrated his feelings by not showing up. It is easier to demonstrate your feelings when you are present. With good reason, Hope was a proud man. But he was also a shy one, and shy pride is easily interpreted as arrogance.

Hope was braver in print, where he really was arrogant. Early in his career a victim of one of his book-reviews committed suicide. After that, Hope softened up as a reviewer, but he was never slow to dismiss whole modern careers. There are plenty of poets who indulge in blanket condemnation. The price of ploughing a lonely furrow is often to mistake it for the only path across the field. But Hope was also a teacher – as professor of English at the Australian National University in Canberra he was at the head of his profession – and he had no business encouraging students to do more of what they will do naturally unless told otherwise: not read. There might have been an excuse for it if his brilliant start as a formal poet had gone on to further triumph. To that question we can now turn, Hope having enjoyed fifty years of scarcely interrupted endorsement since he made his initial impact. Indeed the advent of Dr McCulloch's misconceived opus might well mark the point when endorsement, having decayed into hagiography, needs as much interruption as it can get.

To her, then, we can now say farewell, with a final 'well done' for defending an important artist whose achievement exemplifies everything that Australian ideologists would like to bury about a superseded world of racist, imperialist, sexist culture in plain language, that last property somehow confirming it as the height of elitism. The farewell is made easier to say by the physical discrepancy between Hope's elegant initial book (bound in green and gold by Edwards & Shaw, *The Wandering Islands* was a lovely thing to behold at a time when most Australian books smelled of glue) and a lumbering compendium that drains the spirit even when seen edge-on in the shelf. And I just heard the shelf creak. No, *Dance of the Nomad* will have to go. Hope, who clearly had a personal regard for the author – he wrote a poem to her, which she quotes complete – would have taken one look at it and changed his own name to Despair.

Luckily he never lived to see the day, although he came close. Hope died in 2000, at the age of ninety-three. His stature was never in question and still isn't, but those of us with a regard for his abilities can legitimately ask ourselves why he didn't conquer the world. Nothing could have stopped him doing so except himself. His poems were instantly intelligible wherever English was spoken. Unencumbered with specifically Australian references, populated with an international cast-list of biblical and classical mythology, they could be appreciated by anybody susceptible to his lyrical gift and rhythmic force, which meant just about everyone who read English poetry any-where: people who couldn't tell an iamb from a trochee could still tell that Hope's verse did the business.

And for a while, after *The Wandering Islands*, he got even better. I was at Cambridge in the mid-60s when I happened to see a plush magazine from the University of Texas that carried his long verse letter to Leonie Kramer, 'A Letter from Rome'. Its supple mastery of a playful tone suggested that he might have secretly paid pre-war Auden and MacNeice a lot more attention than he had ever let on. The news-reading properties of *Letters from Iceland* and *Autumn Journal* were in it, and it had a swing to the handling of the *ottava rima* that was not shamed by the rhyme royal of 'Letter to Lord Byron', while proving, from stanza to stanza, that Hope had an even better grasp than Auden of how light verse could develop an argument through comic narrative. The overtly satirical poems of *The Wandering Islands* had usually been called satirical because they weren't really all that funny, but parts of 'A Letter from Rome' were funny, especially about the hard labour of taking in too much art at once.

> I've contemplated all the types of Venus
> Which win the heart or take the soul by storm,
> The modest fig-leaf and the shameless penis
> In every proper or improper form,
> Until the individual in the genus
> Is lost and all exceptions in the norm,
> And fair and foul and quaint and crass and crude
> Dissolve in one vast cliché of the Nude.

On the strength of a tone-control as flexible as that, the way was open for Hope to develop a second line of light verse chronicle that he could have played off against his more overtly serious poetry for the rest of his life, each strand gaining from its interaction with the other. There would have been no one quite like him in the world. But with an open road in front of him, he chose to make camp in a lay-by, and settle in. It could have been that there was no choice. He had to have a job, and the job he got was demanding. He made it more so by turning his professorship into the central point of a whole movement in scholarship that studied and codified the Australian literary past. The results were an unarguable gain for knowledge even if they left the question open of whether the poets at or near Hope's level in the justly entitled Great Generation were really standing on the shoulders of their Australian predecessors or whether, as seems more likely, they had been goaded into emulation by the contemporary literature of Britain and America.

But there could be no question about the scholarly effort involved. It was taxing. Hope spent a lot of time doing what no poet should ever do: reading uninspired stuff because he had to. As a corollary, there was a lot of inspired stuff that he ignored. His reasons for ignoring it were not as good as he thought, or said he thought. It was true that most poets who wouldn't write in forms couldn't really write at all, but some of them could. In Australia, in the long run, the informal poets won out. Les Murray writes almost nothing in regular stanzas. A poet who does – Stephen Edgar is the most accomplished current example – faces the general opinion that an adopted discipline is a restriction on poetic invention, rather than a stimulus to it. Hope's later achievement was strong enough to ward off that general opinion in his own case, but there should never have been a contest. He should have been powerful enough to settle the argument in his favour before it began. Why wasn't he?

I can think of three reasons. The first is that his use of traditional mythology was subject to the law of diminishing returns. Pasiphae could present herself to the bull only so often before she had to yield her place to a more obscure temptress with a less fascinating sexual partner. To put it bluntly, Hope was simply bound to use up what Larkin disparagingly called 'the myth kitty'. In an early poem like 'The Return of Persephone', Hope could count on his readers knowing roughly who Persephone was, or at least knowing where to look to find out: the age had not yet dawned when students would feel discriminated against if asked to pick the difference between a pard and a bard. But by the time of his book-length poem-sequence of 1985, *The Age of Reason*, he had scraped the barrel down to the level of Ophrys and Andrenus: hand on your heart and say you wouldn't have to look them up.

The second reason is closely related to the first. Almost certainly, Hope kept talking about mythical figures because he thought it beneath his high calling to talk about contemporary events, a category in which he included his own personal history. By and large, he left himself out of it, when his range of subject matter could have benefited mightily had he brought himself in. As 'A Letter from Rome' proved, he had the chief weapon that would have allowed him to do so: humour. He could have been funny about growing old, with all his lusts intact in a body falling apart. It is, after all, a universal subject, and there is even dignity in it, if the narrator can admit his failings. But Hope chose to keep his dignity for himself.

The third reason is out on its own, and probably would have decided the matter even without the other two. His technique went haywire. Readers who start with *Selected Poetry and Prose*, edited by David Brooks in the year of Hope's death, will find much to delight them, including a selection from Hope's notebooks modestly presented with no mention of a rhizome. But there is no mistaking the fact that the poems near the end of the book lack the sure-footedness of the poems near the front. A late poem called 'The Cetaceans', an *ottava rima* extravaganza with an enchanting cargo of natural science fact, should have been one of his masterpieces, but there are too many awkward lines, and some of them are jaw-breakers. The days when he could substitute lavishly within a line and still hold it together with a conversational rhythmic impulse were gone. By the standards he had long ago set for himself, he was out of control. His air of authority, always his most precious quality, dissipated as his touch became less certain.

A critic who knew a lot about art and nothing about verse technique could say that Hope had developed a 'later manner', like Titian or Michelangelo, and that he was deliberately leaving undone what he knew too well how to do. But Titian, when he left things half painted, hadn't forgotten how to paint, and Michelangelo, when he left the slaves stuck in the rock, hadn't forgotten how to set them free. Hope either forgot how to compose a line or else he convinced himself that it no longer mattered. Either way, it's a mystery. Luckily the comparative clumsiness of his later work didn't erode the reputation he had already. But it did block off the extra renown he might have earned as a magician transmuting all the experience of

his advancing years into poems that became steadily more rich and
varied. Nobody can know just how good A. D. Hope was who doesn't
regret that his full greatness never quite arrived. He won plenty of
prestige, but you can't recite that.

TLS, May 19, 2006

Postscript

Every couple of years I read Hopkins again – if his musical influence
were not so dangerously magnetic I would read him constantly –
and wonder all over again how Hope could have dismissed him. The
reason might possibly be that Hope couldn't hear very well beyond
the Elizabethan mighty line, which he always set himself to reproduce.
Even early on, he would sometimes injure its rhythmic integrity
when he put in too many hypermetric syllables, and later on he lost
his grip completely. Some of the awkward lines in 'The Cetaceans'
are too embarrassing to quote. It would be an ill service to show his
later work in a bad light when the full measure of his early work
has not yet been universally taken.

ROBERT HUGHES REMEMBERS

Things I Didn't Know, by Robert Hughes (Knopf, 2006)

Among my generation of aesthetes, bohemians, proto-dropouts and incipient eternal students at Sydney University in the late 1950s, Robert Hughes was the golden boy. Still drawing and painting in those days, he wrote mainly as a sideline, but his sideline ran rings around his contemporaries, and his good looks and coruscating enthusiasm seemed heaven-sent, as if the mischievous gods had parked a love-child on us just so they could watch the storm of envy. He still looks the part, which is a bit tough on the rest of us. Unfairly, he still has a full head of hair, and although his once trim and elegant body is now held together with pieces of merely semi-precious metal, his aureate initial appearance has by no means been eclipsed.

The internally-worn pins and bolts that slow his latter-day progress through airport security were made necessary by the celebrated 1999 car-crash in Western Australia that should have written him off. Instead, he writes about it. Evoked with characteristic vividness, the car-crash is the first thing that happens in this autobiography, which thus shares the form of the Ambrose Bierce story about the incident at Owl Creek, whereby the hanged man, after the rope snaps, goes on to be the hero of an escape saga. At the end, we find out that the rope didn't snap at all. But Hughes's rope did. Though he was so badly smashed up that by rights he should have been buried in several instalments, he survived to tell the story of his life.

So now we have the Owl Creek incident plus a long flashback: a brand-new form of autobiography, typical of him in its casual boldness. It is not yet a full account of his life as the leading art critic of his generation. We'll need another instalment for that. This instalment, broadly chronological, traces his Catholic upbringing in the Sydney of the 1940s and 1950s, shading into his university years and his early career as a freelance journalist, first in Australia and then in Europe. The book concludes with his departure for America in 1970. Thirty years into a career spent in that country, he still lives there today. His account of those three decades is going to be the story of an intellectual adventure, so let's hope he is already working on it. But it should still be said that, even though this volume is only a preliminary, it is still detectably sparing with the main drama of his life, which has to do with how he reacted to art with his whole soul, and how the soul became richer because of it.

Mainly because the most thrilling part of his personal odyssey is largely left out, I would place this book only among the second rank of Hughes's achievements as a writer, but that still puts it in the first rank of almost anybody else's. There is a paragraph early on, concerning one of his great-aunts who became a nun, which might have been designed to remind any fellow writer among his readers that the champion is still in town. Try just one sentence of it: 'At the end of these audiences I would be expected to kiss her, which meant craning my neck to get my lips inside her elaborately starched and goffered ruff, its hive-like cells prepared, no doubt, by some wretched, rosary-clicking slavey of a postulant sister with the kind of iron last manufactured in the 1920s.'

Not just a ruff, but a goffered ruff. Nobody since Patrick Leigh-Fermor in his precocious youth has packed in quite so much precisely registered and lexically specified visual detail as Hughes does when he is on song. Although, in this book, he is not on song always, its average of readability would raise it high anyway, and there is more than enough opinionated reflection and generous regret to make the narrative unusual for its scope. If only, instead of just sketching it, he'd put in the full story of his developing response to art, he might have written a stand-alone masterpiece. But perhaps he was too modest, and figured that we could deduce all that from his rack of critical works.

Well, so we can, but that's exactly why we would have liked to hear the personalised version of his early critical career right here and now. The unstoppably voluble Hughes – among a bunch of great Aussie talkers, he looks like being the last one who will ever learn to listen – might seem an unlikely candidate for shyness, but he has been a bit shy on this point, as if he wanted, when it came to questions of the mind, to forgo the heroics. But that's where the heroics are that interest us most. The rest, after all, is just given to us.

About what he was given, Hughes is either compelled to be modest or else he still doesn't realise just how gifted he was. The second thing, I think, is more likely to be true. In Australia, class divisions, though widely believed not to exist, are certainly present to the extent that there are people who feel superior. Very few people, however, feel inferior: a pretty good measure of the prevailing egalitarianism. But Hughes and his background might have been designed to remind his less glossily reared fellow culturati that there was a privileged order.

Hughes emanated from a grand Catholic family far enough up the ladder to inhabit a large house in Rose Bay, one of Sydney's inner eastern suburbs, where the people in the social pages came from. While being careful to point out that his dynastic line was flat broke by the time he came into his share of the inheritance, Hughes is honest enough not to underplay his advantages. His father had been a World War I fighter pilot who later became a papal knight. Hughes was sent to school at Riverview, a scholastically distinguished and spiritually intense little Alcatraz on the harbour foreshore where Catholic boys were expected to get into training for great things. Hughes duly learned his Latin, but in emphasising the formal structure of the system that launched him he rather downplays his inbuilt fitness for his role, a range of qualities which, when he arrived at university, marked him out among the common run of students as if he had a neon halo.

He admits that he had a good memory, for example, but should have said that it was photographic. He admits that he was active as an illustrator for the student magazines and stage productions but should have said that his speed and skill left us flabbergasted. He admits that he flourished as a student journalist but fails to add that the downtown editors stormed the university walls and kidnapped him. He admits that he did all right with the girls but forgets to say – ah, this is the unforgivable malfeasance – that he cut a swathe without even trying.

Brenda, a British ballerina from the touring Royal Ballet, at least gets a mention. I remember her: she was so graceful that you went on seeing her with your eyes closed. The gorgeous Australian actress and future television star Noeline Brown gets a longer mention, as well she might: I knew Hughes well enough to see him in her company many times, and there wasn't an occasion when I didn't whimper from envy. But there was another one, called Barbara, who looked as if she spent her spare time standing in a sea-shell for Botticelli, and she doesn't even get a sentence. I several times sat with her for hours while she waited for Hughes to come out of the school of architecture, where he was staving off expulsion by turning out fifty drawings in a single afternoon. Considering the number of poems I wrote for her without copping so much as a compassionate touch on the wrist, Hughes's omission of her name defies justice. And there were plenty more.

What grates on my nerves in this area is that he probably didn't even have tabs on himself as a Lothario. Of all the young men I knew, he spent the least time glancing into mirrors. He must have just thought it was natural that all these unfeasibly lovely creatures fell into his arms. A certain unawareness of what life is like for ordinary mortals might have been detectable even then by some-one suitably attuned, and is fully detectable now, like those pins of his going through the metal detector as he checks in at the airport for his latest flight to glory. The tendency on the part of the clever to imagine that less gifted people are being wilfully obtuse can have important political consequences, which in the case of Hughes we might keep in mind.

If Hughes nowadays sometimes behaves as if his own country has failed him, we should give him a break and not put it down to snobbery. Sooner or later a man as smart as that will end up believing that the whole world has failed him, unless he is made to realise that a superior intellect, if its owner is bent on assessing the life of human beings in the mass, is more likely to be a handicap than an advan-tage. There are signs that Hughes has been brought nearer to this realisation by the impact of a car coming in the other direction fast enough to break almost every bone in his body, but the job is not yet complete, perhaps because that wonderful brain of his came through in one piece.

Hughes is in no position to say how wonderful the brain was and is, even if he knows, which I suspect he doesn't, quite. But the Australian expatriate writer Alan Moorehead spotted Hughes's cap-acities not long after the art-hungry prodigy, no longer an artist but already causing long-distance ripples as a writer about art, went into self-imposed exile abroad. I should say at this point that the much publicised Australian Expatriate Movement gets far too much attention in Australia and is likely to be misunderstood elsewhere, because it's one of those neat media stories that travel too well, like cheap wine.

In recent years, by media operators and academic drones in Britain and Australia, the story has mainly been written around the adventures, real and supposed, of the so-called Famous Four, a globetrotting group of celebrities comprising Hughes, Barry Humphries, Germaine Greer, and finally, shambling along far in the rear like Sancho Panza, myself. Nowadays the Famous Four get a good deal of approbation in their homeland, partly because of the questionable assumption that they have done something to raise their country's previously supine international profile, and thereby helped to create the climate in which Cate Blanchett, Nicole Kidman and Naomi Watts can be appreciated in their full splendour, as fit female counterparts for the race of supermen represented by Heath Ledger and Hugh Jackman, not to mention Russell Crowe, who in Australia is written up as if he were a dinkum (i.e. genuine) Aussie unless he has recently thrown a telephone at someone, whereupon it is suddenly remembered that he was born in New Zealand. One way and another the expatriates are now, as the Australians say, quids in.

I can remember when it was different, and we were all regularly reviled for having turned our backs on our homeland. (Hughes still comes in for some of this treatment, for reasons we will get to.) But the point to grasp is that this whole thing about a specific expatriate generation is an illusion, because Australia has been producing expatriates since Dame Nellie Melba. It's something that all liberal democracies do, especially in the first flush of their prosperity, when the amount of marketable talent is beyond the capacity of local metropolitan outlets. They start colonising the earth, and Australia has long been sufficiently in flower to spread its pollen on the wind. There were always the theatrical people and the painters, and then, during and after Word War II, came the writers, headed by the war correspondents, of whom the most prominent was Alan Moorehead. Quite apart from his famous books about the Nile, Moorehead wrote a shelf of considerable volumes that it would take a long paragraph simply to enumerate, but sufficient to say that he was ahead of his time in realising that Italy was a perfectly reasonable place for an Australian writer to set up shop, because Australia, which like America had been the product of many of the world's cultures, would inevitably produce cultural figures who were at home anywhere.

Back in Australia, there were still a couple of generations of intellectuals on the way who would be reluctant to agree with that proposition, because they thought that Australia – eternally stricken, poor mite, by its subservient connection to Britain – needed a national identity, which would be sabotaged if talented people opted out. Moorehead, who had just spent several years in a ringside seat as several different national identities tried their best to annihilate each other, knew all that was moonshine, and that Australia's national identity depended on nothing but the quality of its culture, which was more likely to be enhanced than inhibited if some of its young exponents were to spend time abroad. Correctly assessing that Hughes was short of financial resources but was carrying the prose equivalent of what the Australian children's radio programme called the Golden Boomerang, Moorehead invited the loping vagabond to stop by.

One of the many admirable things about Hughes is that he has always cherished his mentor as much as his mentor cherished him. Moorehead was the Virgil to Hughes's Dante. The old hand didn't just teach the youngster which local wine was which, he taught him the importance of not talking a book away – the most important lesson a writer can learn, and the harder to learn the better that he talks. The passages about Hughes's creative sojourn with Moorehead would alone make this book worth the price. 'I found Alan,' says Hughes, 'the kind of father I had never had.' After the bungled operation that left Moorehead with a damaged brain, Hughes pushed his master's wheelchair. Tears of compassion soften the tone, but the style, as always, stays firm. There is never any question about Hughes's ability to find the perfect written equivalent for anything in his range of feeling. There is only ever a question about what he feels.

Whether he feels compassion for his late wife Danne is hard to guess. The safest answer is that he doesn't know what to say. She was too much for him. I knew her too, back when we were all starting off in Sydney, and I had already guessed that she might be too much for anybody. She had a problem vis-à-vis the reality principle that would later be echoed by the second wife of Paul McCartney, still fifteen years from being born when Danne Emerson's tower-of-power beauty was in its launch phase. I can remember how Danne came striding with would-be magisterial slowness through the dining room of Manning House (the cafeteria of the Women's Union at Sydney University) and Germaine Greer said, 'Oh, come *on*, Danne, *relax*.' Germaine was three tables away from me so you can imagine that the comment was quite audible. Danne wasn't fazed. She might have been on something even then.

In London she was on everything and Hughes piercingly describes the consequences. By a paradox mercifully quite rare in the play-power, alternative, Sixties lifestyle, Hughes went and married someone who actually believed in the play-power, alternative, Sixties lifestyle. Why a man who had already had his pick of the world's sane beauties should have teamed up with an insane beauty is a question he doesn't put to himself here, and possibly once again the reason is modesty. Never having grasped the full measure by which he was initially blessed, he doesn't see the irony in how he was subsequently cursed. Anyway, the long episode makes grim reading, and is climaxed by Danne's untimely death and the subsequent suicide of the couple's son, occurrences noted with a lack of comment that surely only permanent and irresolvable bewilderment could make possible. It was tragic fate on a Greek scale, and his benumbed registration of these personal disasters makes it very plausible when he advances the proposition that it takes art to make life bearable.

There is a lot about art here, and politeness demands that we should note the abundance before complaining that there might have been more. Before Hughes left Sydney, he already had an appreciative eye for the Australian art that he would later rank and classify in his pioneering critical work *The Art of Australia* (1966). One of his enthusiasms was for the reclusive genius Ian Fairweather. From an exhibition in Sydney, Hughes bought one of Fairweather's key paintings, *Monsoon*. 'It cost all of three hundred pounds, and I secured it by queuing all night, accompanied by Noeline and ahead of eight or ten other impassioned fans, on the steps of the gallery, with a thermos of rum-laced coffee, blankets, and a sleeping bag, in order to get first pick...' Note the excitement, which, as always with Hughes, is closely accompanied by powers of definition that can evoke even the indefinite. 'It was a large abstraction, predominantly black, brown, and grey, traversed by a violent yet exquisitely harmonious net of swiftly daubed, creamy lines. It gave a sense of lightning flashes piercing tropical darkness . . .'

You will find passages like that all through Hughes's writings (*The Fatal Shore* is especially rich in verbal landscapes of gallery quality) but the thing to grasp here is that he not only felt like that when he was young, he could say it like that when he was young. Saying everything as if he still has the young energy of discovery is what he does. The excitement and the powers of evocation were what Hughes took abroad with him, and his continuing wisdom has been to know that neither works without the other. In this book you can see them working for Duccio, Cimabue, Piero della Francesca, Leonardo, Goya, Bonnard, Sidney Nolan, John Olsen, Robert Crumb, Robert Rauschenberg and others. But not enough others. We would have liked the whole catalogue, because the story of such a brilliant critic's steadily accumulating and interacting enthusiasms, their ever-intensifying interplay of nuance, is his real autobiography. Those were the most important Things He Didn't Know.

Once again, it might be a case of Hughes not quite knowing how rare his gift is. He is ready to risk opprobrium by calling himself an elitist. 'For of course I am an elitist, in the cultural but emphatically not the social sense.' Elitists, however, even such large-minded and non-snobby ones, are never in short supply. What you hardly find anywhere is someone who can do for art what Leonard Bernstein did for music: go on television and become a fisher of men, hauling the general viewers in the direction of a new life. Hughes did it with *The Shock of the New*.

In America the series was successful enough, but from an American viewpoint it is probably hard to estimate the impact that it had in Britain and Australia, where it was shown on the mainstream channels. Here was the kind of survey that the BBC used to be able to do when it still commanded the services of resident grandees like Kenneth Clark and Jacob Bronowski, but now it was being done by an Aussie who had based himself in New York. (Hughes went there in response to a telephoned invitation from *Time* magazine. Immured in his London flat, surrounded by the ruins of his marriage, Hughes was so stoned that he thought the CIA was after him.) He was a new breed: a breed without a readily traceable bloodline. His background invisible in the far distance, he exemplified the biggest advantage the new wave of Aussie expatriates had: they inhabited the cultural world as if they had been born in it, and nowhere else. Culture was their country.

Hughes could, and should, have done a whole chapter about how he got *The Shock of the New* off the ground. Instead, he gives it a paragraph or two, and wastes a whole line recording (correctly, alas) that I warned him about how doing television would erode his reputation for seriousness. It ranks high among the least pertinent things I have ever said, because Hughes's true seriousness is based on exactly that: his ability to transmit the highest level of aesthetic enjoyment through the popular media, one of which, of course, is the bestseller. This book will probably do all right anyway, but it might have done even better if a whole generation who were already grateful to him felt inspired to cram a copy into the hands of their children, saying: here, if you have to go crazy, don't go crazy about Eminem. Go crazy the way this guy did – go crazy about Cimabue.

Hughes did go crazy about Cimabue, before Florence was flooded in 1966, and he went crazier still after the raging waters had done their work. The great Cimabue crucifix in the Museo dell'Opere of Santa Croce was stripped of its paint. At the head of his camera crew, Hughes arrived in time to gather up all the floating specks of pigment and put them in a jar, just in case the resulting mulch might be an aid to restoration. The possibility was never proved, because a workman threw away the jar. The whole episode is as riveting as that: one of the best bits in a book of best bits. But the bits are a bit like the flecks of paint: they belong on a more coherent structure.

There would have been more room for art if there was less stuff about politics. An even more awkward truth is that the stuff about politics could have been more worthy of that superior brain we have been talking about, the piece of Hughes that was left intact after he was comprehensively screwed by his own car. At the subsequent inquest, Hughes got into trouble with the Australian press by suggesting audibly that the proceedings were a circus. Suggesting things audibly is one of Hughes's most endearing characteristics. When young he never had much idea of adjusting his discourse to the audience, and he still hasn't now. But his disinclination to censor himself means that he can easily talk himself into trouble.

What he didn't seem to realise, when the car-crash case was being heard out there in the sticks of Western Australia, was that the national press was already laying for him. Hughes favoured (still

favours) an Australian republic, and had several times flown the
Pacific to speak against those lingering ties with Britain that he
holds to be obsolete. The overwhelming majority of Australia's
intellectuals are Republican like him, but they didn't necessarily think
he was doing their cause a favour. In the referendum of 1999 the
Republicans failed to get their way. Some said it was because of the
manner in which the question was framed, but there were others
who thought that a glittering few of the more prominent Republican
advocates had been counter-productive in their advocacy, simply
because of their 'silvertail' (i.e. privileged) background.

More scintillating than any of these had been Hughes. He would
have a sound right to laugh at the imputation of privilege – I can
remember well how there was so little money left in the family that
his mother had to start a ski-lodge business from scratch – but
there is this much to it: he doesn't necessarily sense the Australian
electorate's reluctance to countenance any measure that might divert
power towards an oligarchy. The question of which interests would
be favoured by a republic popped up quite early in the argument,
and even that vast majority of the intelligentsia who were convinced
that the coming of the republic was historically inevitable were still
ready to question the credentials of a carpetbagger who looked too
eager to scramble aboard the bandwagon.

Almost anybody with a university degree in Australia was, and is,
ready to call the common people a bunch of racists for electing John
Howard. The contempt of the commentariat for a good half of the
electorate is one of the wonders of modern Australia. (At this point,
Americans might need to be reminded that in Australia voting is
compulsory, so half the electorate means half of all the adults alive.)
In theory, the republicans should have agreed with Hughes when he
treated the rest of the Australian population as wrong-headed on the
subject of the republic. But they preferred to think that the visiting
fireman was patronising everybody, themselves included. This opinion of him was reinforced after the accident that turned him into
Evel Knievel, when the press – never helpful to a celebrity on trial
– gave him their standard bucketing and he reacted as if its personnel were out to get him. Undoubtedly some of them were, but in
Australia it would be wise for even Shakespeare to have a fraternal
drink with the Fourth Estate. Suddenly feeling the warmth drain out
of his welcome, Hughes gathered himself up on his crutches, shook

the dust of his homeland slowly from his shoes, and headed off to light up the metal detector at Sydney airport. In the book, he contemplates saying a defiant goodbye forever to the land of his birth.

The land of his birth is unlikely to let it happen. If Australia's too-much talked-about National Identity – that metaphysical abstraction which for so long has been longed for, and longed for so pointlessly because it was always there – means anything at all, it means something that comes with you wherever you go. Hughes spends a lot of time in this book saying what his country never had, and still hasn't got. Actually it's got it, because it's got Hughes. He should give his country a little more credit, if only because it still gives so much credit to him. Nowadays he gets quite a lot of curled lip from the media, but the bitchery is really praise: praise for the larrikin, Australia's eternal prodigal child.

Hughes is the Bastard from the Bush dressed up as the Wandering Scholar. Thousands of bright young Aussies will want to be him, in the same way that thousands of slightly less bright Aussies want to be the cricketer Shane Warne. Hughes is quids in. All he has to remember is that his nation has got some credit coming for helping to form the best part of his brain, the part that wants to share any discovered joy. One doesn't ask him to praise his homeland: just to be fair will do. He is very droll, for example, about the reactionary views of Robert Gordon Menzies, Prime Minister of Australia for most of our youth. But when Hughes accurately recollects the two scholarships he won to Sydney University, and that he wouldn't have been able to go there without them, he neglects to say that his brilliant examination results would have secured him another scholarship, a Commonwealth Scholarship, had he required it: and that the Commonwealth Scholarship scheme – the chief reason why the Australian universities in the late 1950s were teeming with the names that have since become famous – was the invention of the Menzies government.

The Commonwealth Scholarship scheme educated the very generation of intellectuals who were to spend much of their lives vilifying the government that made their education possible. Such ironies are what Hughes should be reporting. I can't believe he misses them out deliberately. I'm afraid they count among the small number of Things He Still Doesn't Know. But they are far outweighed by the

Things He Found Out, and he might consider putting a few more of those into a second edition, in the space left when he removes an elaborate, pages-long confusion between the F2B Bristol Fighter and the SE5. A stickler for accuracy in aeronautical matters – he was a mighty aero-modeller in his adolescence – Hughes will be horrified when he Googles the designations and sees the trick that his magnificent memory has played on him. The better the memory, the bigger the trick: it's a rule in life.

But he can always fill the freed-up space with just one more radiant observation about his field of study and arena of true passion. I drafted this piece in the cafeteria across the street from the Glasgow School of Art, Charles Rennie Mackintosh's great masterpiece. It was registration day, and there were all those young students. I could remember when, in faraway Sydney, they used to be us; and I couldn't look at any of that wonderful building's details without being grateful to Hughes for helping to open my eyes, in those years when I still knew nothing except that I wanted to know everything. He didn't have to find the language for being thrilling about the serious: he had it from birth, which is probably why, in this fine book which should be even finer than it is, he can treat his unrelenting adventure in the arts as incidental. But it's fundamental, to him and to the whole bunch of us: surely he knows that. And as I sit typing this last paragraph in my London apartment, an email from a mutual friend tells me where Hughes is right now. He's in Australia, promoting this book. The Japanese say it every day: I go and I come back.

New York Review of Books, January 11, 2007

Postscript

Naturally gifted critic though he was, Hughes left Australia before he had had time to make a full estimation of how thoroughly the influence of the European refugees had changed the modern culture. His early cartoons were notably influenced by Molnar, a Hungarian immigrant who dominated the *Sydney Morning Herald* in the same way that Osbert Lancaster dominated London's *Daily Sketch*. The European influence was already everywhere. For us natives, it was a matter of seeing what lay too close to be noticed. Later on, with the benefit of exile, Hughes got things in perspective, but by then his early remarks about Australia's isolation had been published and taken hold. A star critic will always need criticism in his turn, but Hughes was so brilliant that no modifying voice could be heard against his own. It was a pity, because the full story of the modern Euro-Australian interchange was one he might have told earlier, and thus helped to save a generation of Australian cultural pundits from a career spent gazing into their own navels. But he had other stories to tell, and they changed the world. *The Shock of the New* was an Australian expatriate achievement on a level with Rod Laver winning Wimbledon five times, Dame Joan Sutherland singing the title role of *Lucia di Lammermoor* at Covent Garden, and Sir Jack Brabham designing the car in which he won the World Championship.

MODERN AUSTRALIAN PAINTING

Delivered as a National Trust Lecture at the State Theatre in Sydney
on June 27, 2006, and later published in a shortened version
by the *TLS*, September 1, 2006

One big advantage of having your name attached for long enough to
Australia's inexorably spreading wave of cultural world conquest is
that you eventually get to meet everyone else. Throw another launch
ceremony on the barbie! Prizes are awarded, exhibitions are opened,
movies and plays are premiered, and sooner or later even the most
dedicated creative loner is flushed out of hiding to loom within reach
of your extended hand. A characteristic sight at any big-time Australian cultural get-together is two life-long recluses falling into each
other's arms. Last time I looked, I was personally acquainted with at
least three of the most illustrious Australian painters of the post-war
generation, the gang who really and undeniably put the Australian
branch of their art-form on an international level.

Admittedly I had met Sidney Nolan and Charles Blackman only
once, and Russell Drysdale and Arthur Boyd not at all. But Margaret
Olley? Jeffrey Smart? Not only mates of each other, but mates, to a
certain extent, of mine. John Olsen? Last had a drink with him at a
big fund-raiser at the Art Gallery of NSW in Sydney when Margaret
Olley was making it surreptitiously clear, with some well-aimed
muttering from the side of her mouth, that she thought her dear
friend Edmund Capon's curatorial campaign to buy a triptych by
Cy Twombley was three kinds of a mistake. Actually I've been in
John Olsen's delightful company for a total of about five minutes,
and although I've been invited to lunch at Margaret Olley's house
in Paddington a gratifying number of times, my only extended
time in the company of Jeffrey Smart was when he was doing the

preparatory drawings for his *Portrait of Clive James* which now hangs in that same Art Gallery of NSW. During the sittings Jeffrey did quite a lot of *sotto voce* complaining about how hard it is to draw someone who has one ear far higher on his head than the other, while possessing eyes almost invisibly small.

I could have wished that there was rather more *sotto* and rather less *voce*, in fact. But I was to discover that in the finished portrait none of these personal details would matter very much. The main study drawing was done in the painter's studio in Tuscany. I thought the drawing of my head rather heroic, with something of a Roman senator about the proportions of the skull, although he would have had to be a Roman senator with an ear-alignment problem. But I didn't see the finished portrait until some time after it arrived in Sydney. I visited the gallery expecting to see a larger version of the drawing, and indeed it was: far larger, as big as a small Paolo Veronese. The actual figure representing myself, however, was extremely small, a dot in an urban landscape, and obviously present only to give scale to the vast buildings. Bending close, I saw with some compensatory benefit to my self-esteem that there was now nothing at all anomalous about the ears: which meant I could have been just about any man my age with small eyes and a neck thicker than his head. And that – on the face of it, as it were – is the evidence of our acquaintance. But if journalists like to conclude that Jeffrey Smart and I must be bosom buddies, who am I to say them nay?

Yes, me and the painters: you can imagine the group photograph. But what's wrong with this picture? Me. I shouldn't be there. I not only never shared their struggle over the long decades, but for most of that time I knew next to nothing about them. The whole upsurge happened without my knowledge. Though the painters eventually changed the way I saw them and have even changed the way I see life, they didn't do it by appealing to my sensitivity. They did it by overcoming my lack of it. And although there were many writers who were less obtuse on the subject than I was, not many of them were in a position to change the general perception of Australian painting by what they wrote. The painters changed it by what they painted.

In retrospect, that was always the main guarantee of the strength of Australian painting: it didn't really need writers to say how good it was. Though the painters cared a lot about what critics said, they cared mainly because critical opinion might affect the sale of their pictures to the public. The law of supply and demand was the measure that mattered. Since the pictures were bought by people who loved them – and that was especially true in the days when the prices were low, because it always takes a real appreciator to buy an artist's pictures before there is an established market for them – the question of where those buyers lived becomes vitally interesting in relation to the larger story of how Australian post-colonial culture relates to the culture of the old imperial world from which it emerged.

But before we start discussing that subject on a large scale, it might be more fruitful to discuss it in the much more restricted terms dictated by my own knowledge of the visual arts in the late 1950s, when I was first a student at the University of Sydney. If only I had been a student of painting. Like students of music, students of painting had to learn something. From the life stories of the Australian painters up until very recent times, it emerges that they all had to submit to the hard disciplines of the craft that underlay the art: they can all prepare canvases, mix colours, apply a glaze. Above all, they can all draw. And those many hours in the life class they all share. If only writers had a shared experience with the same objective standards: they would know their own true ranking much better, and perhaps hate each other much less.

As a student of literature I had to submit to no disciplines at all, and spent an unforgivable amount of time fooling around. But it is, or should be, in the nature of a great university to provide an unwritten charter by which a no-hoper may fool around more constructively than he realises, largely by keeping company with fellow students who are working harder than he is. One of my fellow students was Robert Hughes. A bit older than I, a lot better look-ing, and much more gifted in every respect, Hughes in those days was doing as much of drawing and painting as he was of writing. Nominally he was an architecture student, but he spent most of his time drawing for the student newspaper *honi soit*, for all the other student publications, and, enviably soon, for the first examples of a new wave of serious periodicals that dealt with the whole of culture all at once. Hughes's draughtsmanship was dazzling. He could draw anything and anyone in about ten seconds, like one of those autistic children who can draw whole cities in perspective without lifting the pencil point from the paper. But Hughes's version of autism involved reciting large chunks of *Four Quartets* from memory, and his flying line had mentality and character in every inch. He painted with what seemed to me equal authority, although I was no judge. Hughes was, and the time soon came when he decided he was not original enough, and ought to quit.

He might have been premature in that judgment. Quite often, an original artist starts off looking like every artist he admires, and then his own uniqueness emerges after everyone else's has been absorbed. The future critic might have criticised himself too much. Another reason he might have stopped was that I shot a hole in one of his pictures. At the family house in Rose Bay, he and I were diving around the garden with an air-pistol, making life difficult for the sparrows. When my turn came I tried a deflection shot on a passing spag and the pellet went past the target and on into the garage, where Hughes's latest painting was leaning against a wall. It was a painting of a sad, rather Eliotesque broken king and when we held it up to the light it became evident that the disconsolate monarch now had a hole in one eye. My suggestion that the defeated central figure had thus acquired an interesting new connection with infinity did not go down well. Hughes was as put out as the eye was but he was a generous soul and soon forgave me.

I like to think it was a coincidence that he left for Europe shortly afterwards. Probably his real reason for heading out was a belief that the action in the art of painting, as in the arts generally, was elsewhere, in that distant place we called Overseas. I can remember taking that belief for gospel, even when it came to an art-form that I knew next to nothing about. The first art books with more of their reproductions in colour than in black and white were reaching Australia about then, and I thought I could see from my imported books about Degas and Toulouse-Lautrec that the so-called 'Australian Impressionists' in the Art Gallery of NSW were a secondary event by comparison. Much later on, Hughes the world-famous art critic talked about the effect on Australia's would-be painters of what he called 'the tyranny of the unseen masterpiece'. He took it for granted that for the painters to actually see Europe's heritage of great paintings was crucial. But a loose interpretation of his principle – and a journalistic interpretation, the interpretation that sets the agenda, is almost always loose – tends to neglect the fact that

Australia's post-war wave of painters already knew quite a lot about the European heritage before they went abroad. And they all went. As Hughes himself would now be the first to point out, Margaret Olley, John Olsen and Jeffrey Smart had already made their first trips to Europe while we were still shooting sparrows. But Hughes might not have known that then, and as for me, I didn't even know their names. I had heard of Russell Drysdale because some of his outback scenes had been reproduced in the *Women's Weekly*. Sidney Nolan I knew to be associated in some way with Ned Kelley. But I didn't meet an actual Australian painter until I got to London and found myself living in the same house as Brett Whiteley.

The house, in Melbury Road, Kensington, had once belonged to the pre-Raphaelite crowd-pleaser Holman Hunt. The bunch of recent arrivals that I was with all moved into the ground floor of the house and started being poor. Brett lived in the studio out in the back yard. Brett had obviously already left poverty behind. He had all the signs of success including a blindingly beautiful wife, Wendy. Forty years on, now that my elder daughter is an up and coming painter, I know enough about the harsh economics of the painter's life to realise that Brett might not have been that well off after all. But he certainly got invited out.

It was a tough moment for the rest of us when Brett and Wendy emerged from the studio one spring evening on their way to dinner with Sir Kenneth Clark. Brett, whose tightly curled tea-cosy of a hairstyle was bright blond in those days, a kind of golden helmet, was almost as lovely as his wife. The two of them made us feel very downmarket. But Brett was no snob and seemed not to mind when I spent hours drinking his beer while explaining to him that technique in the arts was a side issue. Brett countered with the argument that one of the reasons Matisse could leave out so much was that he knew exactly how to put everything in. This was a perfectly true statement but I was years away from realising how true it was, because I had never had to sit down and keep reshaping a sentence while the light changed on the verb.

One of the things I most regret about my acquaintanceship with Brett Whiteley was that when he carried out his plan to visit the National Gallery before dawn – he had been given special permission after Sir Kenneth Clark had made the right phone call – I was too hung over to join him on his expedition to watch the sun come up on the Piero della Francescas. (Youth is the time of opportunities neglected: who would want to live through all that waste again?) One of the things I least regret is that I agreed he should do a triptych of nude lovers based on one of my poems. I thought I recognised Wendy in the complicated and lascivious flourish of black ink on the white paper. Anyway the bits that I thought were her were a lot more interesting than my words. After the pictures were framed at Brett's expense (Wendy looked at me very darkly about that, and she was right) he made me a present of them, and I lugged them around for years until I finally left them with a startled landlady in Cambridge as part compensation for being late with my rent. Unless she burned them, I suppose they will turn up one day and fetch a huge price, not because of my lines but because of Brett's line: and that's just how it should be.

British critics were already writing about how Brett had brought his blue sky with him from Australia. I had seen for myself that he got some of his blue sky from Piero della Francesca, but it didn't occur to me that there was a potentially interesting aesthetic question here about memory, perception and inspiration. Nothing about painting occurred to me for some time. At Cambridge I made regular visits to the Fitzwilliam to admire the Rembrandt. The Rembrandt subsequently turned out to be a fake but by then I could tell it was a pretty good one. With my future wife I spent a lot of time in Florence and in the Low Countries, doing the grand tour of the Renaissance. What a busy bunch of guys the Renaissance had been, I joked to myself, but in truth I was duly overwhelmed. I didn't see how anything could compete with that, or even add to it. I liked quite a lot of the new art that was then invading London from America but apart from a few unarguable stand-outs like Larry Rivers I didn't see much that could convince me it was as hard to do as, say, painting the Portinari altarpiece.

Then something big happened, and, as so often happens when something big happens, I wasn't exactly sure what it was; I just felt the thump. There was girl at Girton who wore pop-socks and had that strange, rare, Zuleika Dobson-like gift of being followed around by a troop of prattling young men wherever she went even though she never said anything. One night she invited us all to a party at her father's flat in London. It was in St James's, as I remember, possibly overlooking St James Street itself. I was more than slightly smashed when we all arrived out of the night, but after guessing from the scale of the place that Miss Pop-Socks's father must be loaded, the first thing I specifically noticed was that the walls were covered with paintings which had to be Australian. I guessed this about the Arthur Boyd paintings, and I was certain of it about the Drysdales, which were so numerous that they sometimes hung one above the other.

Overcoming a rush of nostalgia about the *Women's Weekly*, I proceeded to instruct the young company about the rise of Australian culture. Miss Pop-Socks seemed unimpressed, perhaps because she needed no instruction. Her father had backed his appreciation with his money. Or to put it in a less vulgar and ultimately much more useful way, he had backed it with his love. This is an aspect we should note. It wasn't just a case of a pundit-cum-merchant like Sir Kenneth Clark investing in futures as he stocked up on the Nolans and the Whiteleys. It was a case of British art-lovers seeing something that delighted them, and wanting to live with it. That night I got no further than realising that Drysdale delighted me. Yes, that was what a red dirt road looked like, and a town with one pub. Taking it for granted that an Australian painting should have an Australian subject, I could have cried with homesickness.

Homesickness was unrelieved for another ten years at least, until finally the *Observer* sent me back to Sydney on assignment. Until then, I hadn't been able to afford a ticket home. That was the reason, incidentally, why the first trips of the Australian painters to Europe tended to last for years rather than months: it was so expensive getting there that you would have been wasting the money if you didn't stay. I wonder if, nowadays, easy travel really has brought the other side of the world any closer: if you arrive ready to leave again, how much do you learn? How much do you submit, which is the big secret of learning anything?

Anyway, I had been away a long time: long enough for the Opera House to be finished. When I left, it was just a set of foundations. When I got back, it was Sydney's most famous thing since the Harbour Bridge. Before the war, Grace Cossington Smith had painted daringly *pointilliste* pictures of the Bridge when it was being built, but that was as close as art got to engineering. Now the Opera House was there, and it had its own art inside it, including John Olsen's huge painting *Five Bells* inspired by Kenneth Slessor's poem about Sydney Harbour, out onto which the painting looked through the glass: a virtual image observing its reality. The painting knocked me sideways. For a while I thought it was an abstract, until I began to notice that it was composed of natural details. But the natural details were dotted through coloured space, in roughly the proportion of space to object that obtains in a Japanese screen, and with the same touch of quietly ecstatic wit that I had learned to look for in Paul Klee. You will notice that my range of reference had expanded.

Some of these guesses about the kind of art that Olsen has been looking at I was able later to check up on, because with Olsen, as with the other major Australian painters, a useful tradition began of publishing sumptuous monographs in which the reproductions not only got better and better, the text got more and more learned. To the row of Olsen books there has recently been added one called *John Olsen: Teeming with Life, His Complete Graphics 1957–2005*. This book is an education: an education about the artist's education.

In Olsen's prints you get down to the basics of where his big, seemingly boundless paintings such as *Five Bells* and *The You-Beaut Country* got their centripetal strength: detailed drawing. In all the prints of the 1980s that carried images of the now-famous Olsen frog, you can see how he caught the wildlife in motion through letting his line run as fast as it would flow: the frog dives from a branch like a blob of spit. You can also see that all this lyrical freedom must have been the product of a discipline. And so it was. In the early 1950s Olsen worked long hours in the drawing classes of three art schools in Sydney. Two of them were in sight of the Harbour and the third was the fabled East Sydney Tech, where Margaret Olley had already put in what Australians call the hard yakka.

But the extra thing to grasp is that Olsen knew quite a lot about Klee and Kandinsky before he left on the *Orion* in 1956 for his first three years away. He might not have seen many originals, but he saw all the reproductions there were. And the visiting exhibition 'French Painting Today' had taught him a lot, as it taught all the painters a lot, when it toured the Australian cities in 1953. It could teach them so much because they were looking with instructed eyes. And indeed common sense tells us that the Australian painters had never been cut off from the old world, but had been in a constant state of interchange with it, and all the more so because the actual pictures they had seen were so few, and thus so precious. Waiting for a long time under the balcony is not necessarily the worst start to a love affair. But the big difference between Romeo wooing Juliet and an Australian painter saving up for his first European trip was that the Australian painter already had a good idea of what he was going to get.

He, or, of course, she. Before the war, Margaret Preston and Grace Cossington Smith had always had the European heritage on their minds, if not before their eyes. After the war, Margaret Olley might have preferred to have it on her mind for longer. She has always said that she was exposed to the European impact too early in her career. Meg Stewart's excellent biography *Margaret Olley: Far From a Still Life* is a lot better than its title. The book gives us a richly nuanced account of how the girl from Banyan Creek grew up in artless houses but had already seen her first Medici prints while she was at school in Brisbane in the late thirties. We should pause here to remind ourselves, and to inform the incredulous young, of what a Medici print was: it was a very good colour reproduction. What the Australian painters couldn't see of the European masterpieces was the texture. They could see the colour, which meant that they could see almost all of the form. And they saw more of the European modern painters than you might think because there were well-off and cultivated Australians who collected modern art and brought it home, and the same spirit that made the collectors want to own foreign paintings made them want to know young Australian painters. It's the story that's so often left out: the story of the appreciators.

Margaret Olley's real life as a painter began in Sydney towards the end of the war. At East Sydney Tech the young Margaret was soon famous among the artists for her talent and Renoir-pure pulchritude. Drysdale, Donald Friend and William Dobell all painted her, and in 1949 Dobell's Archibald Prize-winning portrait of her, in her white dress of unrationed parachute silk, made her famous throughout Australia: *Women's Weekly* famous, famous in a way that a shy girl didn't really want to be. The journalists, in both senses of the phrase, chased her onto the ship. In Europe, she was overwhelmed by the galleries. We might tend to think that it was because she had no idea. A better interpretation is that she had a very good idea, but when she saw the reality it was too much of what she wanted all at once.

In Paris, all the Impressionist and Post-impressionist paintings that are now coldly housed in the Musée d'Orsay were still splendidly concentrated in the natural warmth of the Jeu de Paume, where, dare one say it, they belong. We can safely deduce that she was thrown for a loop, because a large part of her subsequent career has been devoted to searching through that concentration for its essence. She came back to Australia in 1957 and for twenty years didn't sail again. Nowadays she travels all the time – she doesn't miss a major exhibition anywhere in the world – but for those two decades her journeys were in the mind: for any kind of artist, the journeys that matter most. And just as, when in Europe, she had maintained a presence in Australia – she sent a whole exhibition back to Brisbane from the south of France – she never, when she came back to Australia, ceased to live in Europe. That indeed, was what her journey in the mind was about.

It was conspicuously a journey away from the specifically Australian subject. In her early days, off in the bush at Hill End with Donald Friend, she had painted what was in front of her. Recently there was a rich little exhibition at the National Trust's Samuel Henry Ervin gallery on Sydney's Observatory Hill to prove that Olley and Friend got results a long way beyond the merely decorative. Robert Hughes said that they were two members of the 'Charm School' but the term is dismissive only if you underestimate just how charming charm can be. But now that she was back where she started, Olley painted as if she was still in the Jeu de Paume and the doors had been nailed closed, leaving her there unaccompanied except perhaps by Morandi and Ivon Hitchens. By the time I got to know about her she had been in there for almost forty years.

As I started flying back and forth to Australia more and more often, the question of the duty of the arts to the Australian Identity was taking more and more space in the media. One look at a roomful of Margaret Olley's pictures was enough to prove that the question was a mare's nest. This wasn't Australia being painted, nor was it French pictures being echoed: this was the deep, layered memory of colour and balance being analysed for its coherent force. Mainly the objects in the pictures were items from the flea market that Olley is still running in the Hat Factory, the old name for the annexe of her Paddington house: a flea market where none of the *brocante* is for sale. (The lucky lunch guests, who amount to a long-running *tertulia* of everyone prominent in the Australian arts world, have to get used to being surrounded by knick-knacks recognisable from pictures they have seen and might even own.) But it's doubtful if we should talk about objects at all. Imploding nebulae of colour, her pictures, Australian only in the sense that it's an Australian who paints them, continue to raise the question of whether she is a figurative painter leaving the people out or an abstract painter putting objects in. I tend to the latter view. I think that with her, as with Olsen, there is constant and deliberate adventure into the territory where the subject yields its full material glory by ceasing to matter. But the question, with both those painters, will always remain moot.

With Jeffrey Smart it was settled from the start. There has to be representation, because form is his mainspring. The literature on him is already rich but Barry Pearce's recent *Jeffrey Smart* is the best thing yet, a truly beautiful book. As we have come to expect from the Beagle Press, which is by now setting world standards and not just matching them, the colour reproductions are sumptuous, and because Smart works hard to achieve perfectly flat planes of colour – there has been no impasto for sixty years – every major picture can be not only present but pretty well correct.

The first thing you notice is that hardly any of them are about Australia. Very early on, before he made his first trip abroad in 1948, he painted local subjects, but even then they tended towards the uniquely personal international landscape that his pictures live in now. Blessed like his friend Barry Humphries with original taste, Smart already knew an awful lot about what had happened overseas before he left for Europe via America. Initially, like Margaret Olley, he was stymied by London's National Gallery. But we have to remember that the process of absorbing influence is highly complex. Smart was in search of stillness and proportion. He was already at home with Mondrian, Ben Nicholson, Balthus and Edward Hopper. In Paris, the personal teaching of Léger took him further into a conceptual range of ideal proportion and geometric balance. So when he says that a single ancient mosaic he saw in Naples has had fifty years of influence, he might only be saying that it confirmed what he had already worked out.

In 1951 he came back to Sydney for twelve years, during which time he made a hit as Phidias on the radio show *The Argonauts*. Phidias knew all there was to know about art, both Australian and foreign. Characteristically I managed to miss his every appearance: he might have woken me up a lot earlier. He might have told me in advance that those Australian Impressionists – Streeton, McCubbin, Tom Roberts – were really something. Smart was helping to educate the next generation of art-lovers in the true principle that painting has no nationalism, only painters in different places. But all that time he was getting ready to leave again. One of the reasons is revealed in his autobiography *Not Quite Straight*: Australia was not yet ready for its gay artists.

But another reason can only be called destiny. He was destined not to be caught up in the question of how or what an Australian should paint. He had another country in mind. It wasn't even Italy. He loved Italy, and after a crucial move from Rome to Tuscany he settled down and lived in Italy. He is still there, at the Posticcia Nuova, which must be one of the most beautiful houses any artist has ever inhabited. The exiled Victor Hugo lived in more splendour, but not with such taste. Thus lodged within driving distance of Arezzo, Smart painted Italy, or seemed to. But what he was really painting was a new world; a really new world; the world of Europe's post-war reconstruction, when the colours came out on the sign-systems of the highways and on the cranes above the white buildings. It was a look destined to take over the planet. Whoever said that eventually everyone will live in the Smart country was exactly right.

What he painted was a vision. 'The world', he said, 'has never been so beautiful.' It was the deepest kind of aesthetic perception talking: the kind that can see the formal music of a pre-pyramid Egyptian bas relief and a Giotto Madonna in a late-night diner by Edward Hopper, and see all three in a row of modern apartment blocks half hidden by a hill. But it was a view of the world so contemporary that it was prescient, and he might have gone broke if he hadn't been hard-headed about business. It's a characteristic he shares with Olley, who realised early on that she should put her earnings into houses if she wanted to go on painting. Smart did the same, and his ability to put the painter's inherently boom-and-bust finances on to a stable basis meant that he was able to ward off more than one great danger.

He was never tempted into painting sequences just to fill a too-hastily scheduled exhibition: one of the temptations which, for Brett Whiteley, might have been almost as fatal as heroin. Every Smart picture was, and is, an individual construction. He was also able to ward off the temptation posed by nationalist pressure. Nolan, in my view, fell for both temptations at once when he churned out too many desert landscapes. Smart was not to be forced home, even by his home culture's increasing gravity. Always favoured by discerning Australian collectors who could see that its internationalism was what made the Australian culture boom formidable, he comes home of his own free will, and that's what has made his career a triumph. One of his biggest and greatest pictures, *The Container Train*, now hanging in the Victorian Arts Institute, started to roll in Yugoslavia two years before it reached a forest in Gippsland. There could be no neater way of saying that the old world and its new country are continuous.

You can't read one book about any of these people without running into stories about all the others. Painters have more fun than poets. It seems unfair. Even in the rare cases when they don't get on, the painters are in a club, and quarrels are either settled or become a recognised axis for gossip. (While working on my left ear, Jeffrey Smart told me a scarcely believable story about Dobell and the man in charge of Wiseman's Ferry.) This feeling of fraternity has certainly helped the Australian painters keep the courage of their convictions, the chief conviction being that a painting should be a thing in itself, and not a fleck in a trend. When all else fails, they've got each other, even beyond death. Olsen drew Brett Whiteley in his last years, when the golden helmet had gone dark. After Whiteley died, Olsen made a set of prints acknowledging the everlasting beauty of those early pictures of Wendy in the bath. He drew only the bath, because she was gone, too.

The same feeling extends even further back through time, to foreign painters long gone, whom they might never have met. Margaret Olley, who has always been shy about naming her lucky lovers, is flagrant about her love for Bonnard. A real live Bonnard is one of her many bequests to the Art Gallery of NSW, and there are other, smaller galleries that benefit from her munificence. And, standing out among her many still-lifes, what else is a figurative painting like *Homage to Manet*, with its scrumptiously creamy depiction of Berthe Morrisot, except a cheeky reminder that Margaret Olley, too, had once been painted in white by a great man, and had still managed to lead her own creative life?

Well, it's also a nice picture. And people want pictures. They want poems, too, but they want them in another way, and it's all too easy for poets to get depressed when they discover the deal is never

done, the *fait* is never *accompli*, and the thing is never taken home
to hang cherished on the wall while its creator banks the cheque and
the critics shut up. We who push a pen had just better face it.
Pushing a brush is in every way more satisfactory. But as long as the
results matter, pushing a brush is also a lot harder. Any tribute to
the Australian painters should begin with our gratitude for their
belief that the results do matter. While the writers complained about
being either shut out from the old world or else unable to get free of
it – and there was reason for both complaints – the painters quietly
enjoyed their privilege of helping to build an Australian cultural
identity that the world could not resist. Always separate yet always
together, they created an achievement so exciting for the eyes that it
can make the blind see. I stand here as testimony to the truth of that.

Postscript

This lecture could easily have become a book if time had permitted.
I barely mentioned Charles Blackman, whose accumulated work is
one of the glories of post-war Australian painting. There could be
a whole chapter just on the importance of East Sydney Technical
College, where Rayner Hoff was the tutelary sprit. Hoff's origins
were in England, but after a long spell in the trenches of World War
I, and a period of study in Rome afterwards, he carried a whole
continental heritage with him when he set out for Australia. After he
arrived there in the 1920s, he made a little statue of a lion, which you
can still see in the Art Gallery of NSW. Hoff's lion became the
bonnet ornament of the cars produced by General Motors Holden,
and a version of it is still the logo for Holden today. The cultural
interchange between Australia and Europe began in the nineteenth
century. But then, when you think about it, it began with the First
Fleet. National compartmentalization is a marketable fad in the
minds of commentators who draw a salary for shuffling clichés.
There were Chinese lacquer boxes on sale in the markets of Imperial
Rome. Art travels faster now, but it has always travelled.

A QUESTION FOR DIAMOND JIM

The nickname 'Diamond Jim' fitted James McClelland the way 'Big Julie from Chicago' fitted the gangster in *Guys and Dolls* who rolled spotless dice, with the difference that Diamond Jim wasn't acting. He was really like what his nickname said: spruce, sparkling, charming, the Australian politician with the touch of the patrician, the one whose jacket sat neatly on his shoulders, and who didn't sweat even in the hot weather. In the late 1980s, at a time when I knew less than I should have known about what had been going on in Australia for the previous quarter of a century, I interviewed him for the one and only series of my talk show that I ever taped in Sydney. All the other series were taped in the UK, were broadcast there in the first instance, and appeared in Australia only in syndication. Predictably (predictably in retrospect, that is: if it had been fully predictable beforehand, I would never have made such a blunder), the series I made in Australia was the one greeted by the Australian critics as being, compared with the others, a patronising, sub-standard rush-job designed to lower Australia's repute in the eyes of the watching world.

Actually we took great care with that series, and especially with the casting. Along with the veteran painter Lloyd Rees and the already illustrious poet Les Murray – I think it was the first mainstream television show Murray was ever asked to do – James McClelland was one of the guests I was determined to get on the air. I was pleased that he said yes, and he seemed pleased enough at the level of questions he was asked, but he must have been surprised not to have been questioned more closely about his presence in the blast area during the explosion that has come to be remembered in Australia as the Dismissal. I knew roughly what had happened: Whitlam, as Prime Minister, had incorrectly believed that his appointee as Governor General, Sir John Kerr, would not fire him.

McClelland, a member of Whitlam's Labor government and also a life-long friend of Kerr's, had not guessed that Kerr would push the button on Whitlam. After Kerr duly did so, McClelland had never talked to Kerr again. It was a sore point, but that was no good reason for my steering clear of it. If I had realised just how sore a point it was, I would have asked McClelland about little else. I wasn't there to soothe his ego, which, although nothing extravagant, was immaculately brushed, like his hair.

The truth was that McClelland, the most intelligent of men, had become a walking reminder of just how wrong one man can be about another. In a key sentence from his wonderfully entertaining autobiography *Stirring the Possum* he stirs the possum by putting his elegant finger on the exact nub of the whole Dismissal issue. At this point in his book, McClelland is delivering his assessment of Kerr's *Matters for Judgment*, an embarrassingly limp apologia written by Kerr in the last and unhappiest part of his life. McClelland's key sentence goes like this:

> At no point does he [i.e. Sir John Kerr: CJ] explain why, apart from his fear that it would ensure his own sacking, he did not simply say to Whitlam: If you can't get supply by a certain date I may have to dismiss you.

According to McClelland, the best Kerr can say for himself is that he couldn't warn Whitlam that dismissal might be in the wind, because if he *had* warned Whitlam, Whitlam might have dismissed *him*, Kerr: in other words, it might have been a race to telephone the Queen. As Paul Kelly convincingly shows in his admirable book devoted exclusively to the subject, *November 1975*, the race to the telephone was a mythical scenario: Whitlam could never have got the Palace to dismiss Kerr before Kerr had irretrievably dismissed Whitlam. But those technicalities aside, McClelland hits the point that would have mattered anyway, even if Kerr's warning Whitlam had cost Kerr his job: that Kerr should have been thinking about more than the job. Thinking about more than the job *was* the job, or else the job meant nothing. McClelland quotes devastatingly to show Kerr advancing his own silence as some kind of qualification instead of the opposite. 'I kept my own counsel as to the constitutional rights and wrongs of what was happening until I decided what must be done . . .' But keeping his counsel was exactly what Kerr couldn't do and still be acting according to the Constitution, since the constitutional provisions on the reserve powers stated clearly that among the Governor General's first duties were to advise and warn.

He neither advised nor warned. Kerr resented Whitlam's using him as a rubber stamp. But Kerr had already kept silent on the crucial Loans issue: i.e. he had submitted to being a rubber stamp at the very moment when he should have been asking Whitlam what his government thought it was doing by trying to raise money privately so that it would be able to go on governing without the Senate's approval. By being silent about that, Kerr tacitly encouraged Whitlam to slide further into folly. McClelland rather soft-pedals that last point, as you might imagine; when it came to a choice, he was definitely Whitlam's man and not Kerr's; a preference for which it is hard to blame him. (I should say at this point that I, too, find Whitlam's charm hard to resist: if I had ever worked for him, I would have been no better than anybody else at telling him what he didn't want to hear.) Personal preferences aside, McClelland in his memoirs is as good as any dramatist about the main characters stalking the halls of Canberra in those stirring times – Kerr, whose injured vanity decided the issue; Whitlam, who didn't see the crunch coming; and himself, who should have foreseen it all but somehow didn't. On a detached estimate, however, McClelland can be seen (a) to have got Kerr right, (b) to have been too hard on himself, and (c) to have been nothing like hard enough on Whitlam – or, rather, on Whitlam's government. That government, with McClelland included, belonged to Whitlam to a dangerous extent. By even thinking of raising money to govern without the Senate's approval of Supply, Whitlam was preparing to govern without a parliament – the very thing that the Governor General's reserve powers are designed to stop.

While proposing to govern without a parliament, Whitlam was already governing without a cabinet: scarcely anyone knew about the Loans scheme, which was cooked up in a secrecy that was a tacit avowal of its fundamental unreality. The Loans affair was merely the latest in a series of bizarre episodes that had reduced Whitlam's administration to a wreck. His government had become deeply and deservedly unpopular with the electorate. McClelland is well within his rights when he says that it had already recovered from its low point and might have gone on recovering. (Certainly he himself had

brought a welcome air of competence to his own department.) If an
election had been called for late enough in the following year, Labor
might conceivably have been back with a chance. But here, again,
is a nub, and this time it is a nub that not even the unflappable
Diamond Jim could bring himself to point out with the fine flourish
due to it. Malcolm Fraser, leading the Liberal opposition, was ready
to break the crisis by offering his assent to a double dissolution with
a late election date. Whitlam refused the offer. Whitlam preferred the
crisis: he thought he could face the opposition down. And indeed
he might have done, if Kerr had given him another week. But Kerr's
decision isn't the issue. The issue is how Whitlam got his government
into that situation. He did it by making his isolated will prevail.
There is no point making a fuss about how the Governor General
carried on like an old Queen if one is unable to contemplate that
the Prime Minister carried on like an autocrat. McClelland is ready
to accuse himself of having been bamboozled by Kerr. He is less
ready to admit that he was buffaloed by Whitlam. He can bear the
idea of having failed to guess what the position of *de facto* Head of
State would do to a man of Kerr's character. What he couldn't bear
was having failed to guess how the advent of charismatic leadership
would affect the Labor Party.

Diamond Jim McClelland knew all there was to know about the
Labor Party, but only up until then. In the past, the Labor Party
leaders had been men like Ben Chifley or H. V. Evatt: sometimes
highly qualified, but never stars. In the future, the Labor Party leaders
would be men like Bob Hawke and Paul Keating: stars even when
they were not highly qualified. Whitlam was the transitional figure:
the first star, and thus a man utterly unlike McClelland himself.
McClelland had glamour, but it was not a pose: he was a man of the
people. He was just one of those men who never have to think about
dressing the part, because they have natural taste, and inspire awe for
just that reason. Though both his parents were Irish, only his mother
was a Catholic, which was a flaw in his Labor pedigree, but a minor
one: in all other respects he had an impeccably underprivileged
background, and the arrival of the Depression even ensured that his
precocious admission to university would not distract him from a
lifetime of doing it the hard way. There were no Commonwealth
Scholarships in those days – they were introduced after the war, by
Menzies – so the brilliant young man had to forgo his opportunity.

He joined the work force, and was soon caught up in the radical politics raging within it. With capitalism so obviously on the point of collapse, he gave his allegiance to Trotsky, after the Communists in the Federated Ironworkers had shown him what Stalinism was made of. (The real news about what Trotsky had been made of was at that time harder to come by than it is now.) Having actually read the works of Karl Marx from end to end, he had no trouble arguing the Stalinists out of the room, but always from the premise that it was he who was the true proletarian. Although obvious officer material, he spent the war in the ranks. It was only after the war, with Australia unaccountably booming under the Menzies government, that McClelland enrolled in Sydney University's Law School and began his ascent to the seriously well-cut jacket.

His immaculate grooming never had anything to do with social climbing. For one thing, it is possible, even today, for a man to climb a long way in Australian society while being no better groomed than the Man from Snowy River's horse; and for another, he was too intelligent to restrict his views by forgetting his origins. As his Sydney *Morning Herald* column, written in his retirement, regularly revealed to an enchanted public, he had a capacity to take in the whole texture of Australian life, on all its levels and in all its aspects. He was the kind of natural democrat who charms an audience by treating everyone as a member of an elite, and his later writings – *An Angel Bit The Bride* is the essential collection – can be recommended for the insouciant manner in which they distil the generously sardonic vision that the left-wing intelligentsia in Australia still sorely needs to rediscover in order to be less repellently doctrinaire. He was particularly good about tracing the connection between the deterioration of the language and the corrosion of democratic values. The demagogic tendency to brand grammatical accuracy as elitism was one he spotted early. On the other wing, he was properly alarmed by the cosiness of the alliance formed by the media multibillionaires and the Labor Party hierarchy. Though the prospect of rule by oligarchy didn't put him off a republic, it would have been interesting, had he lived until the 1999 referendum, to find out whether he thought that the same prospect had put the public off a republic.

Unlike many men who have enjoyed power, he had a deep and lasting suspicion of it. Really he thought its concentration should be limited by statute, and he might have pursued the point with more vehemence if he hadn't also thought that the possession of great privilege was its own punishment. In a television studio green room in Sydney one afternoon, Diamond Jim told me the best story about Rupert Murdoch's meanness (what the Americans would call cheapness) I have ever heard. The essence of the story was that Murdoch had stiffed him for the price of a hamburger, but what doubled me up was the way Jim conveyed Murdoch's anxiety that the stratagem might not work, and that he, Murdoch, might actually have to part with money. Apparently Murdoch, to convey the proposition that he had forgotten his wallet, actually patted his pockets. Jim showed me how Murdoch did it: a kind of ritual palpation, as a man might caress something flat with fingers archly surprised that it isn't full. A cat may look at a king, and Jim, always the coolest cat in town, had looked hard at a king among hustlers.

All his life, there wasn't much Diamond Jim missed. But he did miss the significance of Whitlam's overbearing personality: or anyway he missed it at the time, when it mattered. Perhaps, like many clever men – although lawyers are usually proof against this – he had trouble believing that another clever man might be blind to his own impulsiveness. Perhaps, in those hectic hours at the finale, he just lacked time to think: he was a cool customer, but there was fire in the corridors. Perhapses aside, the magnitude of his error is evident from what he could never bring himself to get angry about. He got angry, very angry, about Kerr's failure to tell Whitlam what he had in mind. But he never got angry about Whitlam's failure to ask. If Whitlam, instead of appointing John Kerr as Governor General, had appointed James McClelland, and then patronised James McClelland by not asking his opinion on the Supply crisis, James McClelland would have been no less likely than Kerr to deduce that Whitlam was living in a dream world. The difference between Kerr and McClelland is that McClelland would have raised the issue. But if Whitlam had not listened, McClelland would have had to dismiss him. If I could go back in time to our television interview, that would be the extra question I would ask McClelland: if you had been in Kerr's shoes and Whitlam had ignored your advice, would you have dismissed Whitlam? And if McClelland had said no, I would have asked: then why would you have taken the job?

His answer would have been dazzling. Everything he said was a delight. Kerr died a broken man, and one of the things that broke him must have been his being denied the company of a friend who had always given him what he lacked himself – a pretty wit, lightness of spirit, the unfair ease of personal grace. The last time I saw McClelland was on a summer evening in Blue's Point Road in North Sydney. I was walking down the hill to the harbourside apartment block where I often stay when I'm in town, and I found him lounging suavely at an open-air café with the beautiful television presenter Jennifer Byrne. If she had only her looks to go on, Jenny Byrne would be a prize, but she has excellent literary credentials as well, a virtue she had demonstrated by admiring the prose styles of both myself and Diamond Jim. To put it briefly, she was a protégée of both of us. Though I was old enough to be her father and Diamond Jim was almost old enough to be mine, here were two men who made no secret of their belief that helping to keep a brilliant young lady like this entertained with repartee was a reason for existence. Epigrams flew like darts. Aphorisms rose and fell like swords. Quotations were swung like clubs. It was as if the duty of redeeming fair Amoret had fallen not to Britomart but to Sohrab and Rustum. The names of Voltaire, Hume and Proust were being invoked as the sky grew dark. I remember thinking even at the time – this was years before the Sydney Olympics, although their spirit was in the air – that Australia would be the place to be in the next century. It had always had the substance, and now it was getting the style: and a lot of the style came from people who were fair-minded, fastidious and public-spirited beyond the call of the job – people like Diamond Jim McClelland.

The Monthly, November 2005

Postscript

Putting Denis Healey and James McClelland together in the same book has been a reminder to me that there is a question to be asked about cultivated politicians. In their profession, does a well-furnished mind help, or does it hinder? Certainly it works to better popular effect when well concealed. In the case of Australia, the people enjoy eloquence from their politicians but they seldom trust it. Gough Whitlam's manifest educational superiority doubled the blame heaped on his clever head when events caught him out. The most

powerful weapon Robert Hawke brought to his long reign as Prime
Minister was the ability to persuade, which he learned in the
crushingly boring meetings of the trade unions, and not from
Cicero. Paul Keating, on the other hand, had art-hungry tastes that
all too often expressed themselves as contempt, which eventually
dished him. The Australian intelligentsia as a whole, and the media
commentariat in particular, could never detect John Howard's most
solid advantage as a leader: when he spoke, the people felt that he
was one of them. Plainly he was clever, but he did not sound
different. Somewhere in there a thesis lurks, which might be countered by the fact that Robert Gordon Menzies sounded as elevated as
Pericles. There is a book in it. A measure of Australia's total
achievement as perhaps the most highly developed of the liberal
democracies is that there would be plenty for the author to go on.
Nor would it be a book deprived of colour, clashing characters,
flashing dialogue and slapstick comedy. Many paragraphs could be
devoted solely to the question of how Malcolm Fraser, the born-to-
the-purple patrician among the Australian prime ministers, was
caught in a hotel corridor without his pants.

EXIT JOHN HOWARD

There is a version of American cultural imperialism that infects even the supposedly liberal and artistic. In *Newsweek* recently, some confident dunce announced that France has ceased to produce any great artists who might impress the world. Bernard-Henri Lévy, normally not one of my heroes, commendably flew the tricolour by pointing out that America was not the world, and that it would be enough for the French to go on producing artists who might impress France.

But on the political front, at virtually the same time, there was an even more patronising instance of this kind of cultural imperialism. It made less noise only because the victims didn't realise they were being patronised. According to Hendrik Hertzberg in the *New Yorker*, Australia's long-serving Prime Minister John Howard lost his job in the latest election principally because he committed Australian troops to the invasion of Iraq in 2003. This interpretation is hard to refute – one thing certainly came after the other – but it makes you wonder why, in that case, he didn't lose his job in the previous election, in 2004.

A view less in thrall to geopolitics might suggest Howard lost this time not because he stayed too long in Iraq, but because he stayed too long in office. His successful opponent Kevin Rudd was clever enough to spot that no other issue really mattered except the incumbent's hubristic estimation of his own indispensability. Howard had stepped into the same trap occupied for more than a decade by the Labor Party, which, in one doomed campaign after another, had made everything depend on the one leading role, recast periodically after the previous guy tanked. When Howard, despite murmurings from his own colleagues, decided that nobody except himself could win, he was unmistakeably announcing that he deserved to lose.

The question, now that the Liberal Party has paid a proper

penalty for letting everything depend on Howard, is whether the Labor Party hasn't bought a mass of trouble by letting everything depend on Rudd. Those of us who had long wanted the Labor Party to become electable again, but who think that Rudd has almost nothing to say, will be watching with interest to see how he comes good on the two main issues he said were crucial. These were not, as Hertzberg contends, Iraq and climate change. They were (a) the Future, which would demand New Leadership, and (b) the Educational Revolution. According to Rudd's repeated announcements, the Future lay ahead, and not in some other direction that an older man might seem to advocate or represent. Australia's continuing advance into this Future, featuring New Leadership, would be ensured by an Educational Revolution, in which every school pupil would be issued with a computer.

That Howard was unable to find the words to counter either of these vacuous propositions was in keeping with his inborn reluctance to talk tripe, but was also a clear indication that he had run out of tactical acumen. He should have had a few paragraphs ready to say that a government has no business providing a vision for the future. The job of government is to preserve the freedom and justice that have already been established, while furthering both to the full extent in which one of them does not interfere with the other. Beyond that, the vision of the future will be provided by the creativity of the people. He should also have found a few paragraphs to say that Rudd's scheme of equipping every Australian child with a computer is less likely to guarantee an educational revolution than to provide an incentive for the children to multiply their illiteracy.

A real educational revolution would restore the erstwhile capacity of Australia's young people to read, write and do elementary arithmetic in their heads. In the final minutes of his televised debate with Rudd, Howard started to make that last point, but he had nothing ready except an incoherent sentence, having relied once too often on his faith that the self-evident would make itself obvious. It was already all too obvious that he had forgotten how to fight anyone except the wiser voices in his own party, who had been too timid with their doubts. The voting public saw that the old lion was limping, and down he went. Democracy worked.

Democracy works better in Australia than almost anywhere. An American might usefully tell Australia that it needs a limitation on the number of prime-ministerial terms – if the governmental term remains at three years, then three terms for the prime minister should be enough – but on most other topics the Australians need no instruction from abroad about how to run a country, or about how they might be failing by international standards of morality. To the extent that international standards of morality exist, Australia is doing more to set them than to undermine them: Australia, after all, is the country where immigrant minorities have the best chance, and if the indigenous minority continues to be disadvantaged, it nevertheless has prominent leaders who would like to see their people granted a final freedom – the freedom from being patronised as natural victims. (It was interesting, as the election campaign period got into the home stretch, that Noel Pearson, the most formidable of the Aboriginal leaders and one of the most impressive political analysts in Australia of whatever background, went public with his opinion that Howard was more to be trusted than Rudd. Or it would have been interesting, if Pearson's remarks had fallen into the category of those that the Howard-hating consensus could allow itself to hear.)

Most of Australia's problems – seen by commentators on the spot as proof that the whole of Western civilisation is in deadly danger from the spreading influence of American imperialism – come from conflicting ideas about how to do the right thing. Institutionalised evil is hard to find, and even the corruption is on a small scale, although often inventive. Admittedly it is relatively easy to govern a country whose population is no bigger than that of New York state, but quite a lot of creative thought has been put into the job since Federation in 1901: the creative thought of a political class which has consistently been underestimated by Australia's massed ranks of *bien-pensant* intellectuals, some of whom might have spent too much time bashing Hertzberg's ear when he attended the Sydney Writers' Festival in May 2007. Perhaps they stunned him with the orchestrated confidence of their monocellular opinion that Howard had ruled for eleven and a half years only by trickery. That opinion, with its implied insult to the intelligence of the electorate that had been tricked, helped to keep the Labor Party out of power for as long as its leadership listened to the pundits. When finally a man emerged who had the strength of character either to sidestep or to ignore virtually every issue the pundits had declared vital, his party won.

But let Hertzberg be certain that Rudd ignored him too. Whatever the *New Yorker* and *Vanity Fair* might say in the US – or the *Guardian* and the *Independent* in London – when Rudd is inspired to bring some of the Australian troops home from Iraq it will be because that country has moved closer to being a functioning and reasonably secure democratic state, and not because he disapproved of the invasion. He did disapprove of it, but in this election he didn't make his disapproval a major issue, because he knew it wouldn't fly. In leaving room for the assumption that Rudd thought otherwise, Hertzberg has put the *New Yorker* into the service of a fiction on the very topic about which it is currently most proud of speaking fact.

Fictions are tempting because they give fact shape. Hertzberg has built the best part of his career on respecting the texture of reality, in which facts are recalcitrant. His excellent Penguin collection of political writings, called simply *Politics*, shows that he can pay due regard to conflicting ideas and emotions. During the Vietnam War he served his country in the navy: his war service didn't affect his old-style socialist convictions – which to a large extent he still has, even though his fighting prose is now surrounded by advertisements for furs and jewellery – but it did help to give him the subtlety of nuance by which he could call anti-war polemicists to order if he thought their views simplistic.

With regard to Iraq he has allowed that subtlety to lapse, and it will be interesting to see how fast he can regain it if the news coming out of Iraq continues to improve. We should pay him the compliment of trusting him to greet improving news as welcome rather than otherwise. Hertzberg is a good enough reporter to know how alluring the temptation to shape the facts can be, and many a time he must have had to face the cruel moment when something that sounds good has to be struck out because it might not be so. On a final point, has he asked himself where he got the idea that Howard was 'humiliated' when Rudd spoke 'perfect' Mandarin to the Chinese leaders at the APEC conference in Sydney? Howard is a bit harder to humiliate than that, and would have been well aware that speaking the other chap's language is often the reverse of a qualification: Anthony Eden, after all, spoke perfect Arabic to Colonel Nasser. Howard might very well feel humiliated after losing the election, his seat, and his reputation for infallibility, but all that will pass, and he will be remembered as an outstanding prime minister even by critics who could bring themselves to praise him for nothing except his cunning.

There are a lot of us who sincerely hope that Kevin Rudd will earn a comparable eminence, as the head of a cleanly elected government in a rising country, an ex-colony which, having concentrated and transcended all the virtues of the old empire that gave it birth, is now busy providing an example to the world of what can be done by a bunch of creative people backed up by prudent management and double-entry bookkeeping. That last bit was always Howard's ace in the hole. Often speaking from comfortably subsidised positions, Australia's *gauchiste* commentators called him a money-grubber and condemned the voters for being too easily seduced by prosperity, but more than half those voters ticked the box for him as long as he looked as if he still had his head screwed on.

Certainly Rudd himself never made the mistake of calling Howard anything less than competent. That was one of the ways the new boy won the election: he promised to do almost everything that Howard had already done, but just do it younger. For Howard to answer that one, he would have had to attack Rudd's hairstyle, pointing out the cruel truth: that it's an incipient comb-over, and that time, which improves most men, is the mortal enemy of any man who can't accept it. But Rudd might start looking and sounding less bogus as he gets used to office. Power can do things for you, until the day it doesn't.

The Australian, December 22, 2007

Postscript

Though I had always favoured Howard against the popinjays that the Labor Party put up against him, you will notice that I was careful to give Kevin Rudd credit for a deserved win and to wish him well. The Labor Party, and not the Liberal Party, is, after all, the one I favour by upbringing and conviction. There is plenty of good will for Kevin Rudd and some of it is mine, albeit aimed from a distance. But even during his first year in office – which from the media angle was all honeymoon – he showed himself capable of a level of foolishness that would have disqualified him if it had been generally known before his election, and might well deprive him of a second term later on. His denunciation of the invasion of Iraq had always been a tenable position, and when he brought our troops home he was fulfilling a promise. But when they paraded past him he praised them for having risked paying the necessary price for the defence of freedom. Hypocrisy is bad enough, but inanity is worse. Similarly, it went beyond cynicism, and far into comedy, to tell the old-age pensioners that he couldn't live on their pension either, so he would do something about it the following year, after his experts had reported. What would they report? That thousands of wrinklies had died of hunger? Has he ever heard of Tartuffe? And even some of his media supporters are still wondering why he permitted a story to leak out that President Bush had proved himself ignorant during a telephone conversation. As we go to press, Prime Minister Rudd has still not given a satisfactory explanation of what he was up to, but it seems fair to infer that he was grandstanding. To be Prime Minister of Australia should be a grandstand big enough for anybody. It certainly was for John Howard, who would never have done any of these things; who had a mind of his own with no comb-over to conceal its inner workings; and who might soon be missed even by his sworn enemies. At least, with him, you knew where you were.

ABR 300

The *Australian Book Review*, commonly called the *ABR*,
asked for messages from contributors to celebrate
its 300th issue in April 2008. This was mine.

In Australia, one of the penalties for having survived long enough
as some kind of literary figure is to be asked, in one's senior years,
to write a chapter in the latest distinguished volume devoted to the
history of Australian literature. Such requests, though flattering,
oblige the victim to write a story from which he must leave himself
out. My powers of self-abnegation stop well short of that, so I always
say no. Why should I leave myself out when I have so many
contemporaries to do it for me?

But if I were forced at gun-point to write such a chapter, I would
begin by saying that the growing prominence of the independent
literary magazines in recent years has helped to create an inhabitable
Australian literary world, and that the *ABR* has been in the vanguard
of this development. Long wished for, an Australian literary world
was slow to arrive, partly because it was so keenly awaited: the pot
grew nervous from being watched. Especially in the field of poetry,
the pre-modern era was dependent on the newspapers, with the
Bulletin counting as a kind of amplified newspaper. The requirements
of popularity had some strong results. (Les Murray has always
been right to stress the importance of what he was first to call the
'newspaper poem', and, gratifyingly often, he still writes it.) Looking
back to my own beginnings, I remember the magazines as being few,
thin and hard to find unless you were attached to the same university
as they were.

Actually this memory is inaccurate: it was always worthwhile to
keep a file of *Meanjin*, for example, and when James McAuley started

Quadrant he raised the stakes for everyone. But when I sailed for England in the early 1960s, that was the way the Australian picture looked to me. From here on, my brief account gets personal. Peter Porter, I suspect, has a more informative story about what it meant to become an expatriate Australian poet. He had more reason to think about what was involved, because poetry was his whole endeavour, and the problem of maintaining a spiritual presence in the homeland he had physically left would be a matter of life and death to him. I could never claim that kind of thoughtfulness. Working more by instinct than by strategy, and always more by luck than judgment, I had a big enough task establishing and maintaining a poetic reputation in Britain, where my other reputation as a professional entertainer seemed determined to get in the way. Get caught on screen with your arms around Margarita Pracatan and see what it does to your status as a lyric poet.

But precisely because Britain was in possession of a fully developed literary world, it had room for someone who broke its rules of dignity. In Britain, everyone is aware, even if they hate the idea, that the poet who doesn't fit the picture might be part of the picture. One could be given the cold shoulder – any number of cold shoulders – yet not be frozen out. Even my poems about Australia found space in the literary pages of London. Eventually I found myself writing more and more such poems, and Australian editors – who were still keeping their eye, as always, on the British and American magazines – began asking to reprint them. I was glad to comply, although I hasten to insist that I had no plans for making a *reconquista*. It had long been apparent to me that the expatriate, should he wish for a return, was up against the same difficulties as a space traveller making a re-entry into the Earth's atmosphere: unless he got the angle exactly right, he would burn up, with the implacable Australian press waiting on the ground to interview the fragments. But really my poetry was proof that I had never been away.

It had already proved that to me. Any decent poem begins in feelings so deep that we might as well call them instinctive, and what I had been discovering was the nature of my instinct, which had been formed in Australia and never forgotten it, whatever my conscious mind might have thought. With a whole heart, I can thank the Australian magazine editors for having spotted this almost before I did. At the head of these editors was Peter Rose, who generously made space available in the *ABR* for poems I had published in Britain and America but which might also appeal to Australian readers who had no easy access to the periodicals they first appeared in. Later on there were other editors, and there were poems which had their first publication in Australia, but the *ABR* continued to provide me with my most welcoming landing strip for things I was sending in, or bringing back, from abroad: it was my Edwards Air Force Base. The *ABR* even ran the full text of the address I gave when I received, in Mildura, the Philip Hodgins memorial medal, which remains my sole big literary prize, and the only one I will ever need.

When I published that address as a chapter in a book, I gave the book the same title as the chapter, *The Meaning of Recognition*. Self-dramatising is what I do for a living – everything I write, in whatever form, is an unreliable memoir – but the drama, I would like to think, is not always entirely about me. In writing about the magnificent but cruelly abbreviated achievement of Philip Hodgins, I was an expatriate trying to fulfil what I think of as part of the expatriate's duty: to help give Australia to the world, and to bring a world view to the task of clarifying Australia's position to itself. Laid out as an argument, the full story of how I view that duty would take a book all on its own, but I would be surprised if my work had not been telling the story by implication for these many years. The *ABR* has played a crucial part in helping me to tell it, so I have a personal reason for being grateful for the magazine's existence, and I am sure there has been many a contributor, over the course of its three hundred issues, who could say the same. Finally it comes down to the importance of having a forum in which the concept of intellectual freedom trumps all other political standpoints: a forum in which, wrapped in our separate togas, we can speak our minds to each other without being knifed on the way home. No literary magazine is worthy of its title if it doesn't provide that. The *ABR* does.

THE VOICE OF JOHN ANDERSON

There is a tone of voice that you can hear in the way a sentence is balanced, even if you are not equipped to understand its content. 'What the idealist has, in fact, to show is that there is no real distinction, and the answer is that in that case there can be no real relation.' Thus wrote John Anderson, in *Studies in Empirical Philosophy*, and as soon as I read that sentence I was home. Actually I was leaving home. I read it on the ship to England. At Sydney University I had managed to avoid his lectures, as I had avoided the lectures of everyone else, but his spirit was all around the place. Everyone you met was either an Andersonian or a non-Andersonian. Now, as the Indian Ocean ran slowly past, I was an Andersonian too. Or perhaps a non-Andersonian. Either way, his name was in there somewhere. His name was all over Australia's intellectual world. For good or ill, he was the national philosopher.

If Nietzsche had lived long enough, he would have been horrified at the consequences of becoming the national philosopher of Germany. But to be regarded as a national philosopher is not necessarily a bad thing. For two hundred years, Britain's national philosopher was Hume, and to a great extent he still holds the job, because in the twentieth century none of the attempts to replace him quite worked out. Closely identified with Bloomsbury, G. E. Moore was thought too comfortable by those who were reluctant to accept Bloomsbury as the epitome of civilized Britain. Bertrand Russell was thought incorrigibly silly by anyone who found him less the embodiment of human reason than he did. A. J. Ayer was never thought silly, but he did seem to be having too good a time. For a while, among those serious about literature, Dr Leavis was drafted into the role, but the appointment looked less judicious when he showed signs that he believed it. Uniting all the candidates was a debt to Hume's empiricism, which was still there when all their separate visions frayed. The first embodiment of the national way of thinking remained the best. In Italy, Benedetto Croce achieved the same position. He started much later, but then so did a united Italy. It seems to be one of the characteristics of any nation united by more than power that it will boast one man universally agreed upon as exemplifying its tone of thought. In Britain, the tone of voice is exemplified by Shakespeare and all the poets, but the tone of thought is exemplified by Hume the Scot. If my own country, Australia, has such a thing as a tone of thought –and I think it has – then the man who brought it into being was another Scot: John Anderson.

In his lectures at Sydney University from the late Thirties onwards – he was still there when I was a student in the late Fifties – Anderson carried the torch for realism. The pluralism that he claimed for himself was underpinned by the realism that he claimed for all the philosophers who ever mattered. He influenced whole generations of students, who in turn, because of Sydney University's central place in the tertiary education system, influenced the teachers' colleges, the schools, the broadcasting networks, the emergent media elite, and eventually the entire culture. Plenty of people were against Anderson, especially if they were religious. Catholic archbishops pronounced anathema upon him. My own Presbyterian minister, when he saw that I was going to the Devil, blamed the influence of 'that man Anderson'. In the absence of a ship back to Scotland, his enemies recommended a slow boat to China. Nor were all his enemies on the clerical right. There were plenty on the atheistic left who thought his realistic stance a reactionary denial of the legitimate aspirations of suffering mankind. He was always being attacked from one wing or the other, often on the supposition that he had glossed over a difficulty in his line of reasoning.

He seldom had, but he was easy to misrepresent. Until his last years, he was practically in samizdat. His lectures were his main writings, and they circulated exclusively in note form until he collected them in the only book to bear his name while he still breathed: *Studies in Empirical Philosophy*. Typically I failed to enrol myself in the philosophy school while he was still active: it might have been too useful, too engrossing, too apt to distract me from the essential fields of student journalism, amateur drama, and bad poetry written late at night. But I was surrounded by Andersonians and picked up enough of their acerbic parlance to conceive a thirst for the whole picture. When I went to England the book was part of my luggage. Everything else in my bags might have been ill chosen (as I related in *Falling Towards England*, I was the only Australian ever to arrive in an English winter without a sweater), but I had brought the right book. Looking back on it, I can see my belated immersion in Anderson's lectures as the first step in a long process of coming to terms with the country I had left behind: meaning, of course, that I hadn't left it behind at all, but had embarked on a roundabout way of discovering it for the first time. Anderson would probably not have approved. Although he knew how to let his hair down in old age – I personally knew a famous beauty who had to take to the stairs to outrun him at a party thrown by the Downtown Push – he was no bohemian. He expected his students to buckle down, pass their regular tests in logic, and keep abreast of the background reading. My future wife won the Philosophy Prize for two successive years but she took endless pages of detailed notes while doing so: his powers of compression were a match even for her powers of application. Anderson wasn't for dabblers. He would not have been pleased by the idea of someone reading his work unsystematically as literature. But for those of us condemned by our nature to read him in no other way, there is a lot to go on. Scattered among his dense pages of symbols are plain statements fit to resonate for a lifetime.

For Anderson, realism was the bedrock and idealism the aberration. But since so many kinds of idealism had been so prevalent for so long, the first task of the realist was to combat idealism in all its forms, starting with the pious notion that idealism could annul contention between social forces. This perpetual struggle squared well with his convictions about the necessity of conflict. Later on, when I read Croce, I recognized, in the principles that Croce had inherited and developed from Vico and Hegel, the same emphasis that Anderson had been handing down from his lectern like a renegade Presbyterian minister preaching the inevitability of an unjust world. 'We can't make the world safe for goodness,' said Anderson, 'it exists and develops in struggle with evil.' For Anderson there could be no 'higher' reality: there was only reality, in which the facts were good enough. Realism 'presupposes as the formal solution of any problem the interaction of complex things.' The complex things would not simplify themselves in obedience to a wish, least of all if the wish were a plan.

Anderson's withering contempt for social planning had far-reaching consequences for his political vision. It was not just that he had, like Pareto, a well-developed instinct for the law of unintended consequences. He didn't even much like the intended consequences. The welfare mentality he thought essentially servile. (His view of the welfare state as a control mechanism was his point of contact with the Sydney Libertarians, from whom he otherwise differed in most respects, beginning with his capacity to own a watch, pay his bills, turn up for work on time and fulfil his duties.) Planning, he thought, applied only to commerce, and therefore never to culture, of which he had an entirely non-utilitarian view. If learning wasn't pursued for its own sake then it could not be learning. 'It is true, of course, that social equality is merely a mirage, but devotion to it has still done much to contribute to the destruction of culture.' (The 'of course' was a typically back-handed placing of the banderillas.) Finally he made the idea part of his definition of culture. He said culture had to do with the opposition to levelling.

In retrospect, Anderson might look like part of a war-time politico-philosophical movement that included von Mieses, Hayek, and Karl Popper. In fact, however, he was out on his own, networking mainly with Plato. Perhaps the necessary reaction to progressive social engineering got into the air along with the idea itself. It was no wonder that Anderson was hated on the far left. The wonder was that he wasn't equally despised in the centre, since he held out very little hope even to the mildest ameliorative impulse. Very little became too little when he expressed his contempt for planning. Planning had, after all, helped to win the war against enemies who, had they prevailed, would certainly have included empirical philosophy on their list of activities to be proscribed. With victory in sight, Arthur Calwell planned Australia's post-war immigration policy. Many of the consequences were, naturally enough, strictly incalculable: the law of unintended consequences did not cease to apply. But the calculable consequences worked out quite well, and not just in the field of commerce. The country was transformed, incomparably for the better. Had Anderson lived long enough, he would have been required by his innate honesty to deal with the patent fact that his country – to which he himself had come as a migrant – had planned its future and succeeded in almost all departments, including that of culture. He would have been in the uncomfortable position of a philosopher counting himself lucky that his best pupils hadn't listened.

But they had listened; and being his best pupils they had listened critically, because critical listening was the best thing he taught. Dedicated always to his war against the ideal, he was reluctant to sum up his philosophical teachings: a summary might have smacked of the transcendental unification that his pluralism existed to stave off. But he once let slip that if forced to the point he might say that goods do not conflict. (It is interesting that Isaiah Berlin, himself tentative on the subject, decided that they probably do.) The best evidence that Anderson might have been right on the point could be seen among his pupils. Those with soft hearts for their fellow man were encouraged to develop hard heads. Anderson's toughness of intellect was thus socially beneficial while he was alive. As always happens, there were prematurely middle-aged reactionaries in three-piece suits who were glad to have their prejudices endorsed from the pulpit, but the typical young Andersonians had a thirst for the common good, and were grateful to the magnificent old man that he warned them so convincingly against regarding their mission as a picnic. Beyond that, there was his chastening example to writers of any kind, even if critical enquiry was not their field. In his ability to analyse and punish loose language, Anderson was up there with Karl Kraus. Any writer of expository prose who imagined Anderson looking over his shoulder would soon check his flying pen. Perhaps just as importantly in the long run, for the next generation he left a heritage of scepticism that helped set limits to the influence of international *gauchiste* theorizing, so that the characteristic tone of the Australian realistic voice survived and flourished in the back-waters and bunyip-pools of the media even as the mainstream became a muddy flood. Eventually Gresham's Law took over, but never completely. Anderson's tart remarks set a tone for the bright, and *Studies in Empirical Philosophy* is one of those books that will always attract the sort of reader who thirsts for the acerbic.

The Monthly, July 2005

BEA MILES, VAGRANT

As I recorded in my book *Unreliable Memoirs*, I did a disastrous stint as a Sydney bus conductor to earn money while I was a student. The story about trapping the old lady's head in the folding doors was true. But I did something even worse to Bea Miles. She was the town's most famous eccentric, even more famous than Arthur Stace, the man who wrote 'Eternity'. Everybody in Sydney knew that Bea Miles was allowed to travel free on public transport. The main reason was that she kicked up a tremendous fuss if she was asked to pay. She looked like a bag lady minus the bags but she could kick like the wrestler Chief Little Wolf uncorking his celebrated flying body-slam at Leichardt Stadium. Everyone had heard of her except me. I tried to sell her a ticket and she went for me.

Luckily most of the violence was verbal, at least initially. 'You f***ing c**t,' she explained. After that her language got worse, but I valiantly persisted in trying to extract the fare. The bus came to the next stop and I attempted to ease her out of the back door. It was like trying to shift a grand piano with rusty castors. The driver got sick of waiting and we were off again, while I continued to point out to her that travelling without paying the correct fare was an offence. Finally a Kelly climbed aboard.

The Kellies were the transport inspectors who trailed the buses by car, ever on the alert for a conductor who might supplement his income by taking the money without pulling the ticket. The Kelly on my case must have been some kind of philosopher. Patiently he explained to me that Miss Miles (the appellation Ms was not yet in vogue) was an asset to the city and that any attempt to extract a fare from her was like trying to argue with the Harbour Bridge. Well, I could vouch for that. He praised her to the skies, specifying her individuality, her bravery, and her incarnation of a modern city's success in preserving the spirit of the frontier. She listened to his encomium, nodding her head in approbation at each point, and then called him a f***ing c**t.

In the next few years, as I roamed the city in search of new pubs where a poet in flight from his allotted studies and yet another failed romance might sit and compose masterpieces, I often saw her jumping on and off buses. I was always careful not to be on any bus she might catch, but one night there she was, sitting down beside me. She searched my face with a burning stare, but nothing happened. She had forgotten me. I have never forgotten her. The difference, there, between an upstart and a legend.

Somebody must know the precise day she disappeared. I suppose it is recorded in the register of births and deaths somewhere. Like thousands of people, I only noticed that the days when you didn't see her were accumulating into weeks, then months, then years. When I myself was down and out in London, I thought of her often. I wondered if my true vocation might not be as a vagrant, and wondered also if I had the panache to bring it off. It takes a kind of courage. In New York, which was the world capital of the bag ladies before Mayor Giuliani waved his magic wand, there was definitely a ranking from stardom to nonentity. A run-of-the-mill bag lady had only a few plastic bags full of stuff. A top-echelon bag lady had a shopping cart piled so high with precious junk that she had to periodically shuffle sideways to see where she was going.

But she had confidence that wherever she was going was no less important than where you were going. And of course it's true. We will all come to dust. The derros, as we once cruelly called them, just start early. Some of them do it with style, and become part of the city's everlasting poetry, like the word Eternity. Bea Miles was one of those. Indeed, for a long while she was the only one: a solitary, mobile *memento mori* roaming without a destination, but reminding us that we, too, are going nowhere in the end.

Time Out Sydney, September 10–16, 2008

Postscript

Sydney, like England, is fond of its eccentrics, and both of the two previous subjects ranked in that category. As far as I know, John

Anderson and Bea Miles never met, although they almost certainly saw each other many times in the street as they went about their separate business. Until the advent of Gough Whitlam, Australian official bodies at all levels had a fine time banning books. John Anderson was a stout warrior against censorship, which he thought inimical to culture. But we shouldn't overlook the awkward fact that he thought exactly the same about egalitarianism. He thought that culture depended on privilege, and he had no notion that privilege could be spread by social engineering. John Rawls came back from the war with a belief that a free society could spread benefits to all. According to Rawls's famous Difference Principle, a society should tolerate no discrepancies that did not benefit the worst off. From Anderson, the worst off seldom got a mention. We can't go to him for generosity or imagination. But if we preen ourselves on possessing either of those things, we can still go to him for the dressing down that we probably need. And if we have any bluster left after that, we can go to Bea Miles.

RACING DRIVERS

NIKKI LAUDA WINS GOING SLOWLY

'The secret', said Nikki Lauda, 'is to win going as slowly as possible.' This remark is sometimes attributed to another and even greater racing driver, Juan Manuel Fangio. Perhaps Nikki Lauda was quoting it without acknowledgment. Anyway, I actually heard Lauda say this, at a pre-race press conference in Portugal in 1984, the year he came back from the burns unit all the way to his second World Championship. As far as I know, I was the only reporter who wrote it down. None of the other Formula One correspondents had come to Estoril to study philosophy and neither had I, but even at the time it struck me as a profound remark from someone who had only one race left to snatch the title, and one way or another I have been thinking about what he said ever since. In its specific application to motor racing, the idea is simply right. You can't win the race unless you finish, and the driver who is kind to his car is most likely to go the distance. A Formula One car has very little redundancy in its make-up: it can be hurt by a single missed gear change. In the turbo days the fiercer drivers blew their engines early. Whatever the current specifications of the formula, the tyres are always critical, so the smooth driver will soon be driving a different car to the one wrestled by the less smooth, no matter how spectacular the latter might look.

Fangio, Jim Clark and Jackie Stewart, three of the all-time great champion drivers (Clark might have won more races than the other two put together if he had not been killed in an accident that wasn't his fault), were all kind to the car. Alain Prost, who won more Grand Prix races at a quicker rate than anybody until Michael Schumacher came along, was considered uncanny even by the other drivers for the way his cars held together: it was as if he could hear what was going on in the engine. Prost was the car's friend. Other drivers treated the car no more tactfully than they treated women. I was actually Nelson Piquet's passenger in a Nissan sports car on the *ad hoc* track at Caesar's Palace hotel in Las Vegas when Mario Andretti went past in a similar car. It was supposed to be a demonstration run but Piquet immediately went frantic to catch up: he always drove with passion and that was his problem. He won the World Championship twice but broke down more often than he should have, and when his passion went he could scarcely drive at all.

Stirling Moss, on the other hand, rarely broke down through his own fault. The main reason he never won a championship was that he condemned himself, through patriotism, to inferior machinery; but he could make it look superior by the economy with which he drove it. When I was making a television special about motor racing I needed an ordinary road licence – though always crazy about cars, I had never learned to drive – and we enrolled Moss as my instructor, starting with the very basics. Thus I was inculcated into his principles, which all sprang from his initial precept that the car, not the man, has the power, and the man's job is not to interfere. Moss never, but never, touched the brake pedal unless the car was moving in a straight line. Braking and changing down were all done before he turned into the corner. As a direct result, he rarely span off. Formula One fans often asked me what it was like to be Moss's passenger on an ordinary motorway. The answer is that it was hair-raising, but not because you thought he might be out of control. His personal car was a tiny Peugeot but it had plenty of hidden oomph – it was a wolf in shrew's clothing – and you just couldn't help wondering if all the huge trucks he went zipping closely past were being driven to the same standard.

Nobody who was following the fast cars in the 1950s will ever forget Eugenio Castellotti. But he didn't last long, either in life or in most of his individual races. In the Mille Miglia he drove his Ferrari on the footpath when the road was full of spectators. He was always over the limit, like Jean Behra, another spell-binder who suffered the same fate. In more recent times, the flamboyant Keke Rosberg lived to retire, but it was something of a miracle: in the old days, before carbon-fibre monocoque construction made a crash more survivable, he would have been killed ten times. Rosberg's style thrilled crowds but it strained the machinery. Gilles Villeneuve earned an undeserved reputation for being thrilling to watch. In his time at Ferrari, the car was a monster. He had to fight it all the way, and would have much preferred to look less dazzling: some people wise in the ways of motor racing still think that Villeneuve was the fastest driver ever but that he never had a car to match his talent. As for Ayrton Senna, he was so superior that he could keep the car right on the limit without breaking it. All the drivers in Formula One are superior, even the duffers, but Senna had the full eleven tenths. His winning strategy depended on his ability to go flat out from the jump, with no time wasted playing himself in. The other drivers were meant to be demoralised straight away and usually were, except for Nigel Mansell, who couldn't be demoralised by a pistol held to his head.

The answer to the question of whether Mansell was as quick as Senna is yes, but Mansell was just that crucial bit less easy on the machinery. Senna wasn't killed by a mistake: he was killed by a component failure, and almost certainly it was not caused by any strain that he imposed – apart, of course, from the strain necessarily imposed by driving the car as fast as it could go, all the time. The most convincing proof of Senna's fundamental smoothness was that even the car he drove in his first year at Lotus (a notoriously fragile beast, it was seemingly designed to fall apart before it left the garage) would go several laps before breaking down and sometimes even won.

On the subject of Michael Schumacher, questions answer themselves. As was true of Fangio, if his car is on the pace then there are few races Schumacher finishes that he does not win, and for the same combination of reasons: ability, strategic judgment, and sympathy with the machinery. (Fernando Alonso might have all these things too, but he also has, for the moment, a slightly faster car.) The second and third reasons matter more than the first, although the first makes better copy. In reality, there was never that much difference in sheer driving ability between Schumacher and, say, Michele Alboreto in the period when they were still racing each other. But Schumacher's car got to the chequered flag and Alboreto's went to the junk yard. In journalism, it is more rewarding to talk about Schumacher's supernatural reflexes than to dwell on his capacity to think ahead, and there is no mileage at all in writing about what doesn't show – his gift for preserving the car against its own inbuilt tendency to disintegrate. A racing car is just the most concentrated possible form of a system tending towards entropy. Schumacher understands the second law of thermodynamics. So did Lauda.

That Lauda's principle has a general application to life might seem a truism. Obviously, as long as you get enough exercise, you will live longer if you minimise the time you spend running for a bus. But it gets interesting when applied to the arts. An artist must concentrate, and the more original he is, the more likely it is that he will focus his mental energy beyond the normal tolerance of the human brain in particular or his body in general, let alone the patience of his loved ones. Even if his compensating relaxations do not destroy him, he might well find life difficult. (As we learn from Claire Tomalin's biography of Jane Austen, the greatest novelist in English was put out of action for ten years by an enforced change of residence.) Proust and his friend the composer Reynaldo Hahn were once touring the garden of a large private house. Proust stopped to look at a rose bush. Hahn left him there, slowly circumnavigated the house, and returned to find him still looking at the rose bush. They remained friends, but only because Proust chose his friends carefully. If you spend half your life in a contemplative trance, you must do your best to ensure that the other half is adapted to that activity, or your life will be short. The secret of applying energy is to economise on effort – to win going as slowly as possible.

The Monthly, April 2006

DAMON HILL'S BRAVEST DAY

In his championship year, I wrote and presented a television special in which Damon Hill said a lot of good things, but he was a guest on my weekly studio talk show when he said his best thing: 'What's the hurry?' His frustrating last season was coming to an end. It would have been easy to blame a slow car: the Arrows had some promise, but it was a farm tractor compared with the Williams he was used to. There was no need for him to admit that his motivation was gone. But it was, so he said so. Self-deprecating candour is typical of him, although nobody should ever underestimate his fierce pride: an abundance of confidence was the main reason why he could afford not to bottle up his honesty.

The scene he was evoking was the mad drag between the starting grid and the first corner on the opening lap of a Grand Prix – any Grand Prix. He had lived with that hurtling potential shambles for the whole of his career, and the day had come when he asked himself this question: the day to quit. The great drivers are never suicidal, but in the matter of the time taken between two given points they must have nothing else in mind except the minimum. Damon had his world championship and was unlikely to get another. He had a wonderful family he loved to be with. He had reached the point where he could weigh his achievements against the risks of going on. He had reached the point where he had started to think. Possessing a good, well-stocked brain to think with, he could reach only one conclusion.

The German writer Ernst Jünger drew a distinction between the generals whose broad view of life helped them to fight well and the generals who fought even better because they were interested in nothing else. There was something to it. The principle can be applied usefully to the top rank of British racing drivers since World War II. Jim Clark, the most conspicuously talented even at the level where supreme talent is a common property, was fully focused on driving. So was Nigel Mansell when he wasn't playing golf with Greg Norman. Mike Hawthorn was too much of a gentleman, James Hunt too much of a wastrel: they both had too much to them. Stirling Moss would have won at least one world championship if he had not been a patriot: for a crucial part of his career he condemned himself to the wrong cars just so as to fly the flag, and when he signed for Mercedes the small print said that he had to come second to Fangio.

The principle breaks down, however, when it is applied to Jackie Stewart. Clever and complex enough to run a business empire and a whole racing team of his own, even better at the social round in Monaco than Damon's father, Jackie Stewart was nevertheless the fully equipped, undistractedly dedicated winning animal. Later on he used the position he had gained by his abilities to transform the sport through placing a new emphasis on safety. It is largely due to him that drivers now walk away from the kind of crash that once killed several of them a season. On various occasions which they forgot instantly but which I treasure as fringe-dwellers always do, I have sat down to dine with four drivers who came back from what once would have been certain death: Niki Lauda, Gerhard Berger, John Watson and Mika Hakkinen. Admittedly I also talked with two who died: Gilles Villeneuve and Ayrton Senna. But they both had accidents so freakish that nothing could have saved them. On the whole, anything that can be done for safety in an inherently dangerous sport has been done, and all because of Stewart. This achievement has rather taken the shine off what he was like as a driver. It should be remembered that when he was in the car the last thing he was thinking of was whether the helicopter was properly fuelled up to take him to hospital. He was thinking of nothing except getting in front and staying there: an aim to which he brought such an intensity of motivation that he has ever since been unable to quell it even when a passenger in a limousine – he is a notorious back-seat driver. Any slow car would become faster when he drove it, but that was not a point he was keen to prove. He took the best machinery by right: the mark of the driver for whom coming first comes first, for whom the sport is a means to an end.

Damon wasn't quite like that. If he had been, he would have taken his chance with McLaren after Frank Williams let him go. McLaren offered a relatively low basic salary but a bonus for each win. Though the wins would never have been a sure thing, in the McLaren he might have got them. In the Arrows he couldn't possibly, but he listened to his financial advisers and went for the guaranteed stipend. It made financial sense – with a family to protect against the press, he could not forgo his estate and its upkeep – but it didn't make racing sense. For the true, compulsive winner, no other kind of sense comes into question. Even for Michael Schumacher, who makes more money than anybody, the money is a tool: if Ferrari had not come through for him with a winning car, he would have left them flat.

In his racing years, Alain Prost was a thinker – 'the Professor' was the right nickname – but he never let ratiocination get in the way of winning. Towards the end of his career, when he dealt himself out of a race in Japan because of the heavy rain, it was a sign that he was done with it. Ayrton Senna didn't live long enough to reach the reasonable moment. He had winning like a disease, and one of the secrets of his mastery was the realisation by the other drivers that he would drive right through them if they didn't give him room. He thought it was God's will that he should ram his rival for the championship (it was Prost), remove both Prost and himself from the track, and so, while losing the race, win the championship on points. Schumacher behaved the same way early on, to the cost of Hill among others. Later Schumacher behaved differently, but he still felt the same way. Leaving Nuvolari and Fangio aside, Schumacher is probably the greatest driver we know about, but one of the reasons is that he has so little difficulty imitating an automaton. Even Senna was more complex. At one point Senna interrupted his colloquy with the Almighty and got off with Elle McPherson. The chances of Schumacher doing such a thing are the chances of his being the driver of the next cab you hail.

To my mind, and not just because I am Australian by birth, Jack Brabham was the most interesting of all the drivers because he won championships in a car he had designed – a car that revolutionised the sport. (If you see a list of world-beating Australian expatriates that leaves Brabham's name out, throw it away: its compiler has no imagination.) But that made Brabham interesting as a driver. As a man, he lived in a motor-racing world. The interest of a man like Damon Hill, when he was still driving, was that he lived in a world bigger than his profession. It can be a handicap. Argentina's Carlos

Reutemann, a Williams driver well capable of pushing the car to its dizzy limit, was such a philosopher that he could walk away, look at the sunset, and decide not to race again. Frank Williams found to his horror that he had hired Diogenes. Damon was never quite like that, but life eventually got into his mind even when he had the hammer down, and when life does that it brings the thought of death with it. You can't get one of those cars out of second gear unless you feel immortal.

Not that a great driver is reckless. There have been some quite good ones who were, but they moved into the past tense at an early stage. Usually they got fired before they could get killed, or else just never made it into Formula One in the first place. An F1 car costs millions if you count in its share of the development outlay, and the owners never like to see one of them scuffed up without good reason. As a passenger in the front seat of a car you can afford to buy, I have been driven on the road or on an empty track by several of the F1 drivers. Three of them were world champions: Nelson Picquet, Alan Jones and Damon Hill. Derek Warwick's career was cut short when Lotus reneged on his contract because Senna wanted no rival in the team. (In his last year alive, I missed the chance to be driven by Senna in a Honda NSX: he turned up a day late at Goodwood, and I thought there might be another time.) Warwick drove me on the highway from his hotel to Monza. The following year I watched him at Le Mans driving the Jaguar racing sports car at 240mph on the Mulsanne straight at dead of night, but his driving then didn't look any faster than how it felt to me that day on the highway. It was like being the narrator in Nicholson Baker's *The Fermata*: all the cars we went past seemed stationary. Moss was an education in ordinary English motorway traffic: his little Peugeot threaded between the lorries like a magic bullet through an undulating canyon. On the Adelaide Grand Prix circuit which had been closed down for our appearance, Alan Jones drove me in a Lamborghini Diablo he had never touched before and hated on sight: top gear was the only one he could find except reverse, and I got several chances to study the Armco as we slithered towards it at a hundred plus. Picquet sometimes looked like a madman on the track but on the road he drove as if he wanted to live, so that he could sleep with more women.

What united all the great drivers, when they were driving on an ordinary road with normal human beings, was that they made you feel safe even as the landscape outside the window turned into a smear. They were so in synch with the car that they could let it perform at its optimum while keeping all their attention on the road ahead. I even felt safe with Jones in the Diablo: he had to wrestle the beast, but he knew exactly what was going on. As the great Australian poet Kenneth Slessor wrote about the effect of Captain Cook's navigational magic on his crew, *Men who ride broomsticks with a mesmerist/Mock the typhoon.* The same went double for Damon Hill, who gave me the fastest ride of all. After the Hungarian Grand Prix in his championship year, we were hurrying to the airport to catch a private jet to Bulgaria. There was a police motorcycle escort to clear our side of the road so that Damon could keep his foot down. Though I pretended, on the soundtrack of the documentary, that I thought of nothing but imminent death, the truth was more complicated. He was too good at his job to take even the tiniest risk off the track. On the track, he upped the ante, as they all do until the day comes when they want to get up from the game and go home.

It might even have happened to Senna one day. All the talk about how his early death preserved him in his glory is just bad poetry. It isn't the responsibility of the racing drivers to have our deaths for us. They have their work cut out leading part of our lives for us: the part, deep in our dreams, where the brave not only deserve the beautiful, but become the beautiful. There was a morning in Adelaide when I was crouching beside our camera crew as they got a low panning shot of Senna's McLaren coming out of the garage. There was traffic in the pit lane so he had to stop for a few seconds right in front of me. While the car yelled with the clutch out, he dipped his yellow helmet to my camera. I could have reached out to tap his visor. He gave me a little wave with the tip of his glove. Then there was the heavy crunch of the clutch coming in on the full eight hundred horsepower, and he was gone in a clap of thunder. It must have been like that at Troy, when Achilles came out of his tent. But Achilles could only fight or sulk. A less classical and therefore more civilised breed of hero, Damon Hill had a full life coming to him, and eventually he chose to lead it. It was his bravest day. Of him I remember a hundred moments. In some of them he was racing, but in most he was being human: playing with his children, putting up with the sponsors, or – perhaps the most characteristic – pointing out, in the most polite possible way, that his team had bungled a pit-stop, cost him the race and quite possibly the championship. There was his flaw on full display: he was reasonable and well-mannered when he should have been shouting and screaming. But he always let the car do that.

Sunday Times, March 18, 2007

Postscript

The above two pieces had their origins in the Formula One era that ended with Michael Schumacher's retirement. Since then, the big money, which had grown increasingly important, has taken over almost completely. Fernando Alonso, Kimmi Raikkonen and Lewis Hamilton have all been worthy champions, but in each case the car they drove was hard to catch if it started from the front of the grid, and the amount of money needed to get the car into that position was beyond the dreams of a previous generation raised on the thrill of men in close contest. What we watch now is a race between conglomerates. Talent and character still come into it, but only at the margins. The arts, too, can injure themselves through progress, but as long as they leave room for the lonely freelance to come up from nowhere and win the crowd's favour, they are safe from the blight of a free market tempered by no logic except its own. The parallel between the arts and the sports – one which I have always loved to draw, because the sports, too, belong in the created world – has thus never been exact.

HANDBILLS

GOING ON IN EDINBURGH

Already preparing for my week of solo evenings on the Edinburgh Fringe in August, I check myself out in the mirror. What have I got to offer? Well, physically not a lot. When Hitler conducted a similar self-examination before his next big speech at Nuremberg, he could at least see a pair of sharply focused eyeballs staring back at him, and his moustache had not yet lost its vibrancy. No part of my face remains vibrant. There are veteran quinces with more magnetism. But it won't matter as long as I can still talk. 'All I have is a voice,' said W. H. Auden, who nevertheless could do a pretty good hour on his feet.

Talking solo for an hour on your feet is usually called stand-up, and right there is the first source of fear. The term 'stand-up' is reserved for comedians, and nowadays there are hundreds of them, most of them so technically proficient that they can spend fifty-five minutes telling the story of what they had for breakfast while they roam the stage like wild animals. The last five minutes is consumed by the apocalyptic applause of the audience, uniformly hoarse from too much laughter. Gasping people clap until their hands bleed while the stand-up comedian sticks the microphone in his mouth and imitates a blender. I can't beat that. My only hope is to do something else.

Back in the late 1950s, when I first started paying attention to this kind of thing, there were only about half a dozen people in the world who could just go on and talk. Mostly they sat on a bar stool, so it wasn't, strictly speaking, stand-up. Mort Sahl, my favourite, just talked about life, but put a twist on it. Eventually he disappeared into the mists of conspiracy theory, but he had already been outflanked by another American, Jonathan Winters, who could use the microphone to imitate a tortoise crossing a freeway. Stand-up took off irretrievably into the realm of pure comedy. The subject mattered

less and less, the continuous laughter more and more. You won't
catch me knocking that, but you won't catch me trying it, either.
I want to talk seriously. I just don't want to get lynched while I'm
doing so. How to avoid that is the question.

I started looking for the answer about forty years ago, in Edinburgh. A Cambridge Footlights revue that I had directed was a hit
on the Fringe, partly because I had been sensible enough not to
include myself in the cast, who were all a lot funnier than I was.
Hungry for a share of the limelight, I staged a poetry and jazz show
in the afternoons, with all the jazz devoted to backing my poems and
all the talking done by myself. In the evenings our venue was packed
for the revue. In the afternoons, a thin scattering turned up to hear
me. They had their priorities right, but I couldn't help noticing that
when I went off script and improvised, there was a rapport. The
rapport was especially intense with a small woman in the third row
who wore two overcoats at once and followed me around for several
days reciting her own poems to me while running to keep up. I had
also, however, got the occasional laugh from the normal people.
Nothing to shake the rafters, but still it was heady wine.

The addiction had taken hold, and in subsequent decades I slowly
got better at holding an audience just by talking to them. The scariest
part is that you can always tell when you aren't holding them. They
start to cough, first individually, then in chorus. Finally they are being
conducted by Toscanini. The only way to stave off the coughs is to
say something interesting. For that, part of the secret is confidence.
You yourself have to believe that what you're saying is worth the
crowd's time. It's a hard ask, when you consider that even Mark
Antony needed Caesar's corpse for a prop. The other part of the secret
is to pack the line. As on the page, what you say on stage should give
value for money, bringing a lot in. I learned something about how to
do that when things went haywire in the TV studio and I felt bound
to keep the studio audience entertained until the glitch was repaired.
A warm-up man usually does that job, but I thought we could save a
salary if I did it. To my delight, I found that the audience sometimes
relished what the people at home weren't getting. When I finally left
mainstream television at the beginning of the current millennium,
I went in search of stage audiences who might feel the same.

One of those audiences was in Edinburgh. At the Pleasance, I did
an hour with Pete Atkin, with whom I write songs. He sang the songs

and I talked in between. A whole new generation had grown to maturity since I was last on stage in Edinburgh. In the courtyard of the Pleasance, my daughter's boyfriend was running the World's Smallest Cinema, which could hold an audience of two people. All the same old mad stuff was happening but most of the people were different, and I wondered, when I went on for the first show, whether time hadn't left me behind. The audience at Edinburgh, if you can pull them into the tent, is in search of adventure, but there are limits, and we were a pair of old timers neither of whom resembled Russell Brand. Yet things went gratifyingly well. It was no surprise in Pete's case: he'd been working the clubs for years. But I surprised myself out of my skin. The only man who coughed while I was talking had a genuine case of emphysema. I had no guarantee, however, that I could get away with it all on my own.

Literary festivals supplied some of the evidence that I might. An hour on your feet at a literary festival is usually far removed from stand-up, and most writers very sensibly don't try to put on a show. If V. S. Naipaul started telling tall stories about Ravi Shankar, you'd be worried. But the opportunity to do something other than a straight reading is always there. Over the course of five years or so I tried to develop the author's standard hour into a performance. Cheltenham was a good venue for that, but the best of all, once again, was in Edinburgh, at the Book Festival, where an hour in the big tent turned out to be a hot gig, as they say in the trade. Armed with this new knowledge – I won't call it expertise, because half the time I still didn't know what I was doing – I undertook a tour of Australia last year, playing a total of thirty solo dates all over the country. Finally I went on alone at the Sydney Opera House. The joint was full and it must have worked, because next day I was still in one piece. To disappoint that many Aussies all at once is never wise.

Time, then, to bring the idea back to where it started, under the shadow of Edinburgh Castle while the city teems with ticket-buyers and every spare room in town is a squat for the young and hungry. The only justification for taking some of their limelight is that you, too, are convinced that you are at the start of something. In the afternoons I'll be hosting conversations on stage with some of the Festival stars, which isn't quite the cinch it looks, but after twenty years of doing the same sort of thing on television I would deserve punishment if I couldn't bring if off. In the evenings, though, I'll be going on alone. And it still feels like the start of something new. For one thing, it's something the young can't do, because they haven't lived long enough to reflect on the experience of growing older. But I'm not just after the sigh of recognition from older people in the audience when I make cracks about how I can't get out of my front door without forgetting my Freedom Pass. I want to tell the younger generation about how time will happen to them, and they're lucky if it does. Will they listen? Will they even turn up? Only one way to find out.

Guardian, August 23, 2008

Postscript

Although it sins against chronology, I have put this handbill first in its group because the activity it promotes is the one that makes the others financially possible. If, in these post-television years, I wasn't going on stage alone at regular intervals, I wouldn't be able to absorb the costs of doing anything else without eating further into financial reserves which the global financial collapse of 2008 might well have destroyed already. (I can't be sure: I'm afraid to ring the bank. Will the bank still be there?) The estimable John Sergeant, already a star journalist before he became the *Strictly Come Dancing* superstar who strictly couldn't dance, was the first to notice that his appearances at literary festivals would supplement his income if he transferred them to the theatre. In the light of his example, it suddenly became apparent that anyone who could make a show out of pushing a new book was foolish not to go on the road. Under the lights, I gradually learned that if my preliminary remarks were interesting enough, I didn't even have to read from the book, which could be carried on as a prop and left lying there all evening on the table beside the lectern. It was yet another way of doing stand-up comedy. Stand-up is usually thought of as a young person's game. The young are better at being shocking, and they can yell for an hour without caving in at the knees. A senior citizen, however, can get some useful mileage out of reflecting on experience, if only because he has more of it to reflect on. If he tries his hand, he might be pleased, as I was, to see quite a lot of young people in the audience. Perhaps they find a shuffling oldster a restful change from being shouted at.

GATEWAY TO INFINITY

In 2005 I finally managed to buy my domain name www.clive james.com back from a British pirate. Before the pirate got hold of it, my domain name belonged to another Clive James, a jet-ski instructor in Miami. I waited a long time for him to have his accident, but when I lunged forward to grab the vacant domain name it turned out that the pirate had already bought it. He sold it to me for only slightly less than it would have cost to sue him, but it was worth it. My fledgling multi-media website could now carry my name, an attribute that might come in useful when trying to attract the attention of anyone who remembered it from the days when I had my face on the box in the corner of the room, instead of on the screen of a computer.

By that time my plans for the website were already changing. My first idea was to set up an on-line archive of everything I had ever written. There were practical reasons for doing so. On the Web, your books need never go out of print. They can be made available while occupying no physical space at all: a reasonably humble aim, surely. But I have to admit that megalomania was part of the initial impulse.

I was building a memorial to myself: not a very charming idea even when the pharaohs did it. Luckily I soon realised that the project might be more useful if I included the work of other people. Some of my own work included other people anyway. I was already, in the Video section of the site, running little no-budget television inter- views that I was making in my living room. Jonathan Miller, Cate Blanchett, Terry Gilliam, Julian Barnes, Ruby Wax, Ian McEwan, Martin Amis and others (the complete line-up of twenty-five half- hour interviews is still on the site now, and still growing, with a new series of nine to be uploaded soon) all contributed their services for not much more than a takeaway Chinese meal and cab fare. In the

Audio section, I had been streaming dozens of radio dialogues that I had done with Peter Porter for the ABC in Australia. I had a Gallery section, and all its painters, sculptors and photographers were my guests. (By now there are seventeen of them, with seven pages each.) So why not have Guest Writers and Guest Poets?

Worldwide, there were journalists and essayists who were taking their business seriously. I wanted to help shine a light on their best work. When I was a journalist, I always thought that an individual piece was like an individual poem: if it was well enough done, it deserved to live. On the Web, nothing need disappear. There were poets who deserved a world stage. I wanted to help provide that. If I could load my website with enough permanently valuable material, people from all over the world might visit, not just because it was an example of one writer expressing himself, but because the site itself was expressing a wide range of human creation. A limitless range, in fact: because there were already countless good things glittering among the junk out there on the Web, so a site's grizzled proprietor could turn his years to use by guiding visitors to the treasure.

You could say that this was megalomania taken to a further stage and disguised as altruism. But whatever the motive, after five years of steady construction the site has become the focus of my later life. I used to do several different things for a living. But they were all linked by writing, and now they are all happening in the one place, and I have to do a lot of extra writing to explain what's going on. By the nature of the Web, this explanatory writing has to be terse, but that requirement never hurts.

The site's comprehensive redesign, which has just been completed after months of work, looks a lot less tentative. It looks, as we used to say in television, 'meant'. And so it should, because a lot of people are giving their efforts to it for small financial reward. They are headed by my copy-editor Cécile Menon, who can also converse with computers fluently enough to run the site. Powerfully persuasive for someone no bigger than a *piaf*, she recruits out in cyberspace the ghostly technical experts whose time is worth a fortune. Somehow she persuades them to work, like her, for a pittance. She is also gifted with adventurous taste. Many of our painters and sculptors are found by her. Sometimes she has to convince me, but only by making me look more closely, and invariably they prove to have a quality that my unaided eye might have skated over. Thus my education continues, and I get the chance to write outside my usual frame of reference. In this way, one's mental range is increased. It's the thing I like most about the Web. It can get you beyond yourself.

It can also get you bankrupt, but there is less reason to be afraid of that than you might think when you read press stories about dotcom entrepreneurs going belly up. For a start, you don't have to be an entrepreneur. My aim is not to make money, and I have the account books to prove it. Google has now started advertising in our right-hand margin, but the revenue will probably fall a long way short of paying even for Cécile's croissants. (*J'ai faim!* is her constant cry.) In fact the site was a steady drain on my savings until quite recently. But by now it is almost paying for itself. The drawback of webcasting is that you pay to send the signal, and the cost goes up with the number of viewers, so you can die of success overnight. The cost of streaming the shows could have been fatal, but luckily *Slate* magazine in the US offered to send out the signal and pick up the tab.

The cost of shooting the shows could have been fatal again, but the British cable channel Sky Arts stepped in to pay the bills, and soon, I hope, a further alliance with Times Online will make another season of programmes possible. The bottom line – I love this business talk – is that I not only choose the guests and run the show, I get to run the finished product on the site forever. The same goes for the radio material: all my 'Point of View' pieces that I record for BBC Radio 4 are mine to keep. The Gallery section acquires a new artist every month, and the library of guest writers grows, and . . . well, I'm not exactly planning to install a swimming pool, but there's already the beginnings of a virtual bookshop, although browsers will have to make their own coffee at home. Wandering the gangways of this transparent space vehicle that we have been building as it flies, I try to see it through the eyes of the viewers. There is already plenty for them to choose from. But who are they?

In that question lies the only thing for the aspiring webster to be really scared of. You can throw a party, and nobody might come. As of now, there are at least seven million websites in the world, and about ninety million blogs, and it's already obvious that when everyone on earth is building a personal display case they won't have time to look at anybody else's. As many lone bloggers have already found, their regular audience is only going to be a handful of people like them. Some of the handful are in Iceland or Venezuela, which can be a thrill, but on the whole, no matter how well the bloggers write, if they haven't got a selling point beyond their own opinions they are digging their own graves under the impression that they are putting up a building.

But when I wake up sweating in the night, wondering if I am going broke to no purpose whatever, I can check the viewing figures and remind myself that at any given moment, as the sun comes up around the world, there are people on line to find out what we've got to offer. Not a lot of people, perhaps, but they come from more than fifty different countries. Since most of them, if they decide to browse around, will read as well as look and listen, it's a safe assumption that they are good at English, which they got from books. The fear that the Web necessarily erodes the ability to read is groundless. The Web is fundamentally literate, even if only at a low level.

At an even lower level, alas, it is also frightening, because a huge percentage of it consists of pornography, eked out by master classes in bomb-making, conspiracy theory and religious terror. The word 'jungle' is almost too genteel to apply. But if the whole thing really is a lethally dangerous primeval forest, then a crucial battle will be lost if clearings are not provided in which people can find nothing but civilisation. I suppose the most glittering prize the Web offers is that it gives you a chance to put your life on the line in a constructive way. Even the brightest young people, wherever they come from, are more likely to find an older voice worth listening to if it is talking about something beyond wealth and power. It can talk about value, saying not just 'This is what I have done' but 'This is what others have done, and I find it valuable beyond price.'

I wouldn't want to sound too worthy, because I have never had so much fun since my first trip to the movies. I wish, though, that the Web had been around a couple of decades earlier, because a site on this scale is so obviously the ideal form of self-expression, where you get your name on the gateway to infinity. What would a pyramid be beside that? Just a pointed building sticking out of the sand.

The Times, May 16, 2008

Postscript

My website www.clivejames.com can be defined in two ways: as the first personal fully fractal multi-media archival-critical instrument on the Web, and as an unbeatable method for going broke slowly. The video department is its most money-hungry feature, and to offset the production and transmission costs I have formed various alliances, always with the aim of giving the ally something he needs for the moment while I get something to keep for my Casaubon concordance, my scheme for joining the stars. Forming an alliance with Times Online, I ran the risk of looking as if I had gone to work for its proprietor. But the executives were very kind about allowing me to proclaim my continued independence, and I am grateful to them for giving me the space to do so. Meanwhile, the other departments of the site continue to grow, unhindered by any considerations except those attached to my diminishing supply of time. I wish that last thing were not so pressing, but I would never have started building the site in the first place if I hadn't thought that the day had arrived for getting things together. How to keep running it after I conk out is the big question now. But my Web editor, second-in-command and sole crew member Cécile Menon is already testing an early model of a cyborg boss, which has a close physical resemblance to Gerard Depardieu. It makes strange noises, but so do I.

Back on the Road

This note was included in the programme for a Song Show tour
of Australia in 2004.

The show Pete Atkin and I perform on tour spares every expense. All we need is two chairs, a small table and a piano. If the theatre has no piano, Pete has a portable one in the back of the car. At the start of the show, the curtains are already open. We just walk on. The houselights remain undimmed. There are no theatrical effects. For two hours with an interval, he sings our songs and I do most of the talking in between. Nothing else happens, yet the show is far and away the most fruitful artistic venture I have ever been mixed up in. It wouldn't do for me to go on about how interesting I find it. The audience must judge. But I can say something about how much fun it is to do.

People who see the punishing tour schedule often commiserate with me. I wish they wouldn't, just as I wish young men wouldn't offer me their seat on crowded trains. I actually like being on the road. I was born to be a rock star. I just had to wait a few decades before it all happened: the endless travelling, the anonymous hotel rooms, the soulless existence. I can't get enough of all that stuff. I can't get enough of what it hasn't got. For one thing, it hasn't got complication. On tour, we know exactly what we're doing tomorrow. We're moving on to the next date, and we'll be eating Crunchy Bars in the car while listening to Credence Clearwater Revival's greatest hits. Or anyway, we'll be eating Crunchy Bars while touring Britain. Touring Australia, we might be eating Cherry Ripe chocolate bars. Almost forty years ago, when Pete and I first met in Cambridge, I told him that the greatest taste thrill in every young Australian's life was the Cherry Ripe, eaten chilled from the fridge on a hot day. Over the last two years, as we toured Britain, I have told him many times that although Crunchy Bars are no doubt very nutritious, when we got to Australia he would at last find out what a Cherry Ripe can offer.

I *think* they're called Crunchy Bars. Pete buys them in bulk, and for all I know they're really called Neutrogrit or Yorkiechaff. I have never been able to look at the labels, which carry lists of all the desirable ingredients – sugar, calories, flavour, etc. – that the contents haven't got. This was the second year Pete and I took a song show on a thirty-date tour of Britain. This year's show was entirely different from last year's but the living conditions were the same. Most of the daytime between performances we spent on the motorway, with him driving the car while I changed the CDs and the floor filled up with Crunchy Bar wrappers. (Neutrochaff. That was it.) In Australia, on those occasions when the dates are close enough together to drive between instead of fly, we will both be in the back of a tastefully luxurious chauffer-driven Lexus provided by the sponsor. Cherry Ripe wrappers will be folded up neatly and retained in the pocket. In Britain, most of the nights after performances were spent in one room each of a motorway Travelodge. My room always looked so much like the room of the previous night that I would search it for a missing sock I left a hundred miles away. In Australia we have been promised proper hotel accommodation by our generous impresario, Jon Nicholls, but I have already told him, on Pete's behalf, that we quite like the simple lifestyle of the troubadour and won't mind at all if the taps in the bathrooms of our interconnecting suites are merely gold-plated instead of solid platinum. After all, I'm not Saddam Hussein, nor is Pete Ivana Trump, although there have been lonely nights when I wished he were. In the first few days of last year's tour of Britain I quickly realised why this superficially austere way of life felt so sumptuous. It was because I had been thirsting for simplicity. After too many years in television I was worn out from being looked after. Television isn't the movies, but for anyone with his name in the title of the show the pampering is decadent enough. You never buy an airline ticket yourself. Someone puts the ticket in your hand. You soon get used to the huge basket of fruit waiting for you in the dressing room. You never eat any of it, but if the huge basket of fruit isn't huge enough then your agent will instruct you to eat the furniture, thus to express anger at being slighted. In America it's a huge basket of huge fruit, and the artist's attorney weighs the apples.

Out on tour with our song show, I buy my own apples, and sometimes, even in Britain, I actually eat one, if we have run out of apple-flavoured Fergiecrunch. In Australia I will introduce Pete to the concept of limitless fruit, along with all the fast yet fabulously healthy food that can be bought by the roadside in a nation where not even the shopping malls have yet succeeded in becoming impersonal. It beats being waited on. (For one thing, you can't be waited on without being made to wait: have you noticed?) It's a simpler, saner way of life. I like to think it is matched by what we do on stage. Last year, getting ready for the first tour of our revival phase, we had to choose from more than a hundred songs we wrote in the late 1960s and early 1970s, the period in which Pete released six albums commercially and the record companies could never decide how to promote the stuff, because they didn't know what it was.

Thirty years later, with the blessed Internet having made the music industry less omnipotent at last, we were able to jump to the right conclusion: trust the audience. It doesn't matter what category our songs fall into, as long as people listen. The trick is to make sure nothing gets between the songs and the listeners. So the answer was, in both senses of the phrase, simplicity itself. The word got out, the tour organisers got their money back, and there was an unexpected result. For both of us, being on the road was like being back in our first days in the Cambridge Footlights, when we sat up late in the ratty old clubroom and wrote song after song because there was nothing to stop us except the usual essay crisis. Last year, as if all that elapsed time had never been, we started writing songs again. This new show, the one we are taking all the way to Australia, is largely composed of the new work we have done in the past year, and I am sure that while we are on tour with this show there will be yet more new work getting started, and so on until I am old and grey. But I can just hear Pete saying: 'You already are.' He's a bit like that. A realist. It would be bad manners for me to praise his other qualities, except to say that if my lyrics helped him to discover the melodies of *Winter Spring*, then I have justified my long career of misspent youth. Whether or not my homeland thinks the same I will now find out. I am bringing home my best stuff. Much of it is the sort of thing I am lucky enough to be known for: tall tales about childhood in Australia, unreliable accounts of strange journeys to the magic land of Pracatan. But right at the heart of it is the work I am least known for, but would still like to be, if only as the writing partner of a unique musician. It is the work I have done with Pete Atkin, so I am very glad he has agreed to come with me, to see for the first time the amazing nation that he has heard me talk about so often.

Postscript

An important form of the handbill is the programme note. The audience is already in the theatre, but the programme note helps to orientate them before the lights go down, and after the show they will take the programme home if they think it has enough interesting material in it. A programme taken home works like a handbill, so you win twice. The Australian tour did good business. In the big cities we filled the concert halls, and up country we filled the theatres, the town halls and the function rooms of the hotels. (Only Australia could come up with a title like 'function room': it sounds like a plus-point in a sales pitch for underpants.) Whatever the venue, we were cost-effective, because apart from the two of us we had only our roadie on the payroll. In Australia it was Mark Wilkinson, who has a background in rock music and knows all about sound. Our regular roadie in Britain, Steve Mitchell, has similar qualifications. The sound-check is the most important part of the day, and it's vital to have a man on your side who knows what he's doing. You could leave it to the on-site staff and save money, but only if you felt suicidal. As for the album, *Winter Spring*, it did well enough to make us confident that self-publishing was a viable prospect, and paved the way for a later album, *Midnight Voices*, which is the album I would recommend as a first purchase for anyone who feels the urge to get acquainted with our work. It's still there on Amazon. End of plug.

LURE OF THE LYRICS

When I was still in short pants manufactured in Sydney, Tennessee Ernie Ford's *basso profundo* voice crossed the Pacific like a Boeing Stratocruiser and landed massively in the Australian hit parade. It sang 'I was born one mornin' when the sun didn't shine.' My unwashed ears flapped. 'I picked up my shovel and I walked to the mine.' My unwashed ears came to a point. I just loved the way those words were energised by the music, and I walked around for weeks doing my imitation of Tennessee Ernie Ford. I was a long way from Tennessee and eventually my mother was a long way from sanity, but the pint-sized uproar was a birth pang: a new lyricist was being born.

'Yer load sixteen *tons* . . .' Australia still had tons in those days. Now it has tonnes. This in itself would be sufficient reason for my living here instead of there. Lyric writers cherish their rhyme-words.

If Tennessee Ernie and 'Sixteen Tons' hadn't done it for me, the Four Lads would have. In their hit song 'Moments to Remember' there was a soaring line that went 'The night we tore the goal-posts down', and the way an almost impossibly agglutinated set of consonants like 'goal-posts' could sit so comfortably on the musical notes fascinated me. How could they sing so easily what I could barely say? Imitating a whole barbershop quartet, I sang the line repeatedly, arousing an intense public reaction in the area of Kogarah, my home suburb. Property prices plunged after I made up a few extra lines to fit the same melody. 'The night we kicked the dunny down', I sang, in a mournful serenade to the moon.

More than half a century later, writing song lyrics is my favourite form of writing anything. I've never managed to become famous for it. In fact I'm almost entirely obscure for it, and I fear that being attached to me has done a lot to prevent my musical partner, Pete Atkin, from reaching the degree of celebrity that he deserves. But for me, writing lyrics is up there with writing poetry, the chief difference being that while writing poetry has always paid me little compared with writing prose, writing lyrics has paid me hardly anything at all. There are lyricists who become millionaires. I'm not one of them, but lately I've found myself writing lyrics again, after a long lay-off that was really due to lack of attention rather than lack of income. You can do without armies of raving fans, but not without a certain level of interest. I'm glad to say that the certain level of interest is not only back, but has gone up a notch.

My colleague Pete Atkin, who composes the music for our songs and does the singing, has just brought out a new album called *Midnight Voices*, which Amazon is currently re-ordering hundreds of copies at a time to meet the demand. They can re-order it from him. They don't have to re-order it from a record company, and that's the big difference between now and when we started. Nowadays you can be in business for yourself. Hundreds of copies aren't thousands, nor are thousands millions, but to reach only a minority market is no longer the killer that it used to be, when only the majority market mattered, and if the record company wasn't behind you, there was nothing in front of you except the void.

Today there's a better chance of not being sunk by your own lack of immediate universal appeal. The old mass markets have been replaced by an infinity of niche markets, all reachable through the Net, which also happens to be – by a mechanism nobody can explain – a surprisingly effective method of spreading news by word of mouth. Today you can reach the few thousand purchasers that you need to keep your little fine-arts factory in business. You can always hope for more, but those happy few should be enough to keep a song-writer going if the song, and not the celebrity status, is what he really cares about. This is probably true for all genuine song-writers, and especially for lyricists, who wouldn't be trying such a second-fiddle thing unless they found it so satisfactory to get right. You can hear the click when the words fit. If you find it hard to like Carla Bruni, listen to her first album, the one where she sings her own songs in French: the neatness of the carpentry will impress you even if you're famous in your family for having ordered the *pampelmousse* under the impression that it was a pudding. Maybe the President of France married the right woman after all. You can imagine her singing him a little song. *Vous êtes le Président / Et moi, je suis une enfant* . . .

There was a twenty-five-year stretch back there when Atkin and I didn't write anything together because we thought there was no way of getting through to a public, no matter how small. Pete still did gigs in the clubs, but 'club' can be a big name for the back room of a pub equipped with a sound-system from the Jurassic period. Now the public comes to us. Not a huge public, but they seem to appreciate what we do, even if it has no classification. Back at the start, when we told the record-company executives that what we did was a blend of jazz, rock, pop, Tin Pan Alley, Broadway and anything else except folk, they would purse their lips and suggest that we call it 'Different'. The executive who called it 'Folk' we preferred to ignore, which turned out to be exactly the way he felt about us. A pity: though he had a small brain, he had a large car, in the back of which we would sit with him while he told us that we would get nowhere unless we wrote a hit. He was quite right, but times change.

For me, there was never any doubt that what we were doing was in a tradition going back to the troubadours, who were never in the hit parade either. The words mattered, but the music came first. Long before I had met Pete in the Cambridge Footlights clubroom in the mid-1960s, I was already continuing my childhood researches into the way music gave an extra dimension to the simplest words. There were countless examples of ordinary spoken phrases being made extraordinary when set to music. In his song 'I'll See You Again', Noel Coward transformed the title line by putting the musical emphasis unexpectedly on the word 'you'. Nothing when read, but everything when heard.

When I finally found my own musician, I took delight in leaving him room, by the way I put the stanza together, to try the same thing with a lot of other simple phrases. I might have overdone the supply of phrases that weren't simple at all, but we probably would have been in trouble anyway, because even the most enthusiastic critics didn't know what to call the results. The word *chanson* rang no bells in the English-speaking countries. In France we might have done better. In France, the poets have always written lyrics, and at least one serious song-writer has married the President, as I might have mentioned. We had to settle for less spectacular rewards, but some of them were gratifying. I remember one evening when Stephen Fry quoted one of my own lyrics at me, and I was so pleased I couldn't speak: for me, a rare condition.

Moments like that did something to offset the frustration. The only real cure for frustration, however, is work, and for the quarter of a century we were behind the moon I kept in shape by writing poems, which have their own music, or should have. But I always missed the thrill of hearing a set of syllables being absorbed by a row of notes, in a kind of mid-air mating dance that transmits a new emotion. Then, in the late 1990s, our music came back from limbo. The first generation of fans had found each other through the Net, and it turned out that there was a second generation who had grown up with our songs echoing in the house. We went on tour in both Britain and Australia, and found that the audiences we played to didn't just want to hear the old stuff, they wanted to hear that we were still writing.

No problem there. We couldn't stop, and gradually we realised that we had never stopped. The long hiatus had been part of the process. We had just been gathering our strength in the interim, as a coalminer must sometimes pause and mop his brow. 'If you see me comin', better step aside/A lotta men didn't and a lotta men died . . .' What a lyric! There is still a controversy as to whether Merle Travis wrote it or ripped it off. Either way, it made him a lot of money. Sigh.

Guardian, April 1, 2008

Postscript

When *Midnight Voices*, the first album of the Pete Atkin/Clive James songbook, went on general release in early 2008, the *Guardian* kindly gave me the opportunity to plug its advent by asking for an article about lyrics. Since the disc had no advertising budget whatsoever, the opportunity demanded to be taken, and I would have enjoyed writing such an article anyway. In previous years, when we went on tour in Britain or Australia, I always answered any request for an article from the print media on route. Writing articles was harder than doing interviews but there was a better chance of sticking to the point, which for me was always how the lyrics and the music blended so that you couldn't get them apart. Songwriters can avoid the press if they like, but unless they are massive, stadium-filling stars their fastidiousness will cost them. Jake Thackray, a learned and inventive troubadour in the *chanson* tradition which has so few English contributors, fatally restricted his career by feeling coy about pleasing the crowd, and today he is remembered mainly for his topical songs on the *Bernard Braden* show, which were nothing like his best things. (His 'Remembrance' is an anti-war song that leaves all other anti-war songs in the dust.) Shyness and show business rarely mix. Anyway, the media coverage that we secured for the *Midnight Voices* album couldn't have hurt. At the time of this book's going to press, all six of the early Pete Atkin albums are due for re-release on Demon, Britain's biggest independent label. Once again, sales will probably be small by rock-star standards, but after all this time it's nice to be still in the game.

FIVE FAVOURITES

'You Don't Know What Love Is'

A cocktail piano song of rare power, 'You Don't Know What Love Is' combines a sweet melody by Gene de Paul with a bitter lyric by Don Raye, who started out as a vaudeville hoofer, a suitable background for the man who wrote the peltingly rhythmic words for the Andrews Sisters' swing hit 'Boogie Woogie Bugle Boy'. In this more plaintive number, however, he was out to affect the tear-ducts, not the feet. Billie Holiday was one of the many singers who knew they were on to something great when they sang the penultimate line 'Until you've faced each dawn with sleepless eyes'. The trick is for the singer not to overdo it: the emotion is already in the words.

'I Wonder What Became of Me'

The quiet titan of the American music business, Johnny Mercer sang with big bands from Paul Whiteman through to Benny Goodman before, as the founder of Capitol Records, he became one of the formative talent scouts, a task in which it must have helped to have so much talent himself. His singing abilities probably lay at the heart of his gift for writing lyrics that sound inevitable from line to line. Of the countless songs he wrote with Harold Arlen, none beats 'I Wonder What Became of Me'. A couplet like 'And they pour champagne / Just like it was rain' sounds so simple, but nobody ever wrote like that by accident.

'Every Time We Say Goodbye'

Cole Porter was the man in the velvet mask. As a gay patrician who had to disguise the gender of his feelings, he often wrote regretful lyrics even to his most exultant melodies, and when the melody was regretful the lyrics could be desperate. 'Every Time We Say Goodbye' is the complaint of someone whose heart is being broken not just once, but over and over, so the little flashes of wordplay sound like tears being fought back. 'When you're near there's such an air of spring about it / I can hear a lark somewhere begin to sing about it.' When Ella Fitzgerald sang this song the way it should be sung, plainly and without emphasis, she was up there with Edith Piaf singing '*Et moi*', and Marlene Dietrich singing '*In den Ruinen von Berlin*'. A song can be monumental.

'Folsom Prison Blues'

When the vaunted personal expression of the singer/songwriter movement took over from the old-style songwriters who wrote for anybody, the distance between the best lyrics and the average opened to the width and depth of the Grand Canyon. The time-honoured neatness of the well-crafted professional lyric, however, continued to flourish in an unexpected area: country music. 'Folsom Prison Blues', written as well as sung by Johnny Cash, is only one of hundreds of country songs that become even more enjoyable when you look closely at how they are put together. Cash was especially good at approximate rhymes, which are very tricky to do. 'I hear that train a-comin' / It's rollin' round the bend / And I ain't seen the sunshine / Since I dunno when'. 'Bend' and 'when' didn't really rhyme, but they did when he sang them, because that's the way he spoke.

'Hit Me With Your Rhythm Stick'

A victim of palsy, Ian Dury had a lot more to offer on stage than his exemplary bravery. That twisted body of his was the incarnation of rhythm. One of his most vivid flights of fancy, 'Hit Me With Your Rhythm Stick' hasn't really got a melody, just a relentless forward drive, over which he speaks the lyric rather than sings it. Yet the lyric is perfect in every respect. In a catalogue song that does nothing much except name the names of exotic places, he gets a wonderful air of adventure just out of the precision of his rhymes. 'In the deserts of Sudan / And the gardens of Japan / From Milan to Yucatan / Every woman, every man ...' The effortless way the fragments of French and German are pieced into the lyric is diabolically clever. If only the rap lyricists could write like that. There's no way of telling, but among all the million musical moments on YouTube at the moment, Dury singing this amazing song is probably the single most exciting thing. I tune in half a dozen times a day, wondering what I have to do to make my words even half that good.

Guardian, April 1, 2008

Postscript

Requests from newspapers and magazines to supply lists of favourite things are generally to be avoided. It makes you look as if you think in crumbs. But when a plug is part of the fee, suddenly the prospect looks more attractive. I contributed this list to the *Guardian* as an addendum to the preceding article, just because the editor wanted an eye-catching featurette to offset the comparatively weighty-looking chunk of prose. Back in the 1970s, when I first had off-trail merchandise to publicize, it was made clear to me that editors would like paragraphs as well as pieces. I tried to make a virtue out of necessity and pack the paragraph with as much action as I could. My aim was to write what my young Web colleague Nichola Deane calls the bonsai essay. There was a hidden reward attached to getting better at it. When I finally realized that my website www.clivejames.com could expand infinitely sideways if I wrote enough short introductions to jewels lifted from YouTube and similar sources, the techniques for saying a lot in a short space came in handy. Nowadays, short of time all round, I am usually turning out a few bonsai numbers when not slogging away at something larger, and there is already a strange and previously unheard-of system of echoes building up between what I write for the page and what I write for the Web. The above brief remarks on Ian Dury, for example, were the rehearsal for what I finally set down as his introductory paragraph in the Video Finds section of my website. It will be interesting to see, in the future, how the two kinds of writing converge. Have they a different tempo? I hope they don't have different standards. I won't be here to do the seeing, alas, so it's all in the hands of a new generation of wandering scholars. Starting out from an academic fortress, they have chosen the path of adventure. I wish I was going with them, but I was there to see them off, and half the trick of life is to be as glad for the lives of those who will outlive you as you are for the lives of those you have outlived.

ABSENT FRIENDS

JONATHAN JAMES-MOORE

Upon the untimely death of our old Footlights colleague
Jonathan James-Moore, Pete Atkin wrote the *Guardian*'s principal obituary,
and I wrote a supplementary piece that was published next day.

In his obituary for Jonathan James-Moore, Pete Atkin was right to stress the ability of the young Jonathan, amiable colossus of the Footlights in our late-sixties era, to perform a script at a level beyond the dreams of its writer. Since his performer's understanding of a written line was at the heart of the judgment he brought to his influential career as a BBC radio producer, it might be worth recalling just how good he could be at what we used to call 'doubling the laugh'. The laugh can't be doubled unless the performer understands exactly how the joke works, and there was nobody quite like Jonathan for wanting to know what every comma in the script was up to. One of my own Footlights scripts, called 'Hell Below Zero', was a monologue for an all-purpose BBC winter sports commentator whom we called Alexander Palace. Suitably dressed in a white roll-neck sweater with Olympic rings, Jonathan would get his first laughs as soon as the spotlight came on. The bobble-topped beanie probably helped.

But as the disaster of Alexander Palace's jingoistic commentary developed like a fatuous avalanche, what helped most was Jonathan's capacity to pause after the latest solecism and let the audience enjoy the implications. At one point he had to express his doubts that the British ski champion, who had done a personal best in the downhill, would do quite so well over the same course ('I, for one, would be extremely surprised . . .') in the next day's twin event of the downhill, the uphill. The line got a solid laugh, which pleased me very much. But the laugh doubled when Jonathan's face registered the helpless defiance of a patriotic bone-head who knows that he has got something wrong yet takes pride in his determination to press on regardless. It was a character study, and an object lesson in how to let a line breathe. From then on, I always tried to give the performer time, after getting a laugh with his voice, to get another with his face. In later years the performer was usually me, but I learned how to write it that way from watching Jonathan perform. I could never have learned how to perform from watching him perform: he was just too good.

He had everything as a stage performer except eyesight. Despite those heavy-duty spectacles of his, the world was a bit of a blur even in daylight, and in sudden darkness he was slow to adjust. One night on the Edinburgh Fringe, where his routines were helping to sell out the late-night Footlights revue in the Lauriston Hall (we had to put on extra performances), the lights went out on Alexander Palace's final verbal catastrophe and the black-clad assistant stage manager who had been assigned to go out and get him forgot to do so. A physical catastrophe duly followed. All too aware that the lights would soon be coming up again, Jonathan tried to get off stage by himself. He did, but instead of going off through the door at the side, he went off over the front of the stage and five feet straight down into the audience, where he landed beanie-first. By the time the lights went up again he had included himself in the front row. The two people who made room for him thought it was part of the show, and they were right. Where Jonathan James-Moore was, it was always part of the show, and largely because of his penetrating respect for comic writing, the gift he wasn't given but was born to help bring alive – and that, of course, was his gift.

Guardian, December 2, 2005

IAN ADAM

Ian Adam was the ideal singing teacher. The proof lay in the fact that he could teach a block of wood to sing. I was the block of wood. Around about the turn of the millennium, in the last flickerings of my career on main-channel television, I was running short of puff. Nothing serious, but after a two-day rehearsal for a big show I would sometimes need to breathe again before the end of a long sentence. I was advised that this crimp in the fluency could be taken care of by singing training.

When I pointed out that I couldn't sing even 'Happy Birthday', I was advised that the singing training was meant to help the speaking, not to turn me into Caruso, and that there was a man famous for being able to sort anybody out. I turned up at Ian Adam's door in Chelsea to be greeted by a slightly built, cherubically smiling man who was already flattering me before the door had shut behind me. Showing me into his charming parlour, he told me that as a devotee of radio and television he has been in a state of amazement for years about the richness of my speaking voice. 'Of course all you Australians are natural singers because your voices are placed so far forward,' he said, 'but *your* voice is something special. That lovely deep baritone, but I think you're really a tenor.'

When I assured him that I was neither baritone nor tenor, but fell into a special category that couldn't sing even 'Happy Birthday', he shook his head decisively. 'Well, "Happy Birthday" is actually quite hard,' he said, 'and anyway we're talking about the qualities in your voice that are waiting to be brought out.' By this time he was sitting at the baby grand piano and shaping up to play a few notes that he wanted me to copy. I copied them to the best of my ability, or perhaps not even that. He professed to be delighted. He explained that although the majority of my lower notes were naturally ravishing beyond the dreams of Lauritz Melchior, those higher notes that I couldn't hold had been ruined after my voice broke, and the way to fix them would be to add more notes on top so as to clarify the notes left below. In brief, turning me into a tenor would revive my career as a baritone.

When I said that I had understood the intention was merely to fix my speaking voice, and that I wasn't expecting to be turned into Caruso, he assured me that Caruso, Gigli and Pavarotti had all required training and that in my voice, as in theirs, there would be undiscovered glories that only the correct discipline would reveal, starting now.

Within seconds I was matching him puff for puff in his famous opening exercise, the steam-train chuff. The first part of the steam-train chuff was done with mouth open and the second part – seemingly calculated to shift the contents of the sinuses up into the brain – was done with mouth closed. The stream-train chuff was followed by the airless clack. In the airless clack, the air in the diaphragm was suddenly expelled and the vocal cords were required to make a clucking noise *in vacuo*. Often, sapped by the pressure to perform, they refused to make any noise at all. Ian always confidently announced that they would next time.

Other pupils doubtless had their own private names for these exercises, of which there were about a dozen, all of them dedicated to shifting the centre of breathing downwards and the centre of singing forwards, into the 'mask' of the face. Ian's devoted assistant, Kate Hughes, who filled in for him when he was away, imposed the same regime of disciplinary warm-up, so we all got to reproduce these strange sets of sounds week by week, forever. Before they got to work on that week's song or an aria, everybody had to go through the same preparation.

And everybody meant everybody. If you arrived five minutes early, you could sit in the downstairs kitchen with a cup of tea and guess who was yodelling up there in the parlour at the end of the lesson before the start of yours. If you couldn't guess, you would bump into them on the stairs. At one time or another, they all came through: Michael Crawford, Anthony Andrews, Kenneth Branagh, Jeremy Irons, Emma Thompson, Ron Moody, Patricia Hodge, Maureen Lipman, Terence Stamp, Helena Bonham Carter. Especially among the men, anyone who stunned a West End audience by suddenly revealing a previously unsuspected competence in singing had usually picked up an extra octave from Ian's little academy.

People already famous for singing would drop in to brush up. You just had to get used to the traffic. At one time, waiting outside the parlour, I heard a voice coming from inside that was so beautiful I was already paralysed when the door opened and I was faced with the mind-bending presence of Mary Elizabeth Mastrantonio, who had come in for a pit-stop before she opened a new show on Broadway. Ian never stopped working with real singers. He had known them all personally, all the way back to Maggie Teyte, who had been his own teacher. In the French repertoire that he himself would later favour for teaching, she would make him repeat a phrase until he wept. (He would tell me this story while I was fighting back tears after once again making a shambles of the song by Fauré that he kept me working on for two solid years.)

It was knowing all about the real singers that made him so good with those of us who were only aspiring to that condition. And I was only one of those who never stopped aspiring: long after my breathing had been corrected, I went on turning up for lessons, still battling to get on top of that fiendish long aria in *A Little Night Music* that Sondheim might have designed specifically to drive the star to drink. ('Yes, dear,' Ian would say, 'it is a bit of cow. Even Jeremy took a while to learn this one. Now let's try it again. From the start, I think, don't you? And this time *try not to make it up.*')

Ian was a thrilling teacher because he himself never ceased to be thrilled by the whole business, even at the level where somebody like me was struggling to make the middle section of 'So in Love' sound a bit less like a cat drowning. And the great thing about his method was that it worked. As you added notes at the top, your voice really did start to clarify lower down, and gradually you acquired the ability to do that thing for so long only dreamed of: hold a tune. It took time, but who cared, when going to see him was so much fun, and he would always be there? Now that he isn't, there will be a lot of us, for a long while ahead, who will think of him as we do our exercises, or sing anything, or, indeed, hear anything sung.

Guardian, June 4, 2007

RICHARD DREWETT

Surely destined to be remembered as one of the most inventive television producers of his time, Richard Drewett always had the admiration of his colleagues, but would have been a legend far beyond the borders of the television industry if only the public was able to tell what a producer does. Unfortunately, in the eyes of the general viewer, the competence of a television producer is never visible except when it is absent.

Richard Drewett's competence determined the tone and intelligence of every programme he put to air, so he barely left a trace. He just brought the best out of everyone involved, and they got the credit. Since I was one of them, let me speak briefly for all the others, the hundreds of people who worked with him during a tireless career that never faltered until the day his illness kept him out of the office.

It's in the office, not in the studio or on location, that even the most hands-on producer does the work that makes the difference. Richard was the executive producer for every programme with my name in the title between 1982, when I left Fleet Street to go into television, and the turn of the millennium, when I left television for a retirement which is proving quite busy, but which would be a lot harder for me to make sense of if he had not taught me so much about the fruitful use of time. On top of his charm and good manners, that was the thing he was best at, the thing that ruled all the other things he could do. He was mad about his family and fast cars, but when he was working he was perfectly sane: far too sane to be interested in power, which he could have had, but didn't care about.

He cared only about getting good programmes made. For doing that, his first rule for business was to prepare thoroughly in the office so as to save time in the studio or on location, and thus earn the capacity to pack the air-time tight. Securing the essential early so as to leave room for exploiting the unexpected, he was always able cram the screen with value. A performer like myself, by nature prone to enthusiasm and thus to impatience, could only benefit from his strict sense of priority.

In my raw and uninstructed state, I could hardly have been an enticing prospect when he first took me on. He was in charge of Special Programmes at LWT and I was hanging around the building while various attempts were being made to get me on camera so that I could work off a salary which continued to drop out of the sky because the company still had to pay me even though *Saturday Night People*, for reasons too complicated to go into, was off the air. Though the studio producers were encasing me in several different examples of the classic three-piece suit by that stage, I still looked pretty scruffy, whereas Richard looked dapper and well groomed, with overtones of a military background.

Rendered permanently thin by the kind of metabolism which apparently imposed no necessity to eat anything at all, he looked neatly correct from his fine-drawn features all the way down to his ankles, after which a strange thing happened. He wore white plimsolls, one of which had the top cut away. He never apologised for the odd effect of his footwear and quite a lot of people knew him for years without ever finding out the reason. In my role as brash colonial, I asked him, and was told that the foot in the skeletal plimsoll had been smashed up, the operation on it had been bungled, and any vertical pressure put on it would cause so much pain that he couldn't work.

Work came first. Kindly he listened to my plans for being a literary man and just walking into the studio a couple of times a week to go on air. Kindly but firmly he insisted that it couldn't be like that. If I wanted to do this stuff properly, I would have to work a full week. He set the example by being first into the office every day and the last to leave. From early on, I got a close-up of what it meant to prepare properly. It was the secret of his authority. Since he knew everybody else's job as well, he couldn't be buffaloed by expertise. On the first documentary special we did, *The Clive James Paris Fashion Show*, he could tell from the rushes that Terence Donovan, our director, was skimping on the bread-and-butter coverage.

Richard turned up in Paris and read Donovan the news about the necessity of doing the boring stuff properly if he wanted to make an exciting film. For the task of dressing Donovan down, Richard was wearing real shoes, a sign of how serious the situation was. When standing on his dignity he wanted the right kit. Donovan was a tough customer but he shot the coverage. The scene taught me a lot about Richard and about life. Short on moral courage, I would always avoid telling people what they didn't want to hear. Richard didn't enjoy doing that either but he could do it. Over the next twenty years I didn't see the real shoes very often, but every time I did see them it was for a crucial confrontation that would never have taken place if it had been left to me. I remember one studio director, intent on spoiling the clean effect of the set by adding some superfluous scaffolding, who said, 'It has to look designed.' I thought, 'That's just how we don't want it to look.' But Richard actually *said*, 'That's just how we don't want it to look.'

For the studio shows, Richard was the kind of executive producer that every producer fears most: the kind that never leaves the control room. Most of the producers who had to live with him watching their every move were grateful for the lesson. Directors were often less so, and especially when they were shooting on film out on location – a context in which every young director tends to think that he is Fellini. I always preferred to narrate in voice-over rather than do a walk-and-talk. A walk-and-talk looks so unnatural that only David Attenborough can make it interesting, and mainly because you suspect that he is about to be attacked by a buffalo. But fledgling directors like the shot that moves: the shot that draws attention to itself by smoothly linking things up. I wanted less spectacular shots of single subjects, so that I could narrate at my own pace back in the editing room, without being forced to a thought just because the shot was panning. Richard would appear suddenly out of the sky on various continents and tell the director to stop trying to win a BAFTA. The directors who took the lesson in were the ones who went on to prosper. (One of our directors, Laurence Rees, is currently producing the best documentaries ever made about the Nazi era, and I am sure he would agree that Richard taught him a lot about never letting the technique become the subject.)

Financially, the 'Postcard' programmes were made possible by the weekly studio show. Under various titles on different nights of the week on different channels, the studio show was the one that earned the bread. Most of the many innovations of the studio show have by now been so thoroughly absorbed into the mainstream that everybody has forgotten where they started. One-line captions over photographs, fake commentaries over re-edited news footage, satellite interviews – none of it would have been possible at that time without Richard's ability to run a creative office, because the easier the results looked the harder they were to get. In later years, to get the script, Richard would lock me and our brilliant writing staff, Colin Bostock-Smith, into my office for three days at a stretch. In early years he would lock me in alone, and when I came out to go and buy a takeaway lunch he would have me followed. Everybody knew that Richard was the man in charge, so when Michael Grade moved to the BBC, a phone call to Richard was one of the first he made.

We arrived at the BBC just in time for Grade's resignation, after which we were at the mercy of the managerial revolution. An incomparable scrounger, Richard managed to convert half a floor of the Beeb's new White City building into a special unit devoted to programmes with my name in the title. This was very flattering for me, but Drewett's independence made him a target for re-education into the managerial ethos. He could have taught the managers more than all of them knew put together if they had been capable of learning, but he patiently went off for a whole day per week of the kind of meeting where six grown men work out the best way to lower an egg out of a window with a piece of string.

For once usefully impatient on his behalf, I persuaded him, when the chance came to jump ship back to ITV, to take it. Within ITV's embrace, we started Watchmaker Productions, a company run by us along with Elaine Bedell, one of Richard's many discoveries among the new wave of female production talent. Whether male or female, the production staff at Watchmaker had to spend only a few weeks under Richard's tutelage before they realised that they had enrolled themselves in flying school. Some of the men are now tycoons, having built companies that they could sell for millions. But the blazing career paths of the women alumni are what please me most, and I think Richard felt the same. One day somebody will tell the salient truth about Watchmaker: it was certainly full of knockout females, but they were treated neither as eye candy nor as wage slaves. They got their chance, and an unusually large proportion of them went on to great things. Generally, when we recruited the women, we followed the principle of hiring nobody that we couldn't see ourselves working for when she came to power, and generally the applicants who got the job didn't mind being called the Drewettes. After all, it wasn't Richard who invented the term. It was one of them.

Eventually, as the turn of the millennium approached and television veered inexorably downmarket, Watchmaker was sold to its backers as per contract, and Drewett and I were left with the only real money either of us had ever made in show business. We had always been well recompensed, but on the whole, in television, nobody who cares a lot for the finished programme makes much money out of it, and we cared a lot. Richard cared even more than I did, and for a man who never had much to apologise for he gave me a deep and touching apology when he proved too ill to supervise the editing of the last show we made, at the end of the year 2000. He was right: the show would have been better if he had seen it through to the end. Those of us who knew him well are now feeling the same about our own lives. A great one for catch-phrases, he had a line with which he started every meeting: 'I expect you're wondering why I've asked you all here.' A lot of people will be saying it at his funeral, and smiling at the memory.

Guardian, February 4, 2008

ALAN COREN

Aided by her brother Giles, Victoria Coren was editing *Chocolate and Cuckoo Clocks: the Essential Alan Coren*, a selection of her late father's writings, and she asked me to be one of the panel who would introduce the various sections. They were a distinguished bunch – Melvyn Bragg, Victoria Wood, A. A. Gill and Stephen Fry – so I was honoured to be asked to join them. I got the plum job of introducing a sheaf of Coren's pieces written in the 1980s, which the editors themselves regarded as his golden age. The essay appears here as it did in the book, with no additions, although I could easily have doubled its length. The book was published in October 2008, to deserved acclaim.

Writers of humour often have a bag of tricks, and one day the tricks become recognizable. Eventually even S. J. Perelman could be caught in the act of copying ideas that he had been the first to have. But Alan Coren was so inventive that the new ideas – not just the dazzle on the surface, but the structures underneath – kept on coming, with the seeming ease which invites belittlement from the less blessed. The great Australian swimmer Dawn Fraser's achievements were often taken for granted by the local press, on the grounds that she was 'a natural athlete'. In the same way, Coren was naturally funny. Nevertheless even he had his peak period for minting new coin. He was never better than in the 1980s, when the first flush of youth had been tempered by wisdom and learning.

The learning showed up brilliantly in a piece like '£10.66 And All That', which can be taken as the pioneering instance in any medium of a modern humorist exploiting the probability that the yeomen of olde Englande, while they waded through the mud, exhibited all the whining venality and warped entrepreneurial ambition that we so admire today. As we join the action, the estate agency William & Bastards is about to be 'dragged into the 11th Century'. While we read of how the agency strives to flog a 'property with relatively scum-free well', we can see how Coren was unmatched at the conceit of showing up the delusional sales vocabulary of Now by exporting it to the inappropriate context of Then. Almost every humorist has tried it but Coren could actually do it, at a level of ventriloquism which had been equalled, before him, only by Beachcomber.

Like Michael Frayn in his *Guardian* 'Miscellany' column at the turn of the 60s, Coren always knew that the only way to keep up with Beachcomber's ghost was to cock an ear to the new yet instantly tarnished linguistic counterfeit of the present. This is the secret of Coren's extraordinary feat of mimicry in 'One is One and All Alone', the story of what happened when our current Queen accidentally found herself at a loose end for a whole day. She kept a diary, in which we find that she played I-Spy with Fusebox Pursuivant. ('One won'.) At the end of the day (the kind of dud phrase that Coren always hijacked at the very moment of its ponderously sprightly arrival into the language) Her Majesty is in prison, and obviously grateful for the change of scene.

Nowadays, Google makes it easier to write a catalogue piece that sounds as if it has been researched in a library, but the list of phobias in 'No Bloody Fear' sounds like the inside job of someone who had done a lot of delving in his own head. With Coren it's always important to realise that his vast range of particular knowledge almost certainly included a deep insight into himself. He just never let on. Of all the great British comic writers – among whose number, we must surely see now, he stands high – he is the one whose flights of fancy tell you least about the agonies within. Probably, rather than being defensive, he was just too fascinated with the limitless extravagance of the follies in the outside world: to take them personally would have seemed, to him, disproportionate.

His consolation for a world whose cruelties mocked his mockery – Coren's Idi Amin was a talking doll that spoke from the puppeteer's sense of pity, not from his frivolity – was that the universal madness would always be there, if only because it had been there throughout history. Hence the enchanted insanity of 'Tax Britannica', my personal candidate for the title of Coren Piece for the Time Capsule. The scene, once again, is ancient Britain, but this time very ancient.

The Romans are here. A sniffling tax collector called Glutinus Sinus? Of course. But when I learned that the tax-collector's assistant was called Miscellaneous Onus, I was helpless with admiration as well as laughter, because the name is so exact. Miscellaneous onus equals various jobs, get it? Or, as the skiving Briton in the piece would say, 'Narmean?' Coren was first with that too: transcribing the tormented demotic with phonetic exactitude. Novelists got famous for doing the same. Coren just did it, from week to week, working so far within his abilities that he was the walking, laughing and dancing (he was a wickedly good Lindy Hop dancer) exemplar of a principle: the secret of success in the popular arts is to have power in reserve.

The worst a critic could say of him was that he didn't seem to be trying. There were critics who said the same of Gene Kelly. But although Coren never had to practise a knee-slide that would finish exactly on the mark that the cameraman's assistant had put down on the studio floor, he still had to do an awful lot of technical calculation in his head before he got his effects. He did it so quickly that he could go on a radio programme like *News Quiz* and unreel impromptu lines which were so neatly compressed they sounded as if they had been written. They had been: written instantly, a nanosecond before he said them. Somebody with that kind of gift is always going to be underrated. Coren didn't care. He preferred to make the English language the hero. So generous a writer forms a conspiracy with the reader, as they both revel in the splendour of the tongue they speak. For as long as the spell lasts – and Coren could make it last for a thousand words at a time – the reader can almost persuade himself that he, too, knows how it's done. But it's a secret. Writers who convince you that you share their sense of humour are pulling a fast one. They are celestial con-men. Alan Coren was one of them, and one of the best.

PAT KAVANAGH

Already a star agent in the days before there were any others, Pat Kavanagh had the glamour to reduce most men and not a few women to slavery. She was beautiful, clever and loved to laugh, but she could also have a blunt way with a fool. Since most writers are fools, especially about money, a new client was likely to find his dreams being set straight quite early in the relationship. I can't speak for her other clients – she never spoke about them either – but in general I would be surprised if there were any who were spared a close encounter with brute reality when she first explained to them why it would be unwise to start living like Donald Trump on the assumption that the next advance would be as big as the last one.

Such bluntness could be daunting but it was also reassuring, because the client guessed, correctly, that his new mentor wouldn't be pussyfooting with the publishers either. Pat could make publishers shake in their hand-made shoes. On the appointed day to have lunch with her they always dressed with extra care. Some of the awe she inspired at all levels of the business might have come from the fact that she had a self-assured hauteur and yet was hard to place. She didn't come from any recognizable British social stratum. She was a South African who had sent herself into exile. Like the Australian expatriates of the same generation, she counted as having come from nowhere.

People who had come from nowhere could score an effect if they looked as if they knew something. Pat looked like that. She didn't even have to say anything. At the parties and book-launches that endlessly punctuate the literary round, one babbles to stay alive. Pat never babbled. Her gift for waiting until she had something to say was enough to scare the daylights out of those of us who were busy saying anything at all without waiting for a moment. Julian Barnes, who doesn't babble either, was at a loss for words when he first met her at a party in the old A. D. Peters office. Wisely he sent her a letter saying so, and from then on he was the lucky man. But not even Julian's looming presence could subtract from her individual status. She was always at the centre of a roomful of admiring glances.

On a grand occasion, she had a way of looking unimpressed that could set the assembled company to wondering if they quite measured up. Actually her inscrutability might have had more to do with shyness, but there was no telling for sure even when you knew her. Perhaps you had done something wrong. I once turned up for a book-launch in a flared-trouser all-denim suit that was very wrong indeed, and couldn't help thinking that my appearance might have had something to do with the way she looked into her glass of white wine as if a fly had drowned in it.

But she forgave us all, as long as we kept writing. Pat's client list, always bung full for decade after decade, was a persuasive indicator that she was on the side of the creator. To be effectively on the side of the creator, however, an agent must know the business. Pat did. I can well remember her first explanation to me of why it was better, on a book of memoirs, to have a rising rate on later royalties (the 'escalator' clause) than to inflate the advance, especially if I also wanted the publisher to put out off-trail stuff such as collections of essays and poetry. 'The secret,' she said, 'is to be a long-term asset.'

I wish I could say that the idea had been all mine, but without her deep knowledge of the practical possibilities I would have been stymied. I am sure that there are many other clients who could say the same about their careers. Every literary career is different but the same principles apply, or anyway they ought to. The first principle is to *have* principles. The writer should not expect to have junk published; the publisher should not expect to get away with publishing junk; and the agent should not expect to be praised for extracting a huge advance from the publisher for a piece of junk that will never get the advance back.

Pat saw all this nonsense coming a long way off and she could be very funny about it (she was never more delightful than when pouring on the scorn), but she profoundly disapproved. Everyone in the business knew how honest she was and it must have made some of them uncomfortable. When PFD, of which she had been a stalwart, was taken over, it was an awkward situation for many of us because the literary world in London is quite small and everyone knows everyone. But Pat's clients went with her *en masse* to the new outfit, United Agents, and I doubt if even one of them hesitated any more than I did. I would have gone with her even if I had known that she was soon to grow fatally ill. Every minute of knowing her was valuable. This week many voices will be heard saying the same thing. Being literary voices, they will all say it differently, but there will be common themes: respect, admiration, love, and a racking grief at so cruel a blow, which had an awful quickness for its only mercy.

Guardian, October 21, 2008

Postscript

She died on a Monday morning, and in the afternoon the *Guardian* called me ten minutes before the *Times* did. I had already composed my first few paragraphs, because I knew somebody would be asking, and it was something to do. One of the dubious privileges of sharing your life with famous people is that if you outlive them, you will be called upon to help bury them. Pat was good at fame: disliking the attention intensely, she perfected a natural gift for public privacy. Her lifelong physical beauty announced itself always, but through no fault of her own; and she flaunted nothing, not even her principles. But they were fiercely held, and one of the many things to regret about her unexpected death was that it came just a few days too early for her to see a black man become President of the United States. In her youth, she had left South Africa because of apartheid. The renunciation cost her much regret, which she bore without complaint. I tried to get some of that heroic quality into my piece. In all the pieces – and I suppose there will be more, unless I check out early to be summed up in my turn – I make it my first and only task to catch the character. The standard obituary, with all the biographical details, is beyond me. What I write is what the obit editors call the additional feature. It's easier, but I still wish I didn't have to. The only way out of it, however, would be if your loved ones lived forever: and we can't have that.

BACK TO THE BEGINNING

MUSIC IN THE DARK

All set to go on stage at the Sydney Opera House and do some talking in between renditions of crime-movie music by the Symphony Orchestra, I'll be able to rely on my memory to a remarkable extent. I might have to look up the odd name and date, but mostly the stuff is already in my head. For most of my waking life, I've been seeing almost every notable movie on its first release, and I formed the habit right here in Sydney. Near my home suburb of Kogarah in the late 1940s and the 1950s there were three movie houses (always known simply as 'the pictures') operating full blast. Early on, when I had barely cut my second teeth, my mother used to take me to every change of double bill at the Ramsgate Odeon.

A little later, but while still in short pants, I took myself to the Saturday afternoon matinee at Rockdale Odeon for a couple of action movies, four episodes from different serials, and sixteen cartoons. Long pants having been acquired, I went solo to the Ramsgate double bill in the evening at least once a week, and, on another evening in the same week, to the double bill at the Rockdale Odeon. If the movie had Grace Kelly in it, I could see it repeatedly by chasing it from Ramsgate to Rockdale and back to Kogarah. I saw *Dial M for Murder* five times that way. When the Symphony Orchestra plays the soundtrack music in the Opera House, they'll have to hose me down to stop me singing along.

Is there anything more ridiculous than a young man in love? No, but there is nothing more dedicated either. Time after time in *Dial M for Murder* I was sending thought waves to the screen, warning Grace Kelly that her life was in danger. (Many years later, when I heard the news of her death in a car-crash, I immediately had the guilty thought that I had not sent her a sufficiently powerful message when we were spiritually united in the thrilling darkness of the Ramsgate Odeon.) I even remembered the names on the credits, and so knew from an early age that the spine-tingling score had been composed by Dmitri Tiomkin – two words that I could not pronounce, but they were engraved in my mind as if with a stylus.

My golden-haired beloved was also in *Rear Window*, and once again I sent messages of warning as the music cranked up the tension. She's searching Raymond Burr's apartment for the missing wedding ring! She's found the ring! She's signalling James Stewart but he doesn't know how to tell her that Raymond Burr has come home early! Luckily my own signals reached her in time and she managed to bluff her way out of certain death. The music was by Franz Waxman. I assumed, of course, that he knew Grace Kelly personally.

I had no idea of how movies were made. All I knew was that I couldn't do without a regular supply of them. The experience of watching was closely allied with the experience of eating. In those days I existed on an exclusive diet of sweets and I graded them according to the type of movie on show. At the Rockdale Odeon, when the action films and serials and cartoons were running, I existed mainly on Jaffas and Hoadley's Violet Crumble Bars. Jaffas were ideal for popping like pills during an Eastern Western like *The Golden Blade* in which George Macready threatened Piper Laurie's virtue. Crumble Bars, which imposed a much slower chewing rate, were appropriate when enduring the tension of the latest episode of *Lost City of the Jungle*. In reality, the actors were in no danger except from the set falling down, but I had no idea what the term 'low-budget' meant. For any item on the endless matinee programme, the music could have been by Alfred Newman, who, during a long career, composed for every kind of movie there was. He also composed the Twentieth Century Fox logo theme. 'Da-da-dah, da-da-dah, da-da-DAH!' I could sing it. They'll be playing it at the Opera House to start the show and I'll be singing it right along with them unless they can stop me.

For a high-end romantic movie at Ramsgate, I moved my sweet-eating choices upmarket, culminating in the luxurious Cherry Ripe, still the all-time most sensuous Australian gustatory experience. Either out of lust for Grace Kelly or loathing for Stewart Granger I choked on a Cherry Ripe while watching *Green Fire*. But sophistication was soon to arrive. In the late fifties I expanded my movie-going range. Sydney University had a Film Society whose operating members were drunk at all times. The movies were screened in the old Union Hall (gone now, alas, with all its atmosphere of girls longed for and time wasted) and the screening was always preceded, just before the lights went down, by Bunk Johnson playing 'The Saints Go Marching In'.

Owing to the inebriation of the personnel in the projection box, the reels did not always come on in the right order. Thus my fourth viewing of *The Sound Barrier* was lent a unique dimension. I had already seen it several years before, two nights running at the Ramsgate Odeon and then again at the Kogarah Odeon. I had seen it three times because Ann Todd was in it. She was the British Grace Kelly and in some ways even more attractive, because she made tea for her guests, like my mother. In the movie she falls in love with a handsome test pilot (Nigel Patrick, whose suave sneer was much imitated by me) but he dies in a crash. In the Film Society version, he died in a crash and then she fell in love with him.

Imitating the male stars was a feature of my youth. Though I had no natural gifts as a mimic, I could get closer to a passable impression by seeing the movie several times in a row. Variously rehearsed at both Ramsgate and Rockdale after multiple viewings of *The Wild One*, my Marlon Brando had a startling effect on my mother. When she said that she was getting sick of asking me to mow the lawn, I told her that I would mowmduh lawm domorrow. On the other hand, Brando's Mark Antony in *Julius Caesar* got me speaking in blank verse whatever the occasion. ('Have I not said the lawn will soon be mowed?')

Australia in those years is often accused of provincialism but the truth is that the movies connected us to a wider world. They always had. In the thirties, my mother and father, during those onerous depression years when they could not yet afford to have the child that would grow up to be me, would watch Myrna Loy and William Powell in the 'Thin Man' movies and get a lasting idea of what men and women could be like when they treated each other as equals. And it wasn't just the standard Hollywood and British product that reached us. By the time I was ready to sail, I had seen all the Italian neo-realist movies at Sydney cinemas. But it was an off-trail British movie that knocked me sideways. You couldn't see it in Ramsgate or Kogarah or Rockdale. You had to go 'into town', as we used to say.

It was *Saturday Night and Sunday Morning*, and for three nights on the trot I absorbed the chemicals that transformed me into Albert Finney. By the third night I was talking with a Nottinghamshire accent and humming the themes of the score by Johnny Dankworth. I was ready for England.

Time Out Sydney, September 10–16, 2008

Postscript

Some of the details of my early movie-going in Sydney I put into my book *Unreliable Memoirs*, first published almost thirty years ago and still in print. But I never mind revisiting a theme if there is a new angle demanding to be taken, and here the angle was soundtrack music. There was also the chance to go public with the long-kept secret of my adoration for Grace Kelly, one of the great love affairs of my life, although she never heard about it. The venue for the show, the Sydney Opera House, can be daunting if you are going on alone. On this occasion I had the Sydney Symphony Orchestra with me on stage but I was still the only one speaking. The place, though vast, has a wraparound auditorium and feels, from the performer's viewpoint, quite intimate, but there are so many people looking at you that only a fool would not be scared. Even scarier than a full house, however, is a half-empty one. Unless you can pull in a few hundred people on top of the subscribers, there will be vacant seats, and it takes only a few of those to give the vulture element of the local press a cue to start evoking the spectacle of a lonely old man trembling on the brink of the void. Hence the importance of getting a handbill out to the general public. Luckily the Sydney edition of *Time Out* asked me to be guest editor at just the right moment. Before I caught my flight from London, I wrote about half the magazine just for the chance to get the above article printed. Upon arrival in Sydney, I also appeared on every radio and television show I was asked to do, mentioning my upcoming concert dates in the answer to every question, even if it was about global warming. The combined publicity worked and the hall was full by the third night, but it was a near-run thing. In a subscription house that offers a guarantee, you don't necessarily have to fill the joint to get paid, but Sydney is the town where I made my start, and when I go back I like to get the crowd out if I can, just to prove to them that the runaway made something of himself. It's a primitive urge, which Gore Vidal once defined beautifully when he was asked why he worked so hard to pull an audience for his books: 'None must escape.'

STARTING WITH SLUDGE

It was my third year at Sydney Technical High School, and our English class was being taken by a history teacher while our regular teacher was away ill. Though he conspicuously wore the first Hush Puppies I had ever seen, I can't remember the history teacher's name. But I can still remember everything he said. To keep us in order, he had been asking us what we read at home. I said that I had been reading the collected works of Erle Stanley Gardner. He said there was nothing wrong with that, but that the whole secret with what he called sludge fiction was to enjoy it while you built up the habit of reading, and then move on to something hard. The very idea that there might be something interesting further up the road had not occurred to me before that day. Many years later, I realised that he had chosen his words with care, so as not to crush.

Our knowledge of ourselves is that we are alone, and our dream of ourselves is that we are alone because we are unique. Sludge writers who can tap into that dream are off to a flying start, and the first sludge I knew in my life was flying sludge. It is still airborne in my mind's eye: our house in Kogarah, my little room, and the narrow bed holding up the square squadron formation of my Biggles books, all laid out face up and edge to edge so that I could kneel and worship them as if they were household gods. It wasn't a case of judging books by their covers, because when it came to these particular books I loved their contents, whole chunks of which I could recite by heart, especially when not asked. But my adoration for what was in them had made icons of their outward appearance.

My favourites were the covers with the green background against which, framed by his leather helmet and the heavy collar of his Sidcot flying suit, the features of Biggles loomed with a hieratic numinance which, I was to realise much later, exactly echoed the Nazi sculptures of Arno Breker, much admired by Hitler and his terrible friends as the ideal of Aryan manhood. All the green-covered books had the word 'Biggles' in the title except *Spitfire Parade*, which somehow I treasured even more than the others, perhaps because you had to know it was about Biggles – it was, as I explained to my mother on several occasions, secret information. The narrative paintings on the covers of the later books were a disappointment, as indeed were the books themselves: the post-World War II Biggles adventures had lost focus, not because their hero had aged – miraculously, he never did – but because his author, Captain W. E. Johns, still alive and writing, must have been older than Dr. W. G. Grace would have been if he had been still alive and batting. There was also the possibility that I myself, the ideal reader, was feeling the effects of the passing years, which were soon to propel me into long pants and the necessity to shave.

Bulldog Drummond arrived in my life like a descending testicle, a fair analogy for the size of his brain. By comparison, Sanders of the River was an intellectual. It never occurred to me – though it probably occurred to the author, Edgar Wallace – that Sanders, in demonstrating his mental superiority to all those benighted fuzzy-wuzzies, was the incarnation of the imperial principle. I just liked the way Sanders, having figured everything out in a flash, adjusted his pace so that lesser breeds could catch up. Bulldog had no such resources. But his capacity for ratiocination was never the attraction: it was his Caesarian speed of movement as he went into battle against the all-purpose international heavy Carl Petersen. (Surely it was no coincidence, as the academics say, that John le Carré chose the name Karla for the similarly globe-girdling *eminence rouge* who was later to haunt the squinting imagination of George Smiley.) Acutely potentiated by the hormonal stirrings of pubescence, my feelings for the even more evil Irma Petersen were a giddy cocktail of fear and desire – as, I now suspect, were those of Drummond. The bone-headed crusader would run, swim, drive or fly vast distances at incredible speeds specifically to place himself at her mercy. He always survived her perverted attentions, perhaps because (the thought scarcely entered my adolescent mind, for want, as it were, of a point of entry) she had a thing for him.

The relationship of Irma and Bulldog was duplicated three quarters of a century later in the classically awful British television SF series *Blakes Seven*: no apostrophe in the title, no sense in the plot.

The depraved space queen Servelan, played by the slinky Jacqueline Pearce, could never quite bring herself to volatilise the dimly heroic Blake even when she had him square in the sights of her plasmatic spasm guns. The secret of Blake's appeal, or Blakes appeal, for the otherwise infallibly fatale Servelan remained a mystery, like the actual wattage of light bulb on which the design of Blake's space-ship, or Blakes space-ship, was plainly based. Drummond's appeal for Irma was no secret at all. He was born to jack-boots as she was born to high heels. But the relationship was identical in its balance of forces. In sludge fiction there are only so many situations. It's part of the charm, and part of the importance: these adventure stories by and for childish adults emanate from Jungian archetypes boiling deep below the brain, somewhere in the medulla oblongata. Their thematic templates are practically genetic.

But I didn't know that yet. The Bulldog Drummond books belonged to the parents of my friend Graham Gilbert, down the street. His parents must have inherited them from their parents, because his parents never read anything, with the gratifying conse-quence that the books were in pristine condition, all lined up with yellow wrappers intact – the author's sobriquet 'Sapper' stood out boldly on their spines – in a rosewood cabinet topped off with ferociously polished ornaments of brass and glass. One at a time, I borrowed every volume, immersing myself in their steaming bouilla-baisse of dimwit derring-do and xenophobic snobbery. In retrospect, the jut-jawed, meat-headed Bulldog stands flagrantly revealed as a brawling anti-Semite to whom Julius Streicher would have been glad to extend a sweating paw, but at the time such considerations did not impinge. What counted was the hero's Pavlovian readiness (*Bulldog Drummond Attacks*) to pit himself single-handed against a conspiratorial world. He did the same routines in every book – got tied up loosely by Irma, cut his way free, shot it out with Carl – but still I read them all. Sameness was part of the satisfaction.

Completism was part of the hunger: with print as with food, I was the kind of consumer who leaves nothing on his plate. When I graduated to Ellery Queen and Erle Stanley Gardner – the local lending library came in handy at this point, because there were so many titles by each author that I could never have afforded to own a tenth of them – I read everything by both, even though each repeated himself shamelessly and often verbatim. (Actually Ellery Queen was two people at the very least, but for inventiveness they barely added up to one: whereas Erle Stanley Gardner also wrote copiously under the name of A. A. Fair, thus engendering another few dozen titles to get through.) Nothing, however, could beat actually owning the stuff. Personally doing a lot for the royalties of Leslie Charteris, I bought every Saint book in print, usually in the big yellow Hodder and Stoughton trade paperbacks, although the Pan pocketbooks were more desirable, having the better cover paintings. (On the Pan covers, Simon Templar posed in black tie and pistol plus adoringly draped soignée women: surely the prototype for James Bond's graphic image in later years.) There was no room to arrange all my Saint books on my bed, so I lined them up in rows on the lounge-room floor, in front of the Kosi stove: *Enter the Saint*, *The Saint Steps In*, *The Saint Closes the Case* and (wait for it: the title of the century) *The Last Hero*. Bliss! And boy, couldn't Leslie Charteris *write*, I asked my mother rhetorically, quoting the evidence by the page while she dusted the wax fruit in the brass dish. For the first time in my career as a reader, here were sentences which, when you read them again, got better instead of worse.

Even more than Bulldog Drummond, the Saint was a model for James Bond: years later, I could tell from the first pages of Ian Fleming that he, too, had once thrilled to Simon Templar's savoir faire, his Lobb shoes, his upmarket mistress and his mighty, hurtling Hirondel – a car that would have seen off Bond's Bentley in nothing flat. Unlike Drummond, the Saint, though he packed a narcotic uppercut and could shoot the pips out of the six of diamonds after flicking it through the air, existed on the level of mentality: he was clever, he had wit. He didn't just charge and shoot, he figured things out, like Sanders of the River but without the solar pith helmet. For someone like me – someone who was bringing exactly no sporting trophies home from school, and for whom a reasonable result in English was his sole academic distinction – the idea that brains could be adventurous was heady wine. It was a short step to the most adventurous brain of the lot. Ranging backwards in time but forwards in receptive scope, I submitted to the awe-inspiring intellect of Sherlock Holmes.

In the Sherlock Holmes novels, and even more so in the short stories, almost all the action was in the mind. Though the Saint could outwit his enemies and leave them chastened by his epigrams while they tied each other up and surrendered to the police, he was seldom relieved of the necessity to plug a few of them as well. For Sherlock to carry a pistol was a rare event. In every tenth story, he might discourage an attacking footpad by taking a swipe with his walking stick, but that was about it. Admittedly, and often without informing Watson in advance, Sherlock moved about a lot. Though his favourite posture was one of silent meditation, he was given to sudden disappearances. (This motif was later borrowed by John le Carré: 'Then Smiley disappeared for three days.') After Watson had duly added acute apprehension to his customary unflagging astonishment, Sherlock would just as suddenly turn up in other cities, other countries. But his manoeuvrings were seldom in order to position himself for an attack. They were in order for him to announce in the appropriate circumstances that he had the whole mystery figured out. From this and that he had deduced such and such. Watson, with the same access as Holmes to this and that – the facts in the case – had deduced exactly nothing.

Neither, of course, had the reader, who in this instance was myself, reading far into the night as part of my mental preparation for the mathematics examination next day. But Conan Doyle's trick – a trick raised to the level of sorcery – was to make the reader identify with Holmes instead of Watson. Watson was the same well-meaning dumb-cluck as you were yourself, but Sherlock was your dream of yourself. As a powerful aid towards making the reader imagine himself striding across the moors or along fog-bound Limehouse alleyways in Sherlock's long shoes, Conan Doyle made the master sleuth a bit of a shambles in every department except deduction. Hence his appeal to generations of adolescent boys who couldn't keep their rooms tidy and whose laundry was done by their mothers – a point reinforced, rather than invalidated, by the large number of adult males who even today make a cult out of the Baker Street bohemian. Invariably the Sherlockologists are permanent adolescents retaining all the trainspotting tendencies of youth. When a youth myself and in pursuit of an obsession, there was no aspect of life I could not neglect down to and including personal hygiene. My chief obsession was reading, and for a long while there was nobody else I wanted to read about except Sherlock.

I didn't try to ape his physical mannerisms. A long way from 221B Baker St. London, No. 6 Margaret St. Kogarah was scarcely a suitable dwelling in which to sit around in a dressing gown smoking a meerschaum while gazing into an open fire. I could gaze into the Kosi stove, and my clandestine smoking – ten Craven 'A's a day and sometimes more – was a pretty fair equivalent for Sherlock's drug habit, but otherwise there was no mimetic urge. I never stood in front of the mirror with a deerstalker on my head pretending to be Sherlock, whereas, pretending to be the Saint, I had many times stood in front of the mirror with a sardonic smile, folded arms and a casually tilted Mauser P-38 replica plastic water pistol. For my resident interlocutor, namely my mother, there was no possibility of faulting my logic as I told her why it was necessary, rather than attending to my homework, to disappear suddenly that very evening in the direction of the public library so as to replace *The Hound of the Baskervilles* and *The Sign of Four* with *A Study in Scarlet* and *The Speckled Band*.

It was a phase, of course, and I bless it in retrospect, because Conan Doyle was a real writer providing a free immersion course in the fundamentals of evocation. Conan Doyle was my first case of following a writer along his side-tracks. Previously, not even the authoritative Captain W. E. Johns had been able to do that. Biggles led me to Worrals and Gimlet but not for long, because Worrals never shot anybody down and Gimlet didn't even have a plane. With Conan Doyle it was different. Willing to try Professor Challenger because the same author had invented Sherlock Holmes, I was plunged irretrievably into *The Lost World*, and nowadays I can only pity a generation that gets its dinosaurs from *Jurassic Park* instead of from the magic plateau in whose steamy jungle the Prof and his friends spent so much time on the run. A Steven Spielberg dino is a stunning special effect. A Conan Doyle dino was a dino: it stank. The grunts, smells and yells of fear helped to offset the sneaking suspicion that Challenger was just Sherlock in a pith helmet – i.e. yet another lightning intellect condemned to loneliness among ordinary mortals with slowly churning primitive brains. And anyway, how bad was that?

Like Conan Doyle and Leslie Charteris, C. S. Forester was too good a technician to be classified as a sludge writer *tout court*, but his central character was that same sludge basic: Horatio Hornblower, the best strategic brain in the Royal Navy, was so brilliant that he could work his way to a just preferment only through penetrating the defences of the envious and mediocre. Pretty much like school, really. Saying the minimum like Gary Cooper in *High Noon* or Alan Ladd in *Shane*, resigned to being misunderstood like Christopher Tietjens in Ford Madox Ford's great tetralogy *Parade's End* (a sludge masterpiece daringly masquerading as literature), to whom else was Hornblower designed to appeal except an Australian schoolboy whose class marks were going steadily down the drain?

It was clear to me even at the time that Forester had based Hornblower solidly, not to say shamelessly, on the original of the heroic figure occupying the top of Nelson's Column. Along with the leading character, everything in the Hornblower saga had its basis in historical reality. Forester knew the concrete detail of the period inside out. Years later I wrote myself a starring role in a Footlights sketch as a pirate captain who did nothing but lurch about shouting orders. ('Belay the thwart bollocks and lash down the foreskin!' etc.) I was congratulated afterwards by a yacht owner in the audience who kindly suggested that I must have known the authentic nautical terminology quite well in order to parody it so effectively. Actually my own nautical career had consisted of one terrified trip across Sydney harbour as the other half of the crew of my friend Graeme McDonald's VJ, a journey during which the mere thought of the sharks cruising below froze my hands to the sheets. I got my technical talk from Forester. 'Bumscuttle the larboard strakes, Mr Bush!' I got it from him in full confidence that he got it from reality. But Forester's painstaking verisimilitude should not be allowed to disguise the fact that Hornblower is a fantasy.

I hope I spotted that at the time. For a short while I might have attempted to address my classmates the way Hornblower addressed his first mate, Mr Bush – saying the minimum, asserting his authority, bridling at contradiction – but taciturnity was not my natural style, nor tolerance theirs, so the imposture could not have lasted long, and anyway it was obvious that in at least one vital respect Hornblower was a wish fulfilment. He could steer his ship into the massed broadsides of the whole French fleet and the enemy cannonballs would hit everyone on board except him. They just curved around him. They had been manufactured in the same ordnance factory as the Hollywood bullets that swerved past John Wayne on Iwo Jima. When Hornblower did get hit, he got hit at the edge, leaving all the bits that mattered still working. The same could have been said of Nelson – it must certainly have been said by Lady Hamilton – but Nelson spent as little of his career as possible facing overwhelming odds, whereas for Hornblower the odds had to be overwhelming or he wouldn't bother pointing his bowsprit at them. In recent years the indecently gifted Spanish writer Arturo Pérez-Reverte, taking a tip from Stendhal, has been turning out a wonderful series of novels and novellas about what war was really like in the Napoleonic period. His key trick is to build a central character you can't help sympathising with and then kill him off at random. This is a cruel literary strategy – Tolstoy pioneered it in *War and Peace* when he aced out Nicolai Rostov just after the reader had learned to love him – but in the cruelty lies its truth. War was like that, is like that, and will always be like that, until the day when Full Spectrum Dominance, or whatever the nerds call it, allows a battle with no people in it at all. In reality, flying metal doesn't care what it hits. Least of all can flying metal be staved off by moral stature. An invulnerable character is inviting you to join him in dreamland, the land of flying sludge.

As a war orphan myself, I don't think I ever quite lost sight of the truth about the insouciant randomness of the Grim Reaper's scythe, but there was perhaps an element of compensating for the absent father figure. I think it more likely, however, that I was just fantasising about the possibility of individual initiative and valour having some effect in a world which I already knew to be unjust. Some of my heroes were fascists in all but uniform. My adolescence had taken place after, and not before, the era in which the supermen had done their worst, but I didn't spot the connection: perhaps because I was unusually obtuse, but more likely because adolescence takes place in its own time, and refuses to be pre-empted by history. Putting the best possible construction on it – something we ought not to do for ourselves, but there are times when it is necessary in the interests of justice – I think I admired my collection of superior beings for how they did their duty, not for how they indulged their eminence. From far off, beyond the walls of my bedroom, history had already reached me as a wave of shock. Clearly one was powerless, and yet here were these marvellous people who had power: not power over others – that never really appealed to me, a blessed blank spot on my crowded list of vices – but power over events. The only drawback was that my paragons were fictional.

In my next phase, I moved up to reality, but read about it as if it were sludge fiction. After World War I, the books that told the story of what the war had been really like did not start coming out until about 1928. After World War II, the flood of realistic accounts started almost immediately. In Australia, my generation of schoolboys grew up reading about British heroes: Guy Gibson in Paul Brickhill's *The Dam Busters* and in Gibson's own *Enemy Coast Ahead*, Douglas Bader in *Reach for the Sky* (Brickhill again) and all those resourceful RAF types in *The Great Escape* (Brickhill yet again). Paul Brickhill was an Australian but he might as well have been working for the British Council. I took in all the factual detail but as far as the characters went I was still dealing with Biggles, Bulldog and Sherlock. In *The Big Show* and *Flames in the Sky*, Pierre Clostermann was the French Biggles. When I read Adolf Galland's book *The First and the Last* I was almost sorry the Luftwaffe hadn't won: clearly they would have, if only Hitler hadn't been so stupid about the Me 262 jet fighter's potential. Galland, if not precisely the German Biggles, had a lot in common with Erich von Stahlhein, the caddish but talented gentleman spy and ace pilot who had almost brought Biggles permanently down to earth in *Biggles Flies East*. When I read Desmond Young's *Rommel*, I was overcome with grief that he hadn't won in the desert: clearly he would have, if only Hitler hadn't been so stupid about strategy. My three-colour drawing of Rommel, copied from the dust jacket of Young's book, decorated the wall beside my bed. From my mother's angle it might as well have been a drawing of General Yamashita, but she knew how to wait.

She had to wait quite a while. My hero worship was slow to fade, partly because the cast of characters in the war books had actually been pretty heroic. It hadn't yet occurred to me that they had had the opportunity to cut a dash because their circumstances were favourable. But my voracious reading habit eventually led me to the uncomfortable truth. In *The Scourge of the Swastika*, by Lord Russell of Liverpool, I read my first accounts of another kind of prison camp from which no tunnels led out, and saw the kind of pictures I had no urge to copy. And when I read The *Naked Island*, by Russell Braddon, I got my first close-up of the war my father had been in, and they had all been in: a war to the death, a war in which men were very lucky indeed if they even got the chance to fight, and in which women and children had died by the million. Children like

me. Time to grow up. After that, I continued to read everything that
was real, and I still do. But I got the habit by reading everything
that was false.

TLS, December 16, 2005

Postscript

Any cultural commentator who lives to my age is bound to be
reminded, many times a day, of how his tastes and interests, even at
their most highly developed, began in his childhood enthusiasms,
and of how those in their turn sprang from instinct. Thus the circle
closes, and the mental life that we had thought was linear is revealed
as having no end, because it is joined to the beginning. When I laid
my first books out beside each other so that I could better love
their covers, it was the start of the thrill I feel now, as I decorate
my website with the covers of all the books I have come to favour.
In my library, I see only their spines, but on the Web, they answer
my first desire. Young, naive and knowing nothing, I had no idea,
as I sat absorbed in Hans-Ulrich Rudel's tank-busting adventures as
recorded in *Stuka Pilot*, that Rudel, still alive at the time, was one
of the bunch of unrepentant Nazis in Argentina who always knew
where Adolf Eichmann was hiding. But my clueless fervour was the
beginning of my later capacity to find such things out, and the thrill
of reading was the first and most solid instalment of what Bruno
Schultz called the iron capital of the adult brain. A critical capacity
had already begun, even if it was only on the primitive level of
knowing whether what I read excited me or not. Finally, because
initially, that critical capacity must be innate. Samuel Johnson, who
has been often in my mind during the assembly stage of this book,
invented a worthless critic called Dick Minim. Rising to great prestige
through no other gift but his sensitivity to the direction of the wind,
Dick Minim was devoid of any genuine critical capacity, because he
had not been born with it. Johnson, the most effectively learned man
of his time, had taken in all that mattered of everything that had
been written, but he was sure that his ability to judge it had started
in his blood. 'There is a vigilance of observation and accuracy of
description which books and precepts cannot confer,' he wrote.
'From this almost all original and native excellence proceeds.' He was

talking primarily, at that point, about the scholars and their learned conjectures, but his wonderful *Preface to Shakespeare* is full of precepts equally pertinent for all critics, however general their approach. As he says here, however, the precepts will never mean enough unless we have it in our nature to recognize their truth. Yes, we must read. But first of all we must choose our parents wisely.